D1352211

ROYAL HISTORICAL SOCIETY
STUDIES IN HISTORY
SERIES
No. 16

DENZIL HOLLES
1598-1680
A study of his political career

Other volumes in this series

Copies obtainable on order from
Swift Printers (Sales) Ltd, 1-7 Albion Place, Britton Street, London EC1M 5RE

Denzil Holles Baron of Ifield married 3 Wifes
1. Dorothy is Heir
to St Fr. Ashley by
whom he had 4 Sons
2 Jane Eldest Daughter
& Coheir to Sr Jn Shirley
3 Hesther the
Second Daughter
& Coheir to Gideon
le Lou Lord of
the Mannor
of Columbiers
in Normandy
Dyd October 31.
1677
Aged 79.

Denzil, First Lord Holles

DENZIL HOLLES
1598-1680
A study of his political career

Patricia Crawford

LONDON
ROYAL HISTORICAL SOCIETY
1979

The Society records its gratitude to the following, whose generosity made possible the initiation of this series: The British Academy; The Pilgrim Trust; The Twenty-Seven Foundation; The United States Embassy bicentennial funds; The Wolfson Trust; several private donors.

The publication of this volume has been assisted by a grant from the Australian Academy of the Humanities.

Printed in England
by Swift Printers (Sales) Ltd
London E.C.1.

CONTENTS

vi

ACKNOWLEDGEMENTS

Many people have helped me to write this book. I wish to thank the librarians and archivists in Australia and the United Kingdom who assisted me in obtaining material; the late Duke of Portland, who gave permission to use and copy manuscripts and to the Duchess who kindly allowed the reproduction of the portrait of Holles; the Marquis of Bath for manuscripts at Longleat; Mr. R. Salway for the diary of Seymour Bowman; and the Earl Fitzwilliam and the Earl Fitzwilliam's Wentworth Estates Company, and the City Librarian, for the Wentworth Wood-house Muniments in the Sheffield City Libraries.

My thanks to my colleagues in the University of Western Australia; to other seventeenth-century historians in Australia, especially Wilfrid Prest, who read the manuscript, and George Yule; to historians in the United Kingdom, especially Gerald Aylmer and Donald Pennington; and to my mother and Dianne Hollis for typing. My greatest debts of gratitude are to Professor Valerie Pearl, who encouraged me to undertake this study of Holles and whose stimulating ideas and great knowledge helped me to write it; and to my husband.

April 1979   Patricia Crawford

NOTES ON SOURCES AND DATES

In quoting from seventeenth-century sources, I have modernised the spelling, punctuation and capitalisation. Proper names have not been altered in quotations, but in the text I have standardised on those adopted in the *DNB*. My sole qualm about this has been that Denzil Holles consistently spelt his own Christian name 'Denzell'.

Dates have been cited according to the Old Style, but the year has been taken to begin on 1 January throughout, and not on 25 March. When Holles was in France, dates have been given in both Old and New Style.

ABBREVIATIONS

Add. MSS.	Additional Manuscripts, British Library.
A.P.C.	*Acts of the Privy Council.*
Bodl.	Bodleian Library, Oxford.
BL	British Library.
CJ	*Commons Journals.*
CSPD	*Calendar of State Papers Domestic.*
CSP Ven	*Calendar of State Papers Venetian.*
DNB	*Dictionary of National Biography.*
Do. R.O.	Dorset Record Office.
EHR	*English Historical Review.*
Harl. MSS.	Harleian Manuscripts, British Library.
HMC	*Historical Manuscripts Commission.*
Kent A.O.	Kent Archives Office.
LJ	*Lords Journals.*
N.L. Scot.	National Library of Scotland.
Nott. C.R.O.	Nottinghamshire County Record Office.
Nott. U.L.	Nottingham University Library, Department of Manuscripts.
OED	*Oxford English Dictionary.*
PRO	Public Record Office.
Sheff. C.L.	Sheffield City Libraries.
S.P. Dom.	State Papers Domestic.
TT	Thomason tract, published in London unless otherwise stated.
West. P.L.	Westminster Public Libraries, Archives Dept.

A full bibliography of the primary and secondary sources on which this book is based is held by the Institute of Historical Research, London.

1

INTRODUCTION

Denzil, first Lord Holles, died neither deeply execrated nor greatly loved. The grudging admiration of later observers for the stubborn old patriot would have surprised his contemporaries during the Civil Wars. Then, renowned for his pride and bad temper, he was known as 'Protean Holles', eternally changing. 'A proud ambitious man' he appeared in the 1640s, and with such a cloud on his brow 'a tempest will carry the man into his grave'.[1] Burnet, who first met Holles when the latter was over sixty, found him unable to bear contradiction, and his judgment was sound only when 'not biased by passion'.[2] Holles's temper carried him to such violent altercations that he seemed determined to live up to his motto *Spes audaces adjuvato* (Hope, favour the bold). In 1680 those who remembered his earlier fiery career found wry amusement in the sight of the respectable cortège of the Lord Holles, former Ambassador and Privy Councillor, to which the brass statue of Charles I on horseback at Charing Cross was seen to nod as it passed into the country![3] Holles would not have been amused, for he saw himself as a defender of the subjects' rights and the privileges of Parliament who had, through his long political career, sought also to serve his monarch.

Holles's political career was an extraordinary one by seventeenth-century standards. He first came into prominence in the House of Commons in 1629 and was still active in 1679, a few months before his death, petitioning the King with several prominent peers in favour of a meeting of Parliament. While many lost their lives, fled or retired during the political crises of the seventeenth century, Holles was actively engaged in politics for nearly sixty years from 1620 to 1680. He was remarkable in another way as well. Born the second son of a gentleman, he had his own way to make in the world. His eldest brother inherited lands and an earldom, but Denzil's inheritance was a family name of no particular lustre and £1,000 cash. Nevertheless he died a peer and a wealthy man.

Holles has received only brief notice in the past. Arthur Collins,

---

1 Parliamentary diary of Sir Symonds D'Ewes, BL, Harl. 163, f.291v. (23 July 1642); *Mercurius Pragmaticus*, no. 19, 18-25 Jan. 1648, TT E. 423.21.

2 *Burnet's History of My Own Time*, ed. O. Airy (2 vols., Oxford, 1897), i. 175.

3 *The Life and Times of Anthony à Wood* (World's Classics edn., Oxford, 1961), p. 245.

whose interest was primarily genealogical, gathered much useful information in the eighteenth century. Firth wrote one of his customarily excellent articles for the *DNB* and Guizot prefaced an edition of Holles's *Memoirs* with a biographical sketch.[1] The absence of any detailed study is not altogether surprising, for until recently few studies of individual members of the Long Parliament had been undertaken. Holles's lack of appeal to previous biographers may be partly explained by the absence of a substantial body of family papers.[2] Nevertheless, although there is no body of personal material, his political career can be traced through other sources, chiefly the parliamentary diaries. His own writings and speeches are sufficiently numerous to reveal his ideas and attitudes, and in particular he left a detailed account of his interpretation of the Civil Wars and the crisis of 1647.

The chief focus of this study falls upon the period of Holles's greatest prominence, as one of the parliamentary leaders during the Civil Wars. Singled out by Charles I in January 1642 as one of the five members he would try to arrest, Holles dominated the House of Commons in 1647 and tried to disband the army and settle the kingdom. An account of his policies and actions during these years contributes to an understanding of Civil War politics and of conservative aspirations for church and state. Less attention has been given to Holles's parliamentary career in the 1620s and after the Restoration, because he was then a figure of secondary importance.

Holles's portrait, probably painted shortly after the Restoration, reveals sharp features and thin, grimly-smiling lips.[3] By 1699 when his *Memoirs* were published, the frontispiece portrait engraved by R. White

---

1 Arthur Collins, *Historical collections of the noble families of Cavendishe, Holles, Vere, Harley, and Ogle* (London, 1752); F.P.G. Guizot, *Portraits politiques: Etudes biographiques sur la révolution d'Angleterre* (Paris, 1851); trans. A.R. Scoble and pub. as *Monk's Contemporaries. Biographical Studies of the English Revolution* (London, 1851). Alexander Thompson began a study of Holles, but his projected work was never completed; A. Thomson, 'Denzil Holles his life and political career to the outbreak of the Civil War, 1599-1642', (Cornell University, Ph.D. thesis, 1932). Further information from personal correspondence with Dr Phyllis Lachs.

2 The extant material does not offer the basis for a life study; J. Dollard, *Criteria for the Life History With analyses of six notable documents* (New York, 1935; 1949 edn.). The absence of information about his childhood prohibits any psychological study.

3 See Frontispiece. This portrait, at present in the National Portrait Gallery, is the property of the late Duke of Portland. Holles's second wife, Jane, referred to a miniature of Holles set in diamonds among the bequests in her will; Somerset House, Probate, Divorce and Admiralty Division, Wills, PCC, Jane Holles, 1667. I have been unable to trace this miniature.

subtly altered the image, replacing the grim smile with a more genial expression and rounding out his features. Another eighteenth-century engraved portrait reveals a similarly pleasant expression.[1]

Other images of Holles may be found in published contemporary comments. The seventeenth-century antiquary, Anthony à Wood, described him as 'a leading fanatic in the long parliament'.[2] He was eulogised in a funeral sermon and lamented in an elegy.

> Is Holles dead! the Protestants' best friend,
> Whose zeal and care for *England* had no end;
> Who in these times of jealousy and fear,
> Did shine so bright, transparent, and so clear? . . .
> Then for great Holles, let this word be given;
> He lived and died well, now reigns in Heaven.[3]

His funeral monument in St. Peter's Dorchester, erected by his nephew's son, John Duke of Newcastle, announced that

> All that Denzell's wit or courage, probity or industry, presaged in his youth he made good and exceeded when grown a man, for, as his excellent endowments and abilities made him early known to his prince and country, so he could, by his eloquence and valour, intrepidly defend the liberty of the last without refusing the obedience that was due to the former.[4]

A London plaque declared Holles 'a great honour to his name and the exact pattern of his father's great merit'.[5] During the eighteenth century he continued to be lauded as an illustrious scion of the noble family of Holles, although since the line died out with his grandson he lacked direct descendants who might praise his name and achievements. Nevertheless, Holles's style of politics had its greatest appeal during the eighteenth century, when he was transformed into a classical Whig. In 1750 the *Biographia Britannica* praised Holles as a patriot while dismissing Cromwell as 'that tyrant'.[6] Oldmixon, in the same period, saw him as an heroic champion of parliamentary liberties.[7]

1 *Memoirs of Denzil Lord Holles, Baron of Ifield in Sussex, from the Year 1641 to 1648* (London, 1699); Collins, *Historical Collections;* portrait engraved by Ravenet.

2 Wood, *Life and Times*, p. 245.

3 Samuel Reyner, *A Sermon preached at the Funeral of the Right Honourable Denzell Lord Holles* (London, 1680); *An Elegy on the Death of Denzil Lord Holles, who Departed this Life on 10th day of Feb. 1679/80* [1680].

4 J. Hutchins, *The History and Antiquities of the County of Dorset* (3rd edn. 4 vols., London, 1861), ii. 383.

5 H.B. Wheatley, *London Past and Present: Its History, Associations and Traditions* (3 vols., London, 1891), i. 196.

6 *Biographia Britannica* (6 vols., London, 1747-1766), iii. 2647n.

7 [John Oldmixon], *The History of England, During the Reigns of the Royal*

4

In the nineteenth century, Holles suffered from the popular vogue for the Army and its partisans. A controversy in *Notes and Queries* on the tale of Holles pulling Ireton by the nose reveals more of the contributors' prejudices than their understanding of the protagonists. Holles would not have dared to fight Ireton, said one, little knowing his quarrelsome belligerence. Another launched into a lengthier account:

> Holles was a very weak person, as his *Memoirs* prove, and like many other people of the same sort, was frequently incapable of telling a story correctly . . . It is as wildly improbable that Holles should have ventured to pull Ireton's nose as that he should have dared to pluck a lion by the tail.[1]

One historical writer, J.L. Sanford, thought that Holles's considerable powers of mind were unfortunately weakened by his passions and prejudices. 'His religious views were narrow and intolerant, and his pride and self-appreciation excessive. His private character was high and unblemished'.[2] Moving from these antiquarian, moralistic comments, the seriously-considered historical judgments of Gardiner and Firth were unfavourable. Gardiner found Holles a politician 'of no special ability', while Firth wrote of 'the folly of the Presbyterian leaders' which created a military revolt in 1647.[3]

In the twentieth century, such notice as Holles has received has been chiefly from historians of post-Restoration diplomacy who find him a laughable, unsuccessful figure as ambassador to Louis XIV.[4] Until more recently, historians interested in the English Civil Wars have had little time for the conservatives, the unsuccessful revolutionaries, the Presbyterians, and have concentrated their attention on the heirs of revolution, the Independents, and the protesters against it in the name of social justice, the Levellers, Diggers and so on. Studies of conservative revolutionaries have been unfashionable, and Holles and other Presbyterians have suffered from neglect.[5]

House of Stuart . . . (London, 1730), pp. 107, 328.

1 Contributions by Edward Solley and Edward Peacock, *Notes and Queries,* 5th ser. 7 (1877), 110, 541-2. For a discussion of the incident, see below, p.143.

2 J.L. Sanford, *Studies and Illustrations of the Great Rebellion* (London, 1858), p. 402.

3 S.R. Gardiner, *History of the Great Civil War 1642-1649* (4 vols., London, 1893-4), iii. 216; C.H. Firth, *Oliver Cromwell and the Rule of the Puritans in England* (World's Classics edn., Oxford, 1956), p. 157. See also Firth's article on Holles in the *DNB*.

4 See below, p. 207.

5 I. Roots, *The Great Rebellion 1642-1660* (London, 1966), p. 307 mentions several other important figures who lack recent biographical studies.

2

EARLY LIFE

> His birth and parentage was noble and honourable; he being a
> second son of the illustrious house of Clare . . . My Lord was
> noble by birth, and no doubt he knew it, and did set a due
> estimate upon it. [1]

i.

The Holles family was of some antiquity, although, as Gervase Holles
acknowledged in his delightful *Memorials,* 'we have run some time as it
were under the ground in obscurity'. In the reign of Henry VIII Sir
William Holles raised the family's position when he became a wealthy
London merchant, Lord Mayor of London, and so 'laid the foundation
and groundwork for that greatness our family is now arrived at'. Any
suggestion to Denzil Holles or to his father that their social origins were
in any way inferior aroused the strongest protests, and Denzil's father
was prepared to take issue even with the powerful Lord Burghley, Lord
Treasurer of England, who referred to the above Sir William Holles as
'an abominable usurer'.[2]

Denzil's father, the first Earl of Clare, was born John Holles in
1564. His education followed a pattern which was to become the norm
for the sons of the nobility and of the gentry: he went to Christ's
College Cambridge, to Gray's Inn, and then travelled abroad.[3] In 1591

---

1 Reyner, *Sermon at the Funeral,* p. 19.

2 Gervase Holles, *Memorials of the Holles Family 1493-1656,* ed. A.C. Wood
(Camden Society, 3rd ser. IV, 1937), pp. 12, 93-4, p. 249 n. 11; *HMC Portland
MSS.,* ix. 7.

3 G. Holles, *Memorials,* pp. 88-9. The letter books preserved by John Holles, the
second Earl of Clare, are invaluable in providing family details. Of the five letter
books, one is well known through the publication of the Historical Manuscripts
Commission; *HMC Portland MSS.,* ix. 1-165. The manuscript from the Portland
collections is on loan to the British Library; BL loan 29/239. A complete edition
of these letter books is being prepared by Dr Peter Seddon for the Thoroton
Society, of which the first volume appeared in 1975; *Letters of John Holles
1587-1637,* ed. P.R. Seddon (Thoroton Society, XXXI, 1975). As the edition is
not yet complete, I have cited the original manuscripts, one of which is in the
British Library; Letter-book containing copies of letters written by Sir John
Holles . . . from 1598 to 1617, BL, Add. 32464, the other three in the Nottingham University Library. John Holles, 2nd Earl of Clare, Letter and Commonplace
book (c. 1587-1615), Nott. U.L., PW V 2. Two of the manuscripts are on loan
from the Duke of Portland; Copies of letters to John Holles, later 2nd Earl of
Clare, chiefly from his father, 1st Earl of Clare, 1610-1637, Nott. U.L., Ne C

he married Anne, the daughter of Sir Thomas Stanhope, an alliance which brought him into the struggle raging in Nottinghamshire between the Stanhopes and the Talbots. The Stanhopes were an ancient county family, but only recently had they gained office and influence at Court. Holles's own actions - his marriage into one faction rather than the other and his quarrel with Gervase Markham - added enmity to the main feud.[1] Anne bore him ten children of whom the sole survivors at the Earl's death in 1637 were John his heir, Denzil and an unmarried daughter Eleanor.[2] Of the other children some died young, a son Francis died after a wild youth soldiering in the Low Countries,[3] and a beloved daughter Arbella died in 1631.

Clare, on the deaths of his father and grandfather in 1590 and 1591, inherited the family estates and family responsibilities. His father left him ten items of advice, the first of which concerned the service of God, the other nine the care and nurture of worldly goods, which latter advice he took to heart. There is some difficulty in assessing the precise extent of Clare's inheritance and final worth at his death, but his enlargement of his patrimony is obvious. He boasted that he was worth £5,000 *per annum* in the reign of Queen Elizabeth, and his nephew Gervase believed that by the sale and exchange of lands he advanced his estate to nearly £8,000 *per annum* at his death.[4] Another estimate of the value of the estate in 1637 from one who was anxious to set forth its

15 404; Copies of letters from John Holles, 1st Earl of Clare, to various persons, 1592-1637, Nott. U.L., Ne C 15 405. Unfortunately in all these letter books there are few letters from the Earl to Denzil, and none at all from Denzil to his father. Denzil admitted he had reclaimed his own letters to his father when he was at Haughton in 1637 after his father's death; Sheff. C.L., Wentworth 18, 17 (a), Denzil Holles to Wentworth, 16 Apr. 1638. However, one of the letter books contains many references to Denzil's affairs. Nott. U.L., Ne C 15 404.

1 W.T. MacCaffrey, 'Talbot and Stanhope, an episode in Elizabethan politics', *Bulletin of the Institute of Historical Research* 33 (1960), pp. 74-85.

2 G. Holles, *Memorials*, pp. 108-9. Eleanor subsequently married Oliver Fitz-william, Earl of Tyrconnel. She had the same portion as Arbella, £6,000, but this was handed to Denzil's keeping in 1647 because Fitzwilliam was a delinquent; *CJ*, v. 114.

3 Francis was the black sheep of the family, and doubtless it was a relief to spend £35 on a funeral monument for him in Westminster Abbey to enshrine him among the respectable; 'John Holles, second Earl of Clare: private affairs, c. 1592-1662', Nott. U.L., PW V 4, f. 18.

4 'John Holles, second Earl of Clare: private affairs . . . to c. 1659', Nott. U.L. PW V 5, f. 311; G. Holles, *Memorials*, pp. 89-94, 95. Clare later claimed that his inherited lands were worth only £160 *per annum* in 1590 and were encumbered with £3,000 debt; 'Letter book containing copies of letters written by Sir John Holles . . . 1598-1617', BL, Add. MSS. 32464, f. 146, Lord Haughton to Attorney General Sir Henry Yelverton, 21 July 1617. John Holles, second Earl of Clare, claimed his inheritance was not worth near £4,000 *per annum* and that it was encumbered with a debt of £9,000; *CSPD 1638-9*, p. 491. For a fuller discussion of Clare's estates and his income, see *Letters of John Holles*, introduction.

largest worth was a lesser figure of £6,800 *per annum* plus personal estate.[1] The basis of this wealth was land. Clare consolidated his lands in Nottinghamshire and pursued a policy of acquiring land in London and building thereon. He inherited property in Clement's Inn and Drury Lane from his grandfather, and he purchased more land in Drury Lane and Princes Street. His ground rents from London properties alone in the 1630s have been estimated at £1,200 *per annum*.[2] In the country Clare was interested in the improvement of his land by draining, and his letters reveal constant attention to the details of estate management.[3] Trading and commercial ventures played little part in his increase of wealth.[4]

With his increased wealth Clare advanced his position in society by the purchase of titles. He despised and condemned the Jacobean Court's trafficking in office but he found that other men no worthier than he were, by the purchase of honour, able to leap over his head. Thus 'seeing the market open and finding his purse not unfurnished with it he was persuaded to ware his money as other men had done'. In 1616 he paid £10,000 for the title of Baron Holles of Haughton and although he felt the humiliation of the purchase, he hoped that this would be transient, and his house would be subsequently 'settled in honour'. In 1624 he purchased the title of Earl of Clare for £5,000 but he begged in vain for some office to give justification to the world for his ennoblement.[5]

By education, wealth and ability Clare was qualified to serve his prince, but he failed to prosper under the Stuarts. He was a gentleman pensioner at Elizabeth's Court, but on the accession of James he was

1 Wentworth Woodhouse Muniments, Sheff. C.L., 24-25 no (69), petition of Lady Ashley to the King. Gilbert Holles, grandson to the first Earl, heard that his grandfather left an estate of £7,000 *per annum;* Portland Deposit, Nott. C.R.O. DD 4 P 39/26, Probate will of Gilbert Holles, Earl of Clare, June 1686.

2 G. Holles, *Memorials,* p. 95; L. Stone, *The Crisis of the Aristocracy 1558-1641* (Oxford, 1965), p. 361. Stone does not distinguish the achievements of the first and second Earl in this account.

3 BL, Add. 32464, f.64, Sir John Holles to his servant Richard Shipman, 10 Mar. 1613. Copies of letters to John Holles, later second Earl of Clare, chiefly from his father, first Earl of Clare, 1610-1637, Nott. U.L., Newcastle Manuscript, Ne C 15 404.

4 He had an interest in a coalpit; *HMC Portland MSS.,* ix. 23. T.K. Rabb, *Enterprise and Empire Merchant and Gentry Investment in the Expansion of England, 1575-1630* (Cambridge, Mass., 1967), p. 316, lists investment in the Vancouver Company, Irish Company and Northwest passage Company.

5 G. Holles, *Memorials,* pp. 99-101; BL Add. 32464, f.124, Haughton to his son John, 17 July 1616; *Cabala, Scive Scrinia Sacra, Mysteries of State and Government* (London, 1663), p. 303.

disappointed because of the 'crew of necessitous and hungry Scots' James brought with him[1]. Not until 1610 did he finally achieve office, as Controller of the Household of Prince Henry, newly created Prince of Wales. It was an important office and augured well for the future when the Prince should ascend the throne. Unluckily for Clare, Prince Henry died in 1612 and his household was disbanded. Sadly he found himself once more without office: 'Myself am like a weatherbeaten bark, without mast, sails, and anchor, pulling up and down whither the winds and waves will have me', he wrote to a friend. To his wife a more succinct sentence registered his view: 'well, he is gone, and with him all my hopes'[2]. He began to court the current favourite, Robert Carr, soon to be Earl of Somerset, explaining that he was 'loth to retire to a private condition'[3]. Unluckily again, just as he secured Somerset's support, the favourite was disgraced. Somerset and his wife were both found to have been concerned in the murder of Sir Thomas Overbury in the Tower. Seeking to help Somerset, Clare tried to persuade one of the witnesses to change his testimony on the gallows, for which 'traducing of the public justice' Clare was hauled before Sir Edward Coke in Star Chamber where he received a stinging rebuke and a fine of £1,000.[4] Such obvious support of the declining favourite appeared political suicide, but stubborn loyalty to friends even in the face of adversity was a point of honour: 'I would not neglect a friend supposed in the wane'. To the end of his life he never abandoned Somerset, looking on him as 'the best friend that ever I had'[5].

However, in 1617, when it was clear that Somerset was disgraced, Clare belatedly addressed himself to the new favourite, George, Viscount Villiers, later Duke of Buckingham. In 1617 he thanked Villiers for bringing him to kiss the King's hand and looked for further rewards, but unfortunately his friendship with Lady Hatton brought him into

1 G. Holles, *Memorials*, p. 94.

2 Thomas Birch, *The Life of Henry Prince of Wales, Eldest Son of King James I* (London, 1760), p. 218; *HMC Portland MSS.*, ix. 11 (1613); copies of letters from John, Earl of Clare, to various persons, 1592-1637; Nott. U.L., Ne C 15 405, f.267, Sir John Holles to his wife, 8 Nov. 1612.

3 *HMC Portland MSS.*, ix. 29-30, 129.

4 *A Complete Collection of State Trials*, ed. T.B. Howell and W. Cobbett (London, 1809-28), ii. 1032-4; *CSPD 1611-1618*, p. 601 mentions that Haughton paid £500 in 1618.

5 Nott. U.L., Ne C 15 404, f.244, Clare to Haughton, 27 Feb. 1630 [1] ; *ibid.*, f.240, same to same, 26 Sept. 1630. See also a letter to his brother in July 1615; John Holles, Earl of Clare, Letter and Commonplace Book (*c.* 1587-1615), Nott. U.L., PW V 2, f.216. Sir Walter Raleigh was another old friend Clare did not forget; G. Holles, *Memorials*, pp. 101-2.

direct conflict with the wishes of the favourite.[1] Even so, it was still possible for John Williams, Bishop of Lincoln, to urge Buckingham in 1624 to revive Clare by including him in the Council of War.[2] But Buckingham did not befriend Clare, and after the failure of the scheme to marry Prince Charles to the Infanta of Spain the Earl was further at odds with the favourite, for he was pro-Spanish, and friendly with Gondomar to boot, when the Court became pro-French. Clare's motives for seeking office were mixed. There were financial rewards, for, although his salary in Prince Henry's household had only been £72 *per annum,* Clare admitted that two years in office had 'fully recompensed me for the former eight years'.[3] But more importantly, Clare wanted office because he believed he could serve his prince, and that no other ambition was proper for him.

Gervase Holles, wondering at Clare's lack of success in his quest for office, was told it was due to King James's aversion to those whose hawks and dogs were as good as his own, and to those who spoke as much reason as he.[4] It has been suggested that King James disliked Clare for his Puritan sympathies, and that in Parliament he represented 'political as well as religious puritanism'.[5] The evidence of his religious sympathies is not clear cut. In his letters he expressed conventional Christian sentiments but reveals no deep concern for spiritual matters. He was anti-Catholic, leading an unsuccessful search for priests at Rufford Abbey in 1611 and arguing against the marriage of Prince Henry to a Catholic.[6] In 1602 he wrote to Beza to thank him for favours received during his visit to Geneva.[7] He shared in the more zealous atmosphere of Prince Henry's household, and opposed any 'innovations' in religion, and attempts to use religion as a prop to the prerogative. Puritans might offend in order, but Arminians offended in substance. He mourned Abbot's death in 1633, for though he had been 'a timorous weak man, yet he was orthodox, and hindered much ill'.[8] Gervase Holles believed that the Earl was so orthodox in religion

1 BL Add. 32464, f.137v., Lord Haughton to the Earl of Buckingham, 2 May 1617: Laura Norsworthy, *The Lady of Bleeding Heart Yard: Lady Elizabeth Hatton 1578-1646* (London, 1935), pp. 47-9, 59-60. There are inaccuracies in Norsworthy's account.
2 *Cabala,* p. 308, Lord Keeper to the Duke [of Buckingham], 22 Mar. 1624 [5].
3 Birch, *Prince Henry,* p. 455; BL Add. 32464, f.93, Haughton to John Holles, 29 Sept. 1615; *HMC Portland MSS.,* ix. 143.
4 G. Holles, *Memorials,* p. 100.
5 A. Thompson, 'John Holles', *Journal of Modern History* 8 (1936), p. 155.
6 *HMC Portland MSS.,* ix. 41-6, 47-9.
7 Nott. U.L., Ne C 15 405, f.261, Sir John Holles to Beza, 2 July 1602.
8 *Ibid.,* 404, f.287, Clare to Haughton, 10 Aug. 1633. *Ibid.,* Ne C 14 405, f.142,

that he would never have supported the Parliament in the Civil Wars.[1] But Clare's position was, as will be shown later, almost identical with his son Denzil's. Both appeared moderate Anglicans, but both believed that the bishops, by the Arminian innovations, were destroying their religion. Clare linked the attacks on religion and on the subjects' rights as part of the one design, observing in 1629 that 'peradventure soundness in our religion displeases as much as to be a good patriot'.[2]

Clare's hostility to Buckingham was probably the main reason for his failure to win office. The corollary of his failure to prosper at Court was Court interference with his activities. As a wealthy man, he believed himself a target for Court designs: 'fat geese are worth the pulling', he wrote in 1629, 'this is the Court language'. No matter which way he turned there were courtiers to pluck him: 'every courtier hath power enough to do a countryman a shrewd turn'.[3] He was chased into the country be proclamations and the object of 'sharp proceedings' for dwelling in town.[4] He was prosecuted with others in the Star Chamber in 1629 for some writings he had seen and the prosecution was dropped only on the birth of Prince Charles.[5] He was also in trouble for alleged depopulation.[6] In 1637, threatened by natural disasters as well, he felt thoroughly persecuted: 'the Lord of heaven be merciful to us, all these from heaven, besides ship-money, depopulation, staying in London and a million of projects upon earth'.[7]

Although Clare was increasingly critical of the royal government under James and Charles, he was never so intransigent in Parliament as his son Denzil was later to be. He sat in the Commons in the first two Parliaments of James's reign then took his seat in the Lords. Here too he found himself in conflict with Buckingham. In 1624 his attempt to

---

Clare to Earl of Exeter, 22 July 1627; f.126, 19 Nov. 1626. John Williams, at this date Bishop of Lincoln, was out of favour for his candid criticisms of the foreign policies of Buckingham and Charles. He was to be further in trouble for his ecclesiastical views in the 1630s; article in the *DNB* by S.R. Gardiner.

1 G. Holles, *Memorials*, pp. 107-8.

2 Nott. U.L., Ne C 15 404, f.231, Clare to Haughton, 28 Oct. 1629.

3 *Ibid.*, f.233, Clare to Haughton, 7 Dec. 1629; f.313, same to same, 26 Oct. 1635.

4 *Ibid.*, 405, f.15, Clare to Lord Vere, 10 Sept. 1627. *The Earl of Strafforde's Letters and Dispatches, with an Essay Towards his Life by Sir George Radcliffe*, ed. W. Knowler (2 vols., London, 1739), i. 337.

5 *APC, 1629 May - 1630 May*, p. 177.

6 Nott. U.L., Ne C 15 405, f.189, Clare to Commissioners for Depopulation, 21 June 1637.

7 *Ibid.*, 404, ff. 330-1, Clare to Haughton, 9 June 1637.

defend the Earl of Middlesex was in clear opposition to the wishes of the favourite, and later in 1628 he supported the rival candidate to Buckingham's for the office of Lord Chamberlain, sneering at the bishops who voted for Buckingham's candidate 'as if they had given up their reason and conscience to serve their ambition' and rudely telling them they could not all be archbishops of Canterbury.[1] When Buckingham had one of the peers summoned to the Star Chamber, Clare was privately indignant: 'thus is Parliament, like dirt, trodden under his highness's feet'.[2] He believed that King and Parliament must exist in harmony, that neither could subsist without the other: 'neither the head can live without the body, nor the body without the head'. Consequently he deplored both the high handedness of the Court and the extremism of the M.P.s which led to misunderstandings and trouble. For example, in 1628 he considered that the attempts both to secure the subject's right and property and to grant the King generous finance were 'a better way, than that either King or people be driven to extremes'.[3] Confronted by the power of the Court backed with the law and a new generation of Court preachers, Clare despaired of the outcome of the 1628 Parliament: 'But I hope better, and yet, I believe little in a Parliament; that either it will be, or being, will do the kingdom any good'.[4]

Clare's letter book, over the years from the fall of Somerset to the 1630s, offers a fascinating glimpse of how a man burning to serve his prince turned sour, critical and hostile when his hopes were disappointed.[5] He was disgusted with the rapid re-orientation of the fickle Court around the new favourite in 1616: 'neither wind nor water so moveable as our Court', cynically observing how the reshuffle of office was used for profitable financial ends. The Court was 'as a model of Africk, every day brings forth some rarity'. By 1627 he claimed

1 Bishop Williams, when asked by James to make a party in the Lords to save Middlesex, found 'All shrink and refuse me; only the stout and prudent Lord Holles adventured upon the frowns of the Prince and Duke . . .'; John Hacket, *Scrinia Reserate: A Memorial Offered to the Great Deserving of John Williams* (London, 1693), pp. 189-90; G. Holles, *Memorials,* pp. 103-5.

2 Nott. U.L., Ne C 15 405, f.130, Clare to Lady Hatton, 12 Feb. 1626 [7].

3 *Ibid.,* f.179, Clare to Arundel, Feb. 1625 [6]; f.169, Clare to Earl of Oxford, 28 Mar. 1628. He resented the Court's attempts in 1626 to interfere with the composition of Parliament by choosing their opponents as sheriffs: 'so may this Parliament prove a worse hobgoblin than the former', he wrote to Wentworth who had been so excluded from Parliament, 'such is the guilt of their conscience, that know their cause bad'; Sheff. C.L., Wentworth 22 (b) no. 53, 22 Nov. 1625.

4 *Ibid.,* 22 (a) no. 11, Clare to Wentworth, 24 June 1627 [8].

5 Around 1626 an anonymous observer attributed Clare's disaffection to thwarted ambition: *Cabala,* p. 278.

he never went near it, 'nor near any of Buckingham's haunts'.[1] 'I am no courtier' he boasted, and contrasted himself and his family, 'poor country folks', with his son-in-law Wentworth, 'a powerful courtier'.[2] Not even for causes to which he was sympathetic, such as that of the Queen of Bohemia, was he prepared to stir.[3] Near his death his concerns centred on his family: 'I covet most to govern my own little commonwealth, and to leave the few whom God hath left to my cares, well settled for the time after me'.[4] When he died in 1637 Wentworth admired 'that upright soul of his', and his nephew paid him the tribute of a magnificent portrait in prose.[5] Proud, quarrelsome, ambitious, he was a lively and intelligent man.

ii.

Denzil Holles was born on 31 October 1598 and named after his grandfather.[6] Perhaps it is symbolic of his stormy career that his christening was followed by violence, a further episode in the Stanhope - Talbot feud. Escorting Denzil's grandmother home after the christening, his father met his local enemy, Gervase Markham, in Sherwood forest, and the two fell to fighting. Clare routed Markham, running him 'between the privities and the bottom of the guts up to the hilt and out behind towards the small of his back'. Surprisingly Markham recovered and lived to be an old man,

1 Nott. U.L., PW V 2, f.2, Sir John Holles to son John, 14 June 1616; Nott. U.L., Ne C 15 405, f.44, Clare to Bishop Williams, 1 Sept. 1625; f.124, Clare to Bishop Williams, 13 Nov. 1626; f.130, Clare to Lady Hatton, 12 Feb. 1626 [7].

2 Sheff. C.L., Wentworth 22 (b) no. 58, Clare to Wentworth, 6 Aug. 1629; Nott. U.L., Ne C 15 405, f.213, Clare to Wentworth, 2 Feb. 1632 [3].

3 In 1633 he commented on the Court's expections of volunteers to serve the Queen's cause: 'peradventure in regard of the party and the cause, many voluntaries are expected: but that humour died with Queen Elizabeth ... why should banished men from the state, trouble themselves with it'; ibid., 404, f.287, Clare to Haughton, 10 Aug. 1633.

4 Ibid., 405, f.218, Clare to Bishop Williams, 18 Dec. 1636.

5 Strafford, Letters, ii. 123; G. Holles, Memorials, ch. 12, pp. 88-114.

6 Firth in the DNB and Wood in his edition of G. Holles, Memorials, p. 248 n. 7, both take Denzil's birth date as October 1599. However his father's note of the birthdays of his children dates the birth of Denzil to 31 October 1598; Nott. U.L., PW V 5, f.294. When writing his will in July 1670, Denzil said he was in 'the 72nd year current of my age'; Somerset House, Probate, Divorce and Admiralty Division, Wills, PCC, Bath 1680, f.21. At Holles's funeral sermon after his death on 17 February 1680, his age was stated as 81 years 3 months and 16 days; Reyner, Funeral sermon, p. 1.

but never after ate supper nor received the Sacrament, which
two things he rashly vowed not to do, until he were revenged - a
difficult undertaking . . . having so valiant and circumspect an
adversary.[1]

Although Denzil was probably his father's favourite, he was a
second son, one who would need to use his family's position and his
own talents to make his way in the world, for his elder brother would
receive the earldom and the bulk of their father's lands. Little is known
of Denzil's early years. His father and mother were both cultivated
individuals, and Gervase Holles says that Denzil and his brothers received
an 'education equal to the best and beyond the most of the nobility'.[2] From the papers of Denzil's elder brother, John, it is clear that
the Earl bestowed careful pains upon their education, encouraging
particularly the study of languages in which he himself was well versed.
Even his daughter Arbella benefited: she spoke French and understood
Italian and Spanish perfectly. Although Clare lacked the powerful
Court connections which might have assured his sons' futures, he
wanted them to be reared 'both in the fear of God and good literature'
so that they might be fit to serve their prince.[3] In one of his few
surviving letters to Denzil, Clare urges his son to 'do everything
mannerly, freely, and with good assurance'.[4] At some stage Denzil
was in attendance on Prince Charles when he was Duke of York -
Charles later referred to him as 'old companion and bedfellow'.[5] A
commonplace book compiled some time after 1614 among the Portland
papers is probably his, but contains little more than copies of poems
and current satires.[6]

1 G. Holles, *Memorials*, pp. 91-2. (Clare's version of the quarrel is in *HMC
Portland MSS.*, ix. 2-3.) Wood, in *ibid.*, p. 248, n. 7, questions the connection
of this incident with Denzil's christening, because he thought Denzil was not
born until 1599 and the affray took place in November 1598, but as Denzil
was born in 1598, Gervase Holles's account seems correct.

2 Clare's table was known for the quality of its discourse, *ibid.*, p. 112. When
he embarked on building he borrowed works ranging from Vitruvius to Serlio
and Alberti; *HMC Portland*, ix. 152. Nevertheless the modern commentator
has described his extensions to Haughton as shapeless and dull; M. Girouard,
Robert Smythson and the Architecture of the Elizabethan Era (London, 1966),
p. 177; plate 138. Clare's wife Anne numbered among her books works in several
languages; Nott. U.L., PW V 4, ff.192-4.

3 *Wentworth Papers 1597-1628*, ed. J.P. Cooper (Camden Society, 4th ser. 12,
1973), p. 325. Copy of will of Sir John Holles, Nott. C.R.O., DD 4 P.39/2
(c. 1600).

4 BL, Add. 32464, f.90, 30 Aug. 1615; f.78v., Sir John Holles to Denzil, 4
Mar. 1614 [5].

5 G. Holles, *Memorials*, pp. 106-7. In a letter tentatively dated to 1630 Holles
claims that his younger years were blessed with attendance upon Charles; *HMC
Cowper MSS.*, p. 422.

6 'Holles Miscellanea', Nott. U.L., PW V 3. Among the items are an epitaph

For formal education, Denzil accompanied his brother John to Cambridge in June 1611, and in 1613 he entered Christ's College where he was made a B.A. on the occasion of the Prince Charles's visit and took an M.A. in 1616.[1] While at Cambridge Denzil delivered an oration to welcome the Prince Elector in 1613. In 1614 his father accused him of having 'guzzled, and good-fellowed it more than you have studied, which is neither the end of your being at Cambridge, neither will it provide for hereafter'. He acted the part of the hero Antonius in Ruggle's Latin comedy, Ignoramus, at Clare Hall before King James in 1615.[2] In 1615, following in his father's footsteps, Holles went from Christ's College to Gray's Inn.[3] Foreign travel was intended to complete his education, but although he was granted a pass in April 1618 to travel for three years, he did not use it. In 1623 he again considered travelling abroad, this time to Spain to join the Prince, but there is no evidence of his leaving England.[4]

The marriage of a younger son with his way to make in the world was a most important step. Around 1621, when he was about twenty-three years of age, Denzil met Dorothy, daughter of Sir Francis Ashley, king's sergeant and the Holles family's legal adviser, when she was living with Lady Elizabeth Hatton.[5] Denzil and Dorothy, 'between themselves (as well as they could) made up the match', but neither the Holles family nor the Ashleys liked the proposed marriage well enough to agree

upon Salisbury, satires on Frances Howard and Robert Carr, and a poem 'Upon the Lord Chancellor Bacon's stinking breath'. A copy of an oration delivered to the Elector Palatine in 1613 on his visit to Cambridge is headed 'Oratio mea', and as Denzil was known to have delivered an oration, it suggests his authorship of the book.

1   Nott. U.L., PW V 5, f.197; John Peile, Biographical Register of Christ's College (2 vols, Cambridge, 1910, 1913), i. 278.

2   BL Add. 32464, f.78v., Sir John Holles to Denzil, 4 Mar. 1614 [5]; Nott. U.L., PW V 3, nf. (at end of book); Peile, Biographical Register, i. 278; George Ruggle, Ignoramus: A Comedy (London, 1662). He may also have taken part in a masque at which the King was present in 1621; Sir John Finetti, Philetti Philoxenis, 1656, TT E. 1602, 1, p. 72, refers to 'a son to the Lord Holles'.

3   He was admitted 9 Mar. 1615; The Registers of Admissions to Gray's Inn 1521-1889, ed. J. Forster (London, 1889), p. 137; M.F. Keeler, The Long Parliament, 1640-1641. A Biographical Study of its Members (Philadelphia, 1954), p. 220.

4   APC 1617-19, p. 100; Nott. U.L., Ne C 15 405, ff. 87-8, f.102, Haughton to Gondomar, 22 July 1623, 7 Mar. 1622 [3]. Ibid., 404, ff.153-4, ff.164-166, Haughton to John, 19 Feb. 1622 [3], 19 Mar. 1622 [3]. After wondering where Denzil was, his father found that he had gone to Dorset to visit Sir Francis Ashley, whose daughter he was courting; ibid., 405, f.49, Haughton to Sir Francis Ashley, 24 May 1623.

5   Details taken from the law suits of 1638 (see section iv of this chapter) and Clare letter book, ibid., 404.

to a settlement. On the Holles side, there was some scorn of the daughter of a lawyer, on the Ashley side purported suspicion that a fortune hunter had surprised the affections of 'a giddy girl'.[1] Despite the fact that the contract was made without parental consent, it bound the couple so that Sir Francis was unable to marry his daughter to any other man, although he was still unwilling to consent to the Holles family's demands.[2] Lady Hatton attempted to help by trying to increase Denzil's inheritance. She offered to sell the Isle of Purbeck to Clare at a reduced price, provided he would promise to settle it upon Denzil, to which Clare retorted that this was a poor return for all his kindness, and he would settle his lands on whom he pleased.[3] After Clare received his earldom in 1624, Ashley re-opened the negotiations, and Clare was pleased that 'my little Sergeant . . . now he seeks Den'.[4]

Clare was persuaded to settle on Denzil his lands in Cornwall. Later, after Clare's death, the marriage settlement was the subject of litigation, for Lady Ashley claimed that further lands had been promised. As for the lands in Cornwall which Denzil received, Lady Ashley later said these were worth £2,500 but the Dowager Countess of Clare said that they had been valued at £4,987 around 1606, 'since which time land especially in that country is much improved'. From the Ashleys Holles received lands worth £600 per annum, but future prospects were good, as Dorothy was their sole heir.[5]

The marriage was celebrated on 4 June 1626, and seems to have been a happy one, for Dorothy described Denzil over ten years later as 'a most worthy honest man, which is a most comfortable portion, if I have no more'.[6] She died in 1641 and Denzil later directed he should be buried beside her.[7] Dorothy bore four sons, of whom only one, Francis,

1 PRO, SP Dom. 16/407/13, ff. 29-30; Nott. U.L., Ne C 15 405, ff.45-6, Sir Francis Ashley to Haughton, 21 Feb. 1622 [3].

2 - PRO, SP Dom. 16/407/13, ff.29-30. The Countess of Clare claimed that Denzil acted against his father's instructions, and contracted himself to Dorothy secretly. Nott. U.L., Ne C 15 405, f. 47, Ashley to Haughton, 21 Feb. 1622 [3].

3 PRO, SP Dom. 16/407/13, f.29; Nott. U.L., Ne C 15 404, f.176, Clare to Haughton, 10 Jan. 1625 [6]. Lady Hatton continued her kindness to Denzil, and appointed him one of the executors of her will and bequeathed him £500; copy of will dated 31 Dec. 1645, BL, Harl. 7193, f.21.

4 Nott. U.L., Ne C 15 404, f.173, Clare to Haughton, 16 Dec. 1625.

5 'His Lordship promised to settle a large and competent fortune on his said son', Lady Ashley in 1638; PRO, SP Dom. 16/323, p. 266. (For further discussion of the later disputes, see below, p.28.) Ibid., 16/407/13, f.30.

6 Bodl., Ashmolean 243, f.16v., Holles's horoscope. Wentworth Letter Book, Sheff. C.L., Wentworth 10 (a) p. 139, Dorothy Holles to Wentworth, n.d.

7 Keeler, The Long Parliament, p. 220 and n.460; Somerset House, PCC, Holles, Will, f.5.

16

survived.[1] She probably never won the entire acceptance of the Holles family and claimed in 1638 that she had 'no charity or friendship at all from my alliance' which her brother-in-law, Wentworth was prepared to believe.[2] Nevertheless, there are instances of Denzil's family being kind to Dorothy, particularly in 1629 when he was in the Tower.[3]

During the 1620s Denzil shared his father's critical attitude to the Court and the favourite. At the beginning of Charles's reign in 1625, when his father refused to attend the coronation, both he and his elder brother refused to be made knights of the Bath and he declined an invitation to take part in a masque.[4] Denzil was already thinking upon national ills, and to Thomas Wentworth, who had married his sister Arbella, he wrote bitterly of the effect of the wars on the western counties in 1627:

> That since these wars all trading is dead, our wools lie upon our hands, our men are not set on work, our ships lie in our ports unoccupied . . . land, sheep, cattle, nothing will yield money . . .

In addition, they suffered from the abuses of the soldiers' presence - rapes, robberies, violence - and could obtain no legal redress. After the defeat at the Isle of Rhé, when Buckingham's army was routed, Holles wrote in even greater indignation, of a venture ill begun, worse executed, and a near total disaster.

> This only every man knows, that since England was England it received not so dishonourable a blow. Four colonels lost, thirty two colours in the enemy's possession (but more lost) God knows how many men slain, they say not above two thousand of our side, and, I think, not one of the enemies.[5]

Shortly after, when writs were issued for a Parliament, the corporation of Dorchester made Holles a freeman and elected him as one of their burgesses.[6]

---

1 Funeral Certificate of Denzil, third Lord Holles, Nott. CRO, DD 4 P 40/84. The three who died young were named Denzil, John and Denzil. The diary of Mr. [William] Whiteway of Dorchester, Dorset from Nov. 1618 to Mar. 1634, BL, Egerton 784, f.88v. records the birth of their third son, John, on 25 July 1632.

2 Wentworth Letter Book, Sheff. C.L., Wentworth 10 (a) p. 139, Dorothy Holles to Wentworth, n.d.; ibid., p. 140, Wentworth to Dorothy Holles, 23 May 1638.

3 For example, Clare stayed in London to assist Dorothy; Nott. U.L., Ne C 15 404, f.221, Clare to Haughton, 7 Aug. 1629; Sheff. C.L., Wentworth 22 (b) no. 81, Clare to Arbella Wentworth, 3 Aug. 1628.

4 G. Holles, Memorials, p. 102.

5 Strafford, Letters, i. 40-2.

6 The Municipal Records of the Borough of Dorchester, Dorset, ed. C.H. Mayo (London, 1908), p. 395. Denzil Holles was admitted freeman on 25 Feb. 1628.

iii.

Up to the meeting of the third Parliament of King Charles's reign, and indeed for most of that Parliament's duration, there is little to distinguish Denzil Holles from any other well-born gentleman of the land. He had sat in the 1624 Parliament for St. Michael Cornwall because his brother John was returned for two constituencies.[1] He did not sit again until 1628 when his role before 2 March 1629 was insignificant. However, his participation in the violent and tumultuous scenes in the House of Commons on that day and his subsequent imprisonment and prosecution brought his name before the nation, deeply affected him personally, and more than any other circumstance secured for him a position of pre-eminence when the Long Parliament met in 1640.

The history of the parliaments of the 1620s is more complex than Gardiner and some subsequent writers perceived. Gardiner wrote before much of the critical editing of the parliamentary diaries had taken place, but, more significantly, he saw the history of Parliament in the 1620s in the light of the breakdown between Crown and Parliament in 1642. Some later writers extended this view and assumed a developing conflict between Crown and Parliament culminating in the emergence of an opposition, 'which by 1629 can be called a party'.[2] The recent work of constitutional and political historians has shown that such a view of the Parliaments of the 1620s is mistaken. The Parliamentarians should not be seen as challenging the king's sovereignty but rather as conservative men seeking to regulate the balance between the Crown's prerogatives and subjects' rights. The issues upon which members were divided in principle may not be so insignificant as Dr Russell suggests, but certainly there was no 'opposition' engaged in a struggle for power with a 'government'.[3]

The older view of steadily deteriorating relations between Crown and Parliament obscured the attempts by the Crown to use the Parliaments. Cooperation between the Crown and Parliament was possible in the mid-twenties, when a Puritan group sought to gain their ends by working with the favourite, the Duke of Buckingham. In

---

1   *Members of Parliament.*

2   Williams Mitchell, *The Rise of the Revolutionary Party in the English House of Commons 1603-29* (Columbia, 1957). See a critical review by J.E. Neale, in *EHR* 74 (1959), pp. 528-9.

3   C. Russell, 'Parliamentary history in perspective, 1604-1629', *History* 61 (1976), 1-27.

return for his support for their religious programme, they were prepared to smooth his way in Parliament, and to direct their criticisms at the government generally rather than at him. Among this group was Sir John Eliot, later to be the Duke's most inveterate opponent. This alliance with its prospects of harmony between the Crown and Parliament, broke down in 1625 over a religious issue. The Puritans, alarmed at the tenets propounded by Court preachers, wanted Buckingham's support to attack Montague. When he refused, they denied him their support in Parliament. Relations between Crown and Parliament were thereafter coloured by hatred of Buckingham as the great apostate, the chief cause of all their woes, and the man who misled the King.[1]

The breach between Buckingham and the Puritan group destroyed Buckingham's and Charles's hopes of finance from Parliament, and so they resorted to the dubious expedient of forced loans to finance their foreign ventures. The tale of opposition to the loans and to the forced billeting and martial law which accompanied the foreign expeditions is well known. The Parliament of 1628 met determined to end such abuses. Most of the first session was occupied with drawing up and securing the King's assent to the Petition of Right. Initially Sir John Eliot and Sir Edward Coke led the House in proposing a bill of rights which would formally prohibit the King and Council from imprisoning without showing cause, although a group of lawyers, supported by Sir Thomas Wentworth, John Pym and Sir Dudley Digges suggested a more moderate bill which would simply force the King and Council to state the cause of imprisonment when a *habeas corpus* writ was presented. Since the King made it clear that any bill at all would be unacceptable, the Commons finally decided to proceed by way of petition, to which after lengthy negotiations the King agreed. Gardiner considered this Petition to be of tremendous and far reaching importance by which 'the Commons had stripped Charles of that supreme authority which he believed himself to hold', but subsequent research, in particular by F.H. Relf and Margaret Judson, has modified this view.[2] Through the

---

1   This paragraph is based on *Negotium Posterorum,* in *An Apology for Socrates and Negotium Posterorum: by Sir John Eliot (1590-1632),* ed. A. Grosart (2 vols, London, 1881); I. Morgan, *Prince Charles's Puritan Chaplain* (London, 1957); H. Hulme, *The Life of Sir John Eliot 1592 to 1632 Struggle for Parliamentary Freedom* (London, 1957), and J.N. Ball, 'Sir John Eliot at the Oxford parliament, 1625', *BIHR* 28 (1955), pp. 113-27.

2   S.R. Gardiner, *History of England* (10 vols, London, 1884), vi. 311; Frances H. Relf, *The Petition of Right* (University of Minnesota, Studies in the Social Sciences, no. 8, 1917). Margaret Judson, *The Crisis of the Constitution. An Essay in Constitutional and Political Thought in England 1603-1645* (New Jersey, 1949), especially ch. vi. See also J.N. Ball, 'The parliamentary career of Sir John

Petition the members sought to establish the subjects' rights as part of the ordinary rule of law, not to ask for parliamentary sovereignty or to limit the King's power. The belief in both the absolute prerogatives of the Crown and the legal rights of the subject remained intact at this period, and the struggle for sovereignty was in the future.

In the first session of the Parliament Denzil Holles played little part. He seems to have made only one recorded contribution to debate: after the King declared his hostility to a bill of rights, a short bill to enact the existing statutes was suggested as a compromise which Holles opposed.[1] He was not active in committee work.[2] Relf tentatively suggests that two manuscript diaries of the Parliament may have been his work. On the basis of their provenance and handwriting this seems possible, which would suggest he was at least following the debates with interest.[3]

After Parliament had voted the Petition of Right and the King accepted it, two further issues arose to trouble the Commons before the King prorogued Parliament at the end of June. These were tonnage and poundage, which the Commons considered the King had no right to exact before they granted it, and the religious grievances associated with the unpopular views of the Arminian clergy. The Commons encouraged merchants to resist payment of tonnage and poundage, but those who did were imprisoned and their goods confiscated. Charles delayed the reassembly of Parliament from October 1628 to January 1629.[4] During the recess the King appointed Wentworth to the Presidency of the Council of North, which step from Parliament to office was doubtless one which his brother-in-law Denzil Holles hoped to make in time. When the Commons reassembled on 20 January they proceeded to consider the two issues of tonnage and poundage and religion. Members were divided over tactics. To some, the religious issue was all important: tonnage and poundage could be used as a bargaining counter to persuade the King to curtail Arminian activities in the church. Sir John Eliot disagreed with this view, and Dr Ball has argued that Eliot's insistence on the primacy of the financial rather

Eliot 1624-1629' (Cambridge University Ph.D. thesis, 1953), and J.N. Ball, 'The Petition of Right in the English parliament of 1628', *Anciens pays et assemblées d'état* 32 (1964), pp. 49-51.

1 'Some notes taken in ye Cessions of Parliament . . . 17 March 1627 [8] ending the 26 of June by William Borlase, Knight', BL, Stow 366, f.230v.

2 Holles was named to only one committee (concerning recusants); *CJ*, i. 888.

3 BL, Harl. 2313 and 5324; see Appendix 1 for discussion of authorship.

4 Gardiner, *History of England*, vii. 4.

than the religious issue dissociated him from the Puritan group.[1] Eliot persuaded the majority to support him in his campaign, and it was under his leadership that the whole programme foundered in the extremism and violence of 2 March. In the view of Sir Symonds D'Ewes, 'divers fiery spirits in the House of Commons . . . by whom the truly pious and religious members of the House were too much swayed and carried', misdirected the House and caused a breach on an issue which was 'immaterial and frivolous'.[2]

In this second session Holles was more active.[3] He spoke in support of Eliot's attack on the Customs Farmers who had seized the merchants' goods. The King ordered his principal Secretary, Sir John Coke, to tell the Commons that the Customs Farmers had acted on his own command and direction,[4] but before Coke could inform the House, Eliot reiterated the need for punishing the officers and professed his trust in the King's goodness. Holles spoke after him:

> I fear neither bribing nor terror, nor rock, but I fear to give my voice to anything that I cannot be persuaded of. To proceed to the punishment of offenders: the King not interested in the fault of these men: he commanded them to stay goods, not to seize.[5]

Holles's determination to side step the issue by blaming the King's officers could not have been more clearly stated, but the very next speech was Sir John Coke's statement of the King's acceptance of his own personal responsibility. It cut the ground completely from under the feet of Eliot and Holles, and motions for adjournment followed immediately so that the members might digest this new information.

Parliament adjourned until 25 February when Charles adjourned it again until 2 March. Fearing either further adjournment or a dissolution, Eliot and his friends met at the Three Cranes tavern in the City to plan their tactics so that Parliament would not melt away without any achievement: as one later said 'that we go not out like sheep scattered: but to testify to the world we have a care of their safety; and religion'.[6] These nine men - Eliot, Holles, Valentine, Strode, Long,

---

1 Ball, 'Sir John Eliot' (thesis), ch. 5, especially pp. 311-26.

2 D'Ewes quoted in *ibid.*, p. 326.

3 He was named to another committee concerning recusants, and one concerning a decree in the Court of Wards; *CJ.*, i. 923, 931.

4 Gardiner, *History of England*, vii. 64.

5 *Commons Debates for 1629 Critically Edited and with an Introduction Dealing with Parliamentary Sources for the Early Stuarts*, ed. W. Notestein and F.H. Relf (Studies in Social Sciences, no. 10, Minnesota, 1921), p. 326 (23 February 1629).

6 *Ibid.*, p. 240.

Coryton, Selden, Hobart and Hayman - were subsequently held responsible for the disturbance, and were questioned and imprisoned by the Privy Council. From the Privy Council's investigation, an account of their activities emerged.[1]

Eliot and his friends made their plans carefully. On 2 March Holles and Valentine took the Privy Councillors' seats next to the Speaker's chair.[2] The Speaker announced the King's command to adjourn the House, refused Eliot permission to speak and attempted to leave. Thereupon ensued the famous scene:

> there being a great cry, to have Sir John Eliot heard, and he standing still to speak, Mr Speaker offered to go out of the chair, but was held in by the arms by Mr Holles and Mr Valentine. But notwithstanding he at length got out of the chair, and (divers of the House flocking up towards the table) he was again with a strong hand by them two put into the chair.[3]

When the Privy Councillors tried to free the Speaker, Holles swore 'God's wounds he should sit still until they pleased to rise'.[4] This act of violence did not solve the impasse, for although the adjournment was prevented, the Speaker still refused to allow Eliot to put his paper to the question or to read it. The debate then switched to the question of the Speaker's duty, and Holles was among those who argued that he was the servant of the House.

> If we be a Parliament, and assembled here by the King's commandment, and trusted by those that have sent us hither, you are our servant; and our servants and officers ought to obey us;[5]

Disorder increased. Sir Miles Hobart locked the door and pocketed the key. Finally Eliot spoke to his paper, but as the Speaker persisted in his refusal to act, Selden suggested the clerk should read it. Eliot then announced that he had burnt it and confusion raged once more. Holles brought the House back to the business of the paper:

> I think that gentleman [Sir John Eliot] hath done very ill to burn that paper: But I am of opinion, that it should not be left to the

1 I.H.C. Fraser, 'The agitation in the Commons, 2 March 1629, and the interrogation of the leaders of the anti-court group', *BIHR* 30 (1957), 86-95.
2 Probably they arrived early before the House filled up, since no one records that they moved during the two hour session. In the first copy of the 2 March account, the text refers to Valentine's and Holles's seating: 'the one sitting close to the chair on the one side, the other on the other'; *Commons Debates 1629*, p. 253, n.17.
3 *Ibid.*, p. 253 (2 Mar. account. This was probably the one prepared for the use of the judges.)
4 *Ibid.*, p. 104 (True Relation).
5 *Ibid.*, p. 256 (2 Mar. account). See also another version on p. 240.

liberty of any merchant to pay tonnage and poundage without gift
of Parliament; but if any of them shall pay it, and thereby give
away our liberties, I would have them declared to be enemies to
their country.[1]

Eliot thanked Holles for his reproof, but the debate was diverted as a
message arrived summoning the Sergeant to the King. Sir Peter Hayman
was rebuking the weeping Speaker, Sir John Finch, as a disgrace to the
county of Kent, when Holles once again intervened:

> Since that paper is burnt, I conceive I cannot do my King and
> country better service, than to deliver to this House what was
> contained in it . . .

He read the heads of a paper which he himself had penned but which
revealed his familiarity with Eliot's original:[2]

> Whosoever shall go about to innovate any thing in religion, to bring
> in either popery or Arminianism, or any new doctrine contrary to
> that which hath generally been taught and received by the unanimous
> consent of the divines of our church let him be accounted a
> capital enemy of the King and Kingdom.[3]

He read similar resolutions condemning any who advised the taking
of tonnage and poundage when it was not voted by Parliament as 'a
betrayer of the liberty of the subject, and a capital enemy both to King
and kingdom'. According to some accounts the House agreed to the
Protestation 'with a loud *Yea*' but no formal question was put. About
this time a messenger announced that Maxwell, an usher in the House,
was at the door with a message from the King. On Eliot's motion the
House finally adjourned itself until 10 March,[4] on which day the King
dissolved the Parliament, imputing all the blame for the dissolution to
some 'ill-affected men' only, 'some few vipers among them'.[5]

---

1 *Ibid.,* pp. 259-66.

2 *Ibid.,* p. 105 (True Relation); pp. 266-7 (2 Mar. account); Eliot was sitting
on the back benches, Holles near the Chair, so in the hubbub he would not
have heard Eliot clearly. He presented only three resolutions, although Eliot
had spoken of other matters as well; Fraser, 'Agitation in the Commons', p. 91.
Eliot did not speak of religion, but Holles offered a resolution on this.

3 *Commons Debates 1629,* p. 267.

4 *Ibid.,* p. 105 (True Relation); p. 267 (2 Mar. account).

5 The King's Declaration showing the causes of the late Dissolution, *The Constitutional Documents of the Puritan Revolution 1625-1660,* ed. S.R. Gardiner
(3rd edn. Oxford, 1906), pp. 83-99; The King's speech at the dissolution of the
Parliament, John Rushworth, *Historical Collections* (8 vols., London 1680-1701),
i. 662. 'Viper' to Charles's audience was not just a poisonous snake, but an
unnatural beast which ate its way out of its mother, thereby destroying that
which had given it life; *OED,* meaning 3. The parallel between Charles and his
Parliament would have been obvious.

Before the King dissolved Parliament, the Privy Council summoned the nine men who had met at the Three Cranes, and committed them to prison.[1] Holles, when asked why, contrary to his usual custom, he had placed himself next to the Speaker, above the Privy Councillors, replied

> that he had at other times as well as then seated himself in that place. As for seating himself above the Privy Councillors, he took it to be his due in any place whatsoever except at the Council board, and that he for his part, he came into the House that morning with as great zeal to do his Majesty service as any one whatsoever: Yet nevertheless, finding that his Majesty was offended with him, he humbly desired that he might rather be the subject of his mercy than of his power, To which the Lord Treasurer answered, that he meant rather of his Majesty's mercy than of his justice: I say of his power, my Lord.[2]

Charles wanted to proceed against the nine prisoners in the Court of Star Chamber in April, but when the Attorney-General consulted the judges, their answers showed them reluctant to meddle in the privileges of Parliament. Meanwhile, two of the prisoners were released and the remaining seven sued for bail in the Court of King's Bench. Initially the King refused to allow the prisoners to appear until they improved their behaviour. On 3 October the Court offered bail provided the men be bound for good behaviour, but although in a temporary lapse Walter Long agreed, the other six refused, arguing that this would be an admission of guilt for their earlier behaviour. The judges tried unsuccessfully to persuade Charles to modify his condition, so on 9 October when the prisoners again refused to be bound, they were again returned to gaol where, Judge Hyde warned them, they could stay 'as men neglected until their own stomachs come down'. Finally, in November the Attorney-General decided to proceed against three of them - Eliot, Holles and Valentine - in the Court of King's Bench.[3]

Holles's family and friends did what they could, but as he was a close prisoner in the Tower, they could not visit him. His father badgered the Lieutenant of the Tower about his health, his brother

1 *APC 1628 July - 1629 April*, p. 351. On 4 Mar. the Council ordered that the studies, trunks and cabinets of Holles, Selden and Eliot be sealed; *ibid.*, p. 352.

2 'Answers to the Lords Commissioners by Sir Peter Heyman, Mr Holles, and others of the Lower House, shewing the meaning of their speeches in Parliament, 1628', BL, Lansdowne 93, f.158. There are other versions of this in BL, Add. 30926, f.314, and BL, Harl. 2305.

3 Account based on *State Trials*, iii. 236-87; Gardiner, *History of England*, vii. ch. lxviii; Hulme, *Sir John Eliot*, ch. xiv.

tried to visit him, and both men remained in London hoping that their presence might be of some comfort[1] His wife Dorothy came to London, and Clare conveyed her petition for leave to see her husband to the Earl of Holland in May, but it was not until a cousin, Philip Lord Chesterfield, intervened in October that Dorothy was allowed to visit. Wentworth also offered help, claiming that he could secure Denzil's delivery without any submission from Denzil, which Clare doubted[2] In addition to his family, Denzil's friends tried to visit him. In May John White, a minister from Dorchester, accompanied by one Ferdinando Nicholls of Dorset, 'came under the window of Mr Holles and would have spoken unto him but were prevented by his keeper and put out of the Tower'[3] Two members of Parliament who tried unsuccessfully to see Eliot went to see Holles instead, and although there was a garden between his window and them, they endeavoured to speak to him but were prevented by his keeper. Holles was making sure his health did not decay in the Tower: 'he then showed them his top, and skurdg [scourge?] stick, his weights of [for?] swinging, with them made antic signs and devoted salutations at their parting'[4] Clare had no word of censure for Denzil's rash conduct: rather, he believed Denzil to be the victim of an outrageous exercise of power. Denzil, he considered, suffered 'for righteousness' sake', and he and his fellow prisoners were 'poor state martyrs'. Clare lent no support to the efforts of Denzil's wife and his father-in-law, Sergeant Ashley, who importuned Denzil to be bound for good behaviour. Nevertheless, after his transfer to the Marshalsea on 29 October, Denzil yielded the following day, and Ashley and William Noy (later Attorney General) went bail for him[5] This looks very much like backsliding, for all of the prisoners had refused to be bound, except Long, who later regretted his action.

The case against Eliot, Holles and Valentine opened in the Court

---

1 *CSPD 1628-9*, p. 498; *HMC Cowper MSS.*, i. 383; Sheff. C.L., Wentworth 22 (b) no. 58, Clare to Wentworth, 6 Aug. 1629; Nott. U.L., Ne C 15 404, ff.27, 28 (at end of volume), Mary Vere to Haughton, 4 Apr. 1629, 15 June 1629.

2 *Ibid.*, ff.229-230), Clare to Haughton, 28 Oct. 1629.

3 PRO, Sp Dom. 16/142/52. See pp. 27-8 for further information about John White.

4 *Ibid.*, 'Skurdg stick' probably refers to a whip for the top. 'Scourging the Top' is mentioned in 1581 in the *OED*.

5 Nott. U.L., Ne C 15 404, f.217, Clare to Haughton, 20 July 1629; f.257, same to same, 29 Mar. 1631; ff.229-230, same to same, 28 Oct. 1629; Whiteway, Diary, BL, Egerton 784, f.77; *The Court and Times of Charles the First*, ed. F.R. Williams (2 vols, London, 1848), ii. 36; Rushworth, *Historical Collections*, i. 683; *Court and Times of Charles I*, ii. 40; *De Jure Maiestates or Political Treatise of Government (1628-30) and the Letter-book of Sir John Eliot (1625-1632)*, ed. A.B. Grosart (2 vols, London, 1882), ii. 74.

of King's Bench on 25 January 1630. The Attorney-General accused them of conspiracy in Parliament but the three men refused to plead, claiming that the Court had no jurisdiction for offences committed in Parliament. Consequently they were judged on a *nihil dicit* as guilty, and on 12 February they were sentenced to imprisonment during the King's pleasure, Eliot was fined £2,000, Holles 1,000 marks, and Valentine £500.[1] Holles later said that he did not pay his fine immediately, but made an escape and lived a banished man, until, he paid his fine in 1637.[2] It is not altogether clear what happened to him immediately after the sentence: some writers have taken his comment to mean he fled to the continent, but in fact he seems to have stayed out of prison on bail, and lived in Dorset and Wiltshire during the 1630s.[3] Meanwhile Eliot, Valentine and Strode remained in prison, from whence in June 1631 Eliot wrote a friendly letter to Holles - Denzil in reply referred to it as a 'loving letter' - commending Holles's virtue.[4] (Eliot's biographers, nevertheless, refer to Eliot's magnanimous silence on Holles's desertion.)[5] Eliot died in the Tower in 1632 and Valentine and Strode remained in prison until January 1640.[6] At some date after the scene in Parliament on 2 March, Holles addressed a most humble letter to Charles asking for pardon and favour: if 'in anything he may have failed, it hath been through misfortune, and the error of his judgment' he confessed, begging Charles in fulsome terms to accept the sacrifice of his sorrowful heart, 'a heart burdened with a sense of your Majesty's displeasure, prostrate at your royal feet with all humble submission waiting till your Majesty will reach out the golden sceptre of princely compassion to raise me out of this lowest dust'.[7] Holles's 'great stomach' had come down. When he told Charles 'it was the height of his ambition to end his days in your service' he spoke the truth. What other service was there? No concept of a parliamentary career could be entertained in the early seventeenth

1 *LJ*, xii. 165; the value of marks: 13/4 to each £ sterling; *OED*.

2 Denzil Holles's account to Parliament, 27 Aug. 1646, Bodl., Tanner 59, f.507; printed in *Memorials of the Great Civil War in England from 1646-1652*, ed. H. Cary (2 vols, Oxford, 1842), i. 149-51; *State Trials*, iii. 329.

3 For example, H.B. Butler and C.R.L. Fletcher, *Historical Portraits 1600-1700* (Oxford, 1911), p. 98. Holles wrote letters from Dorset, and his third son was born there in July 1632; Whiteway, Diary, BL, Egerton 784, f.88v.

4 Printed in J. Forster, *Sir John Eliot: A Biography. 1590-1632* (2 vols, London, 1864), ii. 644, 23 June 1631; p. 645, 26 Sept. 1631.

5 Eliot, *Letter Book*, p. 74.

6 Gardiner, *History of England*, ix. 87.

7 Letter tentatively dated to 1630. It is in general terms, and may well have been penned after the judgment in King's Bench, *HMC Cowper MSS.*, i. 422.

century, and although Denzil posed as a sufferer for the liberties of Parliament his real aim was to serve his King.

What is the significance of the events of 2 March and the subsequent prosecution? The resolutions passed were of no constitutional significance - Holles acting as Speaker was completely irregular - and many were disturbed at the disorder and violence in the House. 'Never was there such a morning as that which occasioned the dissolution'.[1] The scene on 2 March gave Charles some justification for his decision to call no more Parliaments until men were in a better temper.[2] However, the harsh prosecution and unyielding hostility of the King diverted attention from the members' misconduct, and even in 1629 they were said to be feeding themselves 'with popular applause'.[3] Eliot's death in the Tower confirmed the air of martyrdom surrounding the members, and subsequently the Short and the Long Parliaments took cognizance of their sufferings, although their actual vindication waited until 1667.[4]

Holles's role is interesting. His contribution to the scene of 2 March was a practical one, since he offered leadership which the House accepted. His violent restraint of the Speaker caused an uproar, but he played an important part in putting Eliot's resolutions before the House, thereby ensuring that Parliament did not dissolve without some protest. Though the resolutions seem futile, reverting to Eliot's earlier untenable position that the King was not involved with the conduct of his officers, their supporters saw them as having a propaganda value for their county communities, testifying to the world, as Strode said, that 'we have a care of their safety'. Holles's pride and high spiritedness — what his cousin Gervase called his 'great stomach' — sustained him through the ordeals of questioning and trial, and enabled him to return defiant, memorable answers. That done, he disappeared from the public contest, and while Eliot died in the Tower, Holles lived on, to fight another day.

iv.

After his marriage in 1626 Denzil retained only a sentimental link with Nottinghamshire and the north of England. His interests and

---

1 *The Life and Letters of Sir Henry Wotton,* ed. L.P. Smith (2 vols, Oxford, 1907), ii. 318-9.
2 A Proclamation for suppressing of false rumours touching Parliament, Rymer, *Foedera,* viii. pt. 3, pp. 36-7, 27 March 1629.
3 *CSPD 1629-31,* p. 26.
4 The Short Parliament began investigations, and the Long Parliament men-

estates were in the west, chiefly in Dorset and the town of Dorchester. Dorset was a prosperous county at this date, with 'a self-sufficiency of all commodities necessary for man's temporal well-being'.[1] Its chief town, Dorchester, was described in 1613 as a thriving centre:

> one of the principal places of traffic for western merchants, by which means it grew rich and populous, beautified with many stately buildings and fair streets, flourishing full of all sorts of tradesmen and artificers; plenty with abundance revelled in her bosom, maintained with a wise and civil government . . .[2]

Despite the setback of two fires, the town presented the same prosperous air to Bulstrode Whitelocke when he rode on the Western circuit in 1628: 'The town standeth upon a rising, at the foot of which the river runneth. The merchants here in quiet times grow rich by traffic with France'. Prosperity was based on the cloth trade, and with its 'quick markets and neat buildings', and the number of its inhabitants, many of great wealth, Dorchester could claim pre-eminence in the shire.[3] The town was first incorporated in 1610, and a new charter was issued in 1629. The corporation was active in regulating the commercial life of the town and in supporting the propagation of religion. Although Denzil's father-in-law, Sir Francis Ashley, was the town's first Recorder from 1611 to his death in 1635 and was one of the burgesses in the 1620s,[4] Denzil had no business interests in the town and took no part in the corporation's affairs.

Dorchester was renowned for its religious activity under the direction of the minister, John White, known as the 'Patriach of Dorchester'. According to Fuller, he 'absolutely commanded his own passions and the purses of his parishioners, whom he could wind up to what height he pleased on important occasions'. Sir Francis Ashley held White in high regard. He was interested in White's schemes for colonisation, and in his will testified to his appreciation of White's labours for him and his family by a bequest of £100.[5] Although Holles

tioned the sufferings of the members in the Grand Remonstrance. However, the proceedings in the Court of King's Bench were not reversed until Holles introduced a writ of error into the House of Lords in 1667; *LJ*, xii. 166, 223.

1 Thomas Fuller, *The History of the Worthies of England* (London, 1662), p. 277.

2 Contemporary pamphlets, quoted in W.H. Barnes, 'The Diary of William Whiteway 1618-1634', *Dorset Proceedings* 13 (1957-8), 78.

3 Bulstrode Whitelocke, Annals, BL, Add. 53726, ff.34-35v.; John Coker, *A Survey of Dorsetshire* (London, 1732), p. 69.

4 *Municipal Records of Dorchester*, pp. 384, 56, 435, 452-4.

5 Thomas Fuller, *The Worthies of England*, ed. J. Freeman (London, 1952), p. 469; Somerset House, Will of Sir Francis Ashley, PCC, Pile 44.

was not associated with White's colonising schemes, he shared his concern with the Protestant cause in Europe and the fate of the Queen of Bohemia.[1] White's chief work, *A Commentary upon Genesis*, published posthumously by his son in 1656, was dedicated to Denzil Holles, as White had intended, 'as an acknowledgement of your friendship, and the several courtesies he had received from you'.[2] White's own parish organisation — a disciplined Protestant community with which the civil power co-operated — may have given Holles some insight into how a Presbyterian type of church government might function.

On the death of Sir Francis Ashley in 1635 Holles inherited estates worth £1,200 *per annum*.[3] He was not so fortunate on the death of his own father in 1637, for the only will which could be found was over thirty years old and bequeathed Denzil only £1,000. His mother-in-law, Lady Ashley, contested this, alleging that she and her husband had consented to Denzil's marriage to their only daughter solely upon the understanding that a further settlement of over £1,000 *per annum* would be made. The case was a difficult one, since it involved a son against his mother and brother, and both sides petitioned the King to prevent legal suits.[4] The Privy Council proposed a hearing before a Commission, but as this was unacceptable to the Dowager Countess, the Privy Council directed Lady Ashley to complain to equity, declaring that after the evidence was taken, the Commission would then give a judgment. The bills of complaint and answers are among the Chancery Papers, but no decision was ever made and the Earl's will was never proved.[5] Unfortunately there are no family papers for this later period to indicate what practical settlement was made, nor how family relationships were affected. Gervase Holles says that John and Denzil had fallen out even before their father's death, due to the Earl's preference for his second son, that their jealousy was fanned by a dispute between their wives at cards, and that both brothers were

1 F. Rose-Troup, *John White the Patriarch of Dorchester and the Founder of Massachusetts 1575-1648 . . .* (New York, 1930), p. 43.

2 John White, *A Commentary upon the First Three Chapters of the First Book of Moses called Genesis* (London, 1656).

3 Collins, *Historical Collections*, p. 105.

4 Sheff. C.L., Wentworth 24-5 (69), Petition of Lady Ashley to the King, [1638]; (70), copy of Petition of Dowager Countess of Clare to the King.

5 PRO, SP Dom. 16/323, p. 267; PRO, PC 2/49, ff. 215-6, 25 May 1638; PRO, C.2. Charles I, A. 51/76, C.2. Charles I, H. 98/63; Nott. U.L., PW V 4, ff. 284, 285, Clare to Charles Bate, 19 Dec. 1662, says the will was 'not suffered to be proved'; Clare to Clarendon, 4 Oct. 1662, says it was 'never proved, nor suffered to be so'.

'of great stomachs'. Their brother-in-law, Wentworth, considered John and Denzil 'unruly, loving themselves on both sides something further than moderation, without that equal respect we ought all to observe towards others'.[1] Although there are instances of co-operation between the two brothers during the Civil Wars and after the Restoration, there is no evidence of any strong bond between them,[2] and in Denzil's own will of some thirty years later there is a passage about the evil consequences of bitter disputes between relations over wills, 'God's curse commonly attending those unnatural divisions and animosities in families'.[3]

One interesting development from the suits over the late Earl's death was that Holles ended his estrangement from his former brother-in-law, Wentworth, who was now the powerful Lord Deputy in Ireland. The warm friendship between the Holles family and Wentworth had faded after Wentworth accepted the Presidency and received his Viscountcy, but there was no breach until after Arbella's death in 1632. Holles wrote to Wentworth in April 1638 in an attempt to enlist his support in the disputes over Clare's will.[4] Wentworth refused to take sides, but wrote to Laud endeavouring to patch up the difficulties. He anticipated that this would be fruitless, as indeed it was. Although the friendly correspondence and free exchange of the early days was never resumed, formal relations were established and visits were arranged for Arbella's children.[5] The situation was such that when the Long Parliament opened, Denzil Holles would not be among those who hounded the Lord Deputy to his death.

In 1638 Holles quarrelled with the Earl of Salisbury, his landlord for the manor of Damerham south. The Earl complained that Holles had

1 G. Holles, *Memorials*, p. 109. The Earl's preference for Denzil was the subject of debate in the suits. Dorothy Holles declared to Wentworth that 'the world knows [Denzil] was the son of his love'; Sheff. C.L., Wentworth 10(a), f. 139, Dorothy Holles to Wentworth, n.d. [early 1638]; Strafford, *Letters*, ii. 172.

2 Their sons travelled together in 1646, and there are hints of co-operation in Whitelock's Annals. Denzil helped his brother over the recordership of Nottingham in 1662; Nott. U.L., PW V 4, pp. 286-7. However John did not name Denzil as an executor of his will, and chose instead his brother-in-law Sir John Wolstenholm; Somerset House, PCC, will of John Holles, 1666-73. In 1663, when Holles was ambassador in France, a letter of John's suggests that the two did not correspond; Nott. U.L., PW V 5, f.356, Clare to Frecheville Holles, 3 Nov. 1663.

3 Somerset House, PCC, Will, Holles.

4 Sheff. C.L., Wentworth 18 (17a), 16 Apr. 1638.

5 Lady Burghclere, *Strafford* (2 vols, London, 1931), ii. 103. Wentworth was troubled at the suits; *HMC Various MSS*, vii. 420; Strafford, *Letters*, ii. 172, 379. Denzil's brother John was present at the creation of Strafford in January 1640; *HMC D'Lisle MSS*, vi. 224.

taken more than the £250 worth of timber which was his due,
demanded satisfaction, and advised Denzil to mend his ways 'otherwise
I must be enforced to seek the preservation of my inheritance in a legal
way'. At the receipt of this letter, Denzil's outraged self-importance
dictated a furious reply. He berated the style of address, suggesting that
it must be the work of a secretary since the Earl 'better do know how
to write to the son of one of your own rank', abused the Earl's house
as 'a rotten house not fit for a gentlemen to live in', implied that
Salisbury was a 'nippy landlord', and concluded by declaring he
would take trees again if he felt he needed them. He signed himself 'as
you use me, at your service, Denzell Holles'. Not surprisingly, the
Earl complained to the Privy Council, who considered Holles should
offer satisfaction for his insults. Should he refuse to kneel to
acknowledge his fault, he should be committed until he did. Nearly
thirty years later Holles admitted he had been glad enough to ask
pardon to end the dispute.[1]

Meanwhile Dorset, like other counties, was suffering from the
grievances of ship money, impressment and monopolies. Although
under a cloud for his conduct in 1629, Denzil was not completely
isolated from public life in the 1630s. He was a captain of the Dorset
militia in 1636, and a member of the Dorset sewers commission in
1638.[2] However, he continued his contumacious behaviour, refusing
the second levy of ship-money in 1635, until the sheriffs complained to
the Privy Council, and abetted his mother-in-law, Lady Ashley, in her
resistance to distraint of goods after her failure to pay. On this occasion
it was he who complained to the Privy Council. When the Crown-licensed
men arrived to dig his dovecote for saltpetre in 1637, he abused them
and chased them from his land. In 1639 he refused to contribute to a
loan for royal expenses in the north.[3]

The county of Dorset was divided into two geographical sections at
this date. In the west, the gentry were under the influence of the
Digbys, but in the east, where there was no such ruling family, a group
of gentry resorted weekly to a bowling green, 'well placed for to

1 PRO, SP Dom, 16/393/54, f.98, 25 June 1638; *ibid.*, 16/400/2, 1 Oct. 1638;
CSPD 1638-9, pp. 84-5 [Oct. ? 1638]. 'I . . . was sent for by a messenger about
100 miles out of the country, and made to wait a good while before I could be
discharged, and was glad to be friends with his good Lordship'; PRO, SP France
78/121, f.2, Holles to Arlington, 11/1 July 1665.

2 J.P. Ferris, unpublished article on Denzil Holles. (I am grateful to the Institute
of Parliament Trust for allowing me to consult Mr Ferris's work.) Keeler, *The
Long Parliament*, p. 220.

3 *CSPD 1635*, p. 523; *CSPD 1636-1637*, pp. 287, 437, 449; PRO, PC 2/48,
f.611; Rushworth, *Historical Collections*, iii. 913.

continue the correspondence of the gentry of those parts'. The Earl of Suffolk was the man of highest social standing, but next in precedence came two younger sons of peers, Henry Hastings and Denzil Holles.[1]

National events became even more pressing at the end of the 1630s. After his unsuccessful attempt at forcing the Scots to accept the English Prayer Book, Charles sent out writs for a Parliament to meet in April 1640. The elections in Dorset were keenly contested. Lord Digby was returned as a knight of the shire only when Sir Walter Erle, who received more voices, stepped down.[2] In Dorchester, the Court interest was firmly resisted. Before the issue of the writ 'the most part of the Company did declare their opinion that the fittest men to be chosen for burgesses of Parliament, if any writ come, to be Denzell Holles, esqr., and Mr. Dennis Bond'. Later when a servant of the Earl of Suffolk asked the Mayor if the town would choose Sir Dudley Carleton, 'The company thought fit that the best answer was to give that Mr. Mayor had talked with divers of the town and company and they resolve to choose townsmen, and some refuse to declare their opinions of choice until the time of choice'.[3] Denzil Holles and Dennis Bond were returned.

Charles hoped for money from his Parliament, but as the members wanted remedy for their grievances, the Parliament was soon dissolved and Charles launched a second attack on the Scots which was even more disastrous than the first. The Scots' army entered England and occupied Newcastle.[4] Charles had no choice but to send out writs for another Parliament to meet in November. Again Dorchester chose Holles and Bond to represent them. There was an advantage in choosing townsmen, for they could be expected to look after the town's interests.[5] However, although Holles and Bond did assist on

1 Shaftesbury, Autobiography, printed in *Memoirs, Letters and Speeches of Anthony Ashley Cooper, First Earl of Shaftesbury*, ed. W.D. Christie (London, 1859), pp. 21-6. Shaftesbury was hostile to Holles at this date, for he had been cheated of his inheritance by his uncle, Sir Francis Ashley, whose heir Holles was; K.H.D. Haley, *The First Earl of Shaftesbury* (Oxford, 1968), pp. 17-20. J.P. Ferris, 'The gentry of Dorset on the eve of the Civil War', *The Genealogists' Magazine* 15 (1965), 105.

2 Transcript of Chronology made by Dennis Bond, Esq., of Luton in the Isle of Purbeck of the years 1100-1658, Do. R.O., D.53, p. 30. Richard Rogers received 942 voices, Sir Walter Erle 902, and George, Lord Digby, 800. In 1620 Sir Francis Ashley had stepped down for the Treasurer; Hutchins, *Dorset*, ii. 356.

3 *Municipal Records of Dorchester*, pp. 435-6.

4 For the Scottish background see D. Stevenson, *The Scottish Revolution 1637-1644 : The Triumph of the Covenantors* (Newton Abbot, 1973).

5 For example, the corporation wrote to Bond for assistance in January 1641;

occasions,[1] they would be far more concerned with national than with local issues in the 1640s, and the townsmen were forced to make and execute many of their own decisions during the war without aid from Westminster. Holles and Bond were very different individuals, for although both would support the Parliament, Holles was foremost among the political Presbyterians while Bond was active among the political Independents, and supported the Commonwealth. Bond was a Dorset man, a woollen draper who played an active part in the corporate life of the town. His view of the second Scots War was quite plain: 'for my part I paid not a penny to the taxes nor would furnish a man'.[2] Like Holles, he was influenced by the minister White, and in 1643 a hostile author termed him 'Patriach White's own disciple'.[3] In 1640 Bond was little known to national politics, while Holles was already a figure of some importance.

In explaining Holles's importance in 1640 several factors should be taken into account. His family background was respectable, and his social position and wealth were enhanced by the activities of his father, the first Earl of Clare. His marriage with a Dorset heiress established his position with the gentry of that county, who respected his birth and wealth. He came into contact with the men of the opposition through his father's circle of disgruntled place seekers who were critical of the Duke, and his geographical situation surrounded him with hostile observers of Buckingham's foreign ventures. His own actions in the Parliament of 1629 placed him among the foremost of this opposition, and although he did not remain in prison for so long as the other members of Parliament, his defiance of the Council was remembered. At the opening of the Long Parliament in 1640 observers recognised him among the foremost members. He was, says Clarendon,

> as much valued and esteemed by the whole party as any man, as he deserved to be, being a man of more accomplished parts than any of them, and of great reputation by the part he acted against the Court and the duke of Buckingham in the Parliament of the fourth

Do.R.O., Corporation Minute Book, B 2/16/4. In return, the corporation voted payment for their members. £200 was set aside for this in 1647; *Municipal Records of Dorchester*, p. 629. Bond collected all this money; Do.R.O., C.9 (dated 1648).

1 For example, Holles and Bond assisted the corporation in 1647 to purchase Fordington Parish from Walter Yonge; *Municipal Records of Dorchester*, p. 629.

2 *DNB*; Keeler, *The Long Parliament*, p. 111; Bond, Chronology, Do.R.O., p. 31; *Municipal Records of Dorchester*, p. 715.

3 *A Letter from Mercurius Civicus to Mercurius Rusticus, or, London's Confession but not Repentence*, Oxford, [25 Aug.] 1643, TT E. 65.32, p. 31.

33

year of the King . . . and his long imprisonment and sharp prosecution afterwards on that account; of which he retained the memory with acrimony enough.[1]

[1] Edward, Earl of Clarendon, *The History of the Rebellion and Civil Wars in England* (Book III, 35), ed. W. Dunn Macray (6 vols, London, 1888), i. 249.

3

THE FIRST SESSION OF THE LONG PARLIAMENT, NOVEMBER 1640 – SEPTEMBER 1641

Some did not look far before them but did what they thought was best at the present.[1]

i.

When the Long Parliament first assembled in November 1640 the members were strongly united in their condemnation of the King's government. No opposition 'party' actually existed, but contemporaries recognised that there were leaders in the House, men who were in each other's confidence. Clarendon considered that the 'great contrivers' in the Lords were the Earl of Bedford, Lord Saye, and Lord Mandeville, with the Earl of Essex as a convert, and in the Commons, John Pym, John Hampden, and Oliver St. John together with Nathaniel Fiennes, Sir Henry Vane junior and Denzil Holles. Clarendon judged that Holles's refusal to take part in the prosecution of Strafford did not interrupt his friendship with this group, and that 'in all other contrivances he was in the most secret councils with those who most governed'.[2] However, in his earlier account of the events of 1641, Clarendon gave a more qualified picture of Holles's relationship with the opposition leaders.

> In the Lords' House the earls of Essex, Bedford, Warwick, the lords Saye and Kimbolton, were the governing voices, attended by Brooke, Wharton, Pagett, and such like. In the House of Commons Mr. Pym, Mr. Hampden, Mr. St. John, Mr. Holles, and Mr. Fiennes absolutely governed, being stoutly seconded upon all occasions by Mr. Strode, sir John Hotham. . . sir Walter Earle, young sir Harry Vane, and many others of the same tempers and dispositions; but truly, I am persuaded whatever design either of alteration or reformation was yet formed, I mean in the beginning of the Parliament, was only communicated between the earl of Bedford, the lords Saye and Kimbolton, Mr. Pym, Mr. Fiennes, Mr. St. John, who together with the earl of Rothesse and the lord Lowden [of the Scots' commissioners] managed and carried it on; and that neither the earl of Essex, Warwick, nor Brooke himself, no, nor Mr. Holles or Strode, or any of the rest, were otherwise trusted than upon occasion, and made use of according to their several gifts.[3]

1 *Richard Baxter. Reliquiae Baxterianae, or Mr Baxter's narrative of the most memorable passages of his Life and Times*, ed. R. Sylvester (London, 1696), p.25.

2 Clarendon, *History*, (Bk. III, 25-35), Macray, i. 241-50 (This account is taken from Clarendon's *Life). (Ibid.*, (Bk. III, 35) Macray, i. 250. (for a further discussion of Strafford's trial see below, p. 36).

3 Clarendon, *History*, Macray, i. 263 n.1. For a discussion of the relative merits of different passages in Clarendon's *History of the Rebellion* see C.H. Firth, *DNB*, article on Hyde.

There is other evidence to support the view that Holles was not completely identified with the opposition leadership. Historians have long known what the members of the opposition did not want — ship money, arbitrary church courts, and the like — but they have found it much harder to perceive what they did want. Time was short, and the work of destruction and the preparation for war occupied so much of this. Yet Professor Trevor-Roper, in a stimulating essay, has argued that there was a positive philosophy shared by the opposition leaders; that is, a belief in reform on the lines advocated by Bacon, and publicised by Samuel Hartlib and John Dury.[1] Sharing a common vision of an enlightened society, a group headed by John Williams, Bishop of Lincoln, Lord Brooke and John Pym, and probably including Mandeville, invited the Czech philosopher Comenius to come to England in 1641 to prepare plans for the reform of society. Comenius arrived in September and set to work but before Parliament could consider his plans, the Irish rebellion broke out in November. Thereafter as Parliament's struggle with the King intensified, the time seemed unpropitious for reform and Comenius decided to leave England.[2] Denzil Holles was not among those connected with Comenius or his visit, although his father had been friendly with Bishop Williams, which suggests that Holles had little interest in educational and social reform — an impression confirmed by his later life — and thus was detached from the opposition leaders' philosophical ideas.

Another bond between the opposition leaders was the colonising schemes of the 1620s and 1630s, in which there is no evidence of Holles participating, despite his friendship with John White, the founder of the Massachusetts Bay Company.[3] At the meetings of the Providence Island Company in the 1630s the Earl of Warwick, Lord Saye, Lord Brooke, John Pym, Sir Gilbert Gerard, Sir Benjamin Rudyerd, Sir Thomas Barrington, Oliver St. John, John Gurdon, John Robartes, John Hampden and Sir William Waller kept in touch with each other, but Holles was not a member of this group and did not share their interest in colonisation.[4]

1 H.R. Trevor-Roper, 'Three foreigners: the philosophers of the puritan revolution', in *The Crisis of the Seventeenth Century: Religion, Reformation and Social Change* (New York, 1968), pp. 237-93.

2 R.F. Young, *Comenius in England* (Oxford, 1932), pp. 38-9, 42, n.4, 43-4.

3 Rabb, *Enterprise and Empire*, Appendix p. 316.

4 A.P. Newton, *The Colonising Activities of the English Puritans: The Last Phase of the Elizabethan Struggle with Spain* (New Haven, 1914), suggested that the leaders of the parliamentary opposition learnt to work together in their joint schemes of colonisation. More recently, C. Thompson, 'The origins of the Politics of the Parliamentary Middle Group', *TRHS* 5th ser., 22 (1972), 72 argues that it was not their colonising activities which kept the group together, but rather their common ideas and political principles.

What Holles shared with the other opposition leaders was experiences of the 1620s. Like Pym, Hampden, St. John, and others, he had lived through those years when the Antichrist seemed to triumph in Europe, when the Palatinate cause was abandoned by England, and England abroad was generally inept and ineffectual. It has been observed that in the Civil War the Parliamentarians were on the average older than the Royalists, and this difference in age probably reflects a difference of generation and experience. The men of the 1620s had lived through a gruelling time.[1] Now Holles, as a veteran Parliamentarian, was extremely useful to the common cause, but while his lack of interest in educational reform and colonisation did not detach him from the opposition leaders when the work of destruction was in progress, it would be significant later when a new society was to be built.[2]

ii.

The first and most important of the King's evil counsellors to be destroyed was Strafford, who had supported the King for so long in his rule without Parliament. Eight days after Parliament opened, on 11 November, the attack on Strafford was launched. The Commons named a 'close' committee of Pym, Strode, St. John, Holles, Digby and Clotworthy to prepare for a conference with the Lords to charge the Earl, but the next day the House accepted Holles's withdrawal from the committee.[3] In the following months as the Commons' impeachment of Strafford proceeded, Holles did nothing to stem the tide against him, beyond occasionally intervening when the debate became too heated. For example when Clotworthy inveighed against Strafford saying that his answers consisted of 'shameless denials or frivolous shifts', Holles stood up 'to desire that all such speeches touching any man's person might be forborn', and on other occasions he vouched for the authenticity of a petition presented by Strafford.[4] The trial opened in March, but when it appeared that the Lords would not convict him the Commons resorted to an Act of Attainder.[5] Holles was not among those

1 D. Brunton and D.H. Pennington, *Members of the Long Parliament* (London, 1954), pp. 14-15.

2 Out of a total of 547 M.P.s 328 had never sat before the Short Parliament; Keeler, *The Long Parliament*, pp. 15-16 and n. 75.

3 *CJ*, ii. 26, 27.

4 *The Journals of Sir Symonds D'Ewes from the Beginning of the Long Parliament to the Opening of the Trial of the Earl of Strafford*, ed. W. Notestein (New Haven, 1923), p. 410 and n.5; p. 515 n.8.

5 Manuscript notes on a printed copy of the articles against Strafford and his replies have been attributed to Holles; 'The printed Dispositions and Articles

known as the 'Straffordians' who voted against the Attainder,[1] as some of Strafford's other relations were,[2] but when it was proposed that some provision should be made for the payment of Strafford's debts and for his wife and children, Holles 'spoke himself on the behalf of those innocents, as he called them'.[3]

Initially, Strafford's friends and more moderate supporters seem not to have realised that the Earl's life was sought.[4] Holles may have expected Strafford to be disqualified from the King's service, but when he realised that his former brother-in-law might well forfeit his life and goods, he exerted himself.[5] Two sources discuss his attempt to save Strafford's life. Firstly, Laud says that an offer was made to Strafford

> That if he would employ his power and credit with the King for the taking of episcopacy out of the Church, he should yet have his life . . . The man that sent him this message was his brother-in-law, Mr Denzil Holles, one of the great leading men in the House of Commons.

According to Laud, Archbishop Ussher heard this directly from Strafford, and Laud believed it because he did not think Strafford would lie against his own brother while preparing to leave the world.[6] The second account is from Burnet, who recounts what Holles told him over

against Thomas Earl of Strafford, February 1640 interleaved with large Remarks and Observations of what passed at his Trial', BL, Harl. 6865, f.107. A pencilled note in the BL Manuscript Room copy of the *DNB* attributes these notes to Denzil Holles. The handwriting in the manuscript appears identical with that of Holles at this period. If the work were by Holles, it would suggest that he followed the trial with very close attention.

1 *Verney Papers: Notes of Proceedings in the Long Parliament*, ed. J. Bruce, Camden Society 31 (1845), pp. 57-8.

2 For example, Sir Gervase Clifton, whose relationship with Strafford was even more distant than Holles's, as he had married a sister of Strafford's first wife, voted against the attainder. He was later a Royalist.

3 D'Ewes's diary, BL, Harl. 163, f.43. The act contained no such provisions. Holles had been active also on behalf of Strafford's secretary, Sir George Radcliffe; T.D. Whitaker, *The Life and Original Correspondence of Sir George Radcliffe, Knight*... (London, 1810), p. 223 (8 May 1641).

4 'Copies of documents relating to the negotiations with the Scottish Commissioners . . . connected by a short narrative and concluding with an account of the impeachment and imprisonment of the Earl of Strafford', BL, Add. 15567, ff.32v. — 33. (See p. 39, n.3 for a comment on authorship).

5 Here I disagree with C.V. Wedgwood, *Thomas Wentworth First Earl of Strafford 1593-1641. A Revaluation* (London, 1961). The cited evidence of Strafford, *Letters*, ii.417 and Clarendon, *History* (Bk. III, 35), Macray, i. 249-50, points not to an attempt to stop the impeachment, but only to detachment from the prosecution and an attempt to save the Earl's life.

6 *The Works of the Most Reverend Father in God, William Laud* (7 vols., Oxford, 1847-60), iii. ed. J. Bliss, p. 442.

twenty years later, after the Restoration, according to which the King
sent for Holles and asked him how he could save the Earl. Holles
pointed out that although Charles could lawfully pardon Strafford, he
did not advise this, and instead suggested that Strafford should petition
for a short respite, which petition the King should take to the Houses
with a prepared speech 'and Holles said to him [Charles] he would try
his interest among his friends to get them to consent it'. Up to this
point, the story seems plausible, but thereafter the details become more
confused. Holles told Burnet that he had 'prepared a great many'
members to believe that Strafford would become wholly theirs, so that
if the Court party had backed them they might have saved Strafford,
but the Queen, fearing that Strafford would turn against her, dissuaded
Charles from going to the Parliament himself and persuaded him to add
the miserable postscript which wrecked the appeal: 'If he must die, it
were charity to reprieve him till Saturday'. She also ensured the Court
party were against the scheme. However, as Airy points out, this story
of the Queen's intervention is unsubstantiated by any other evidence.[1]

Strafford had a scheme of his own and possibly Holles was associated
with this. He suggested that the King should object to passing the bill
of attainder because of the presence of parties in the House, the posting
of the names of members who opposed the bill, and the tumults.
According to this scheme, Firth believes, Charles should have offered
some guarantee that Strafford would possess no political authority.
Strafford suggested that if the King moved the Lords individually and
some of the principal Lower House men, and meanwhile kept the
Tower in safe custody, 'it is thought the Earl might yet be saved'.[2] This
scheme failed because Charles assented to the bill. Another plan was
proposed by the King to the Earl of Bedford, whereby offices would be
given to him and his friends if he would save the Earl, and as Holles was
mentioned as one of those to benefit from Bedford's scheme, possibly
this was the basis of Ussher's and Burnet's stories.[3] Although as Clarendon pointed out, Holles was not involved in the most important business
before the Parliament, it did not affect his standing with the opposition.[4]
Clarendon saw his detachment in terms of family loyalty, and the
members could accept such a plea, as they could even excuse Bulstrode

---

1 Burnet, *Own Time*, i. 50-1; 51 n.1. There are details of this story which are
characteristic of Holles, such as an over estimate of his own political ability, and
a blaming of other persons or events for his failure.

2 'Papers relating to Thomas Wentworth, First Earl of Strafford from the
MSS. of Dr William Knowler', ed. C.H. Firth, in *Camden Miscellany 9* (1890),
21-5.

3 For a further discussion of Bedford's plans, see below, p. 40.

4 Clarendon, *History* (Bk.III, 35), Macray, i. 249-50.

Whitelocke from participating in the prosecution of Laud, because Whitelocke owed his education to Laud.[1] Besides, even while Holles was dissociated from Strafford's case, he was active in Laud's, and in other opposition business.

Holles's detachment would have created a favourable impression on Charles, who was unable to reconcile himself to those who had opposed Strafford.[2]

iii.

Prior to the Long Parliament's first meeting, the opposition leaders were said to have met together to consult about

> how to direct their parliamentary resolutions in order to a present redress and future security, and it was conceived by them to be the most certain way, and most consistent with the duty and allegiance of subjects, to fix their complaints and accusations upon evil counsellors . . . rather than upon the personal failings and maladministrations in the King.[3]

Historians have long recognised the central importance of the appointment and control of the officers of the Crown. The accepted political theory was that the King could do no wrong, and that his ministers were responsible for his actions. This was not completely unrealistic in that it recognised that the King was advised, but it ignored reality in shifting responsibility for decisions from the King to his advisers. In 1640 the M.P.s blamed evil counsellors for misgovernment; John Pym, in the first serious address to the Long Parliament, moved that they should find out the authors of their woes and punish them.[4] Even after Strafford's death, the M.P.s were not allowed to think that the work was complete, for the opposition leaders used the disclosure of the Army plot in May 1641 to remind them of the prevalence of these evil men. In his formal speech urging the Lords to join with Commons

---

1 Whitelocke, *Annals*, BL, Add. 37343, ff. 277-8. Nevertheless, Lord Digby claimed that his own backwardness in the prosecution of Strafford was ill taken; *The Lord Digby his last Speech against the Earle of Strafford*, [21 Apr.] 1641, TTE 198.1, pp. 2-3.

2 B. Manning, 'The aristocracy and the downfall of Charles I', in *Politics, Religion and the English Civil War* (London, 1973), p. 68.

3 BL, Add. 15567, ff. 30-30v. This manuscript has been attributed to the Earl of Manchester, but this seems unlikely since the tone of the account is hostile to the parliamentary opposition. A pencil note in Add. 15567 suggests Lord Falkland was the author, although Add. 35838, is actually catalogued as 'Collections out of a Manuscript entituled Memoires written by the late Earle of Manchester . . . under his own hand . . .'.

4 *D'Ewes*, ed. Notestein, pp. 7-8.

in a Protestation, Holles blamed evil counsellors for all the nation's ills:

> we must conceive, they must be ill counsels which have brought us into this condition. These counsels have put all into a combustion, have discouraged the hearts of all true Englishmen, and brought two Armies into our bowels, which (as the vulture upon Prometheus) eat through our sides, and gnaw our very hearts.[1]

The Commons believed that misgovernment would cease if the King were rightly advised, but their problem was how to secure this. Professor Roberts suggests that broadly five solutions were open to the Parliamentarians. They could make ministers accountable to Parliament by the process of impeachment, they could participate in schemes to 'undertake' the King's business in Parliament, they could persuade the King to appoint Privy Councillors in whom the nation could confide, or they could insist on the King accepting ministers of parliamentary nomination. These ideas were put forward by different groups at different times.[2] Holles considered at least four of these alternatives. Family loyalty detached him from the impeachment of Strafford, but he was not opposed to the process, for he carried the impeachment of Laud to the Upper House, and in the second session he proposed the Commons impeach *all* the bishops.[3] He was associated with the abortive scheme by which the Earl of Bedford was to undertake the King's business in Parliament and gain revenue for him, in return for which the King was to appoint a group of new advisers. Bedford was one, Clarendon believed, who 'only intended to make himself and his friends great at Court, not at all to lessen the Court itself'.[4] Charles's habit of taking men from the parliamentary opposition into his service was generally known, although his friends disapproved. On 29 January 1641 Charles had appointed St. John his new solicitor general, and on 19 February named seven new Privy Councillors — Bristol, Bedford, Essex, Hertford, Saye, Mandeville and Savile.[5] Late in April it was rumoured that he would make a whole series of new appointments, among whom Pym was to be Chancellor of the Exchequer, and Holles

---

1 *A True Copie of the Speech, Made By The Honourable Denzell Holles, Esquire, At a Conference . . . Concerning the Protestation . . .*, [4 May] 1641, p. 2.

2 Clayton Roberts, *The Growth of Responsible Government in Stuart England* (Cambridge, 1966), p. 100 and ch. 3, 'The Failure of Impeachment (1640-1642)', *passim*.

3 *CJ*, ii. 54; *The Diurnal Occurences or Dayly Proceedings of Both Houses*, 3 Nov. 1640 3 Nov. 1641, TT E.523, p. 386. 'Master Holles thinks fit that the bishops should be accused of high treason, and gives several reasons for the same, both by precedents and otherwise'.

4 Clarendon, *History* (Bk. III, 25), Macray, i. 241.

5 Gardiner, *History of England*, ix. 264, 292.

a Secretary of State.[1] But Charles insisted that in return for these places Bedford should save Strafford's life, and since he was unable to promise this, and died from smallpox within a few days of Strafford, the whole scheme came to nought.[2] In May Charles created Lord Saye Master of the Court of Wards, and it was rumoured that he would confer Windebanke's vacant Secretaryship of State on Holles.[3] In July there were further rumours: Nicholas, clerk of the Council, reported on 15 July that Holles, Hampden and Mandeville were rivals for the Secretary- ship, but on the 29th said the office would go to Holles.[4] Chief Justice Bramston and Sir John Temple had also heard the rumour that Pym was to be Chancellor, Holles Secretary.[5] Yet since nothing materialised for Holles, he had no inducement to moderate his conduct in Parlia- ment. Charles's whole policy of taking men into his service from the opposition was doomed from the beginning, because his purpose was to persuade men to act for him in the Parliament, while the opposition's purpose in accepting office was to persuade the King to accept reforms in church and state. Furthermore, once the opposition leaders did accept offices in the King's service, their credibility in the Parliament was weakened.[6] Even the rumour of impending office made Bedford an object of suspicion in December 1640.[7] The Commons were so fearful that men would sell out to the King that there was an abortive self- denying bill proposed in June 1641 by which members would be 'debarred from being capable of any honour, dignity or service under the King, Queen or Prince during this Parliament or any ensuing Parlia- ment unless it come by descent or the leave of both the Houses'.[8]

Hyde and his friends later wanted the King to appoint Privy Coun-

---

1 Clarendon, *History* (Bk. III. 191), Macray, i. 333.

2 Roberts, *Growth of Responsible Government*, pp. 102-4. Laud's biographer, Heylin, considered that the King changed his mind. His not preferring any of these persons, 'so exasperated them who were concerned in this designation, that they prosecuted the Earl of Strafford with the greatest eagerness'; P. Heylin, *Cyprianus Anglicus: or, the History of the Life and Death, of William [Laud]* (London, 1668), pp. 477-8.

3 Clarendon, *History* (Bk. III, 20), Macray, i. 238.

4 *CSPD 1641-3*, pp. 53, 63.

5 *The Autobiography of Sir John Bramston, K.B. of Skreens, in the Hundred of Chelmsford*, ed. T.W. Bramston, Camden Society 32 (1845), 81; *HMC D'Lisle MSS.*, vi. 406.

6 Roberts, *Growth of Responsible Government*, pp. 104-5. In different circum- stances in 1679 Charles II took the opposition into his Privy Council, and the scheme failed for both these reasons. Charles did not heed the advice of his Council, and the Councillors lost credit with parliament (see chapter 11).

7 *Letters and Memorials of State*, ed. A. Collins, (2 vols., London, 1746), ii. 664.

8 D'Ewes's diary, BL, Harl. 163, f.256 (3 June 1641).

cillors in whom the nation had confidence but there are no signs that Holles ever supported such a scheme. Instead, he seems indirectly associated with the proposal that Parliament should control the King's appointment of officers. The Scots had included among their demands of Charles that he would appoint none of the great officers of state in Scotland without the assent of Parliament.[1] A similar demand gradually developed in England. On 24 June the Commons passed propositions including a request that the King remove evil counsellors and confide in good ones. The Commons' vote of 30 July that all office holders should take the Protestation Holles commended as an attempt to impose a negative test on officers.[2] On 9 August Holles formally requested the Lords to ask the King to appoint the Earls of Salisbury and Pembroke as Treasurer and Steward respectively.[3] There are signs, too, that Holles was prepared to advocate even more radical measures, for in May 1641 he and William Strode proposed that some particular officers, commissioners for the collection of tonnage and poundage, should be responsible to the Parliament.

> Mr Holles and Mr Stroud spoke very vehemently and very often that it might be granted to commissioners in trust for the King . . . and that the liberty of the subject might be asserted which hath been so long oppressed and that now we may plainly show that it is in the power of the subject to grant it either to his Majesty or to others for a defence and guarding of the sea.

Although the House was prepared to appoint commissioners, they could not agree on the persons, so the scheme fell through.[4] This was the most radical of the plans for replacing the King's evil counsellors with good men with which Holles was associated. When he argued that Parliament should appoint officers, he moved well beyond the traditional belief in blaming evil counsellors for misgovernment.

The King and his supporters later claimed that the opposition had

---

1 Minutes of the Treaty between the English and the Scots, held at London; from 10 Nov. 1640 to 12 Aug. 1641; by Sir John Burroughes, BL, Harl. 457, f. 77.

2 *CJ*, ii. 185, 230; pub. 30 July 1641, TT 669. f.3 (10); *The Speech of Denzill Holles Esquire, at a conference with the Lords on Tuesday the third of August 1641*, 1641, p.4.

3 *CJ*, ii. 248. Carrying a message was not necessarily indicative of support of a policy, for on occasions the House forced members to carry messages despite their personal opposition to the policy. For example, Sir Ralph Hopton opposed the Grand Remonstrance, but the House insisted he be one of those who presented it to the King; *The Journal of Sir Simonds D'Ewes from the first recess of the Long Parliament to the withdrawal of King Charles from London,* ed. W.H. Coates (New Haven, 1942), p. 223 n.1.

4 D'Ewes's diary, BL, Harl. 163, f. 243v. (28 May 1641); f. 252, f. 305 (1 and 10 June 1641).

simply created trouble so that they might force the King to take them into his service. They wanted, Clarendon said, 'to bring those persons into place and power about his Majesty who had principally for that end contrived these mischiefs'.[1] While the correspondence of the Earl of Northumberland with the Earl of Leicester at the opening of Parliament showed that members were aware of how they and their friends could use their parliamentary activities to secure office, this does not mean that the opposition was motivated by self-interest alone.[2] Charles, with his attempts to come to terms with the opposition by taking them into his service, encouraged its members to hope for places. Rumours that he would be taken into the King's service gave Holles no reason to moderate his parliamentary behaviour.

iv.

Any discussion of Holles's religious views in the first session of the Long Parliament must take into account the context of the religious debates. The most significant factor affecting Parliament's discussion of religion and episcopacy was the Scots' demand for uniformity in religion published on 24 February 1641.[3] The Scots' demand, which involved the abolition of episcopacy, coloured the whole discussion thereafter,[4] for the English opposition leaders depended upon the Scots' friendship for the continuance of Parliament. They had been frank in their expression of dependence on the Scots' army. 'They confess that army is their own', wrote Baillie, 'and a most happy mean

1 An Account delivered to Mons. D'Harcourt [1643] printed in *State Papers, Collected by Edward, Earl of Clarendon . . .* , ed. R. Scrope and T. Monkhouse (3 vols., Oxford, 1769-1786), ii. 158; See also *Good English; or, Certain Reasons Pointing out the Safest Way of Settlement in this Kingdom,* 2 May 1648, TT E. 441. 10, p. 14: 'The aim of the English Presbyters, was the quelling of their opposites at Court, and supplanting them in their offices . . .'.

2 *Letters and Memorials,* pp. 663-6. Obligation did not win the Earl of Leicester to the King's service, nor, as Clarendon pointed out, did it win anyone; Clarendon, *History,* Macray, i. 479 n.1.

3 The Scots said that they drew up a paper to justify themselves against the public slander that they 'waxed cold' against episcopacy, which was printed without warrant; N.L. Scot., Wodrow MSS. Fol.xxii. n.f., Scots commissioners in London to Scots commissioners at Newcastle, 27 Feb. 1640 [1]. For a discussion of the Scots demands, see C.L. Hamilton, 'The basis of Scottish efforts to create a reformed church in England, 1640-41', *Church History* 30 (1961), 171-8; Stevenson, *Scottish Revolution,* ch. 7; M. Mendle, 'Politics and political thought 1640-1642', in C. Russell (ed.), *The Origins of the English Civil War* (London, 1973), pp. 234-6.

4 For example, *A Modest Advertisement Concerning the Present Controversie about Church Government,* (London, 1641), discussed the objection that unless England received the 'new discipline' there would be 'heart-burning' between them and the Scots; pp. 16-17.

for all their desires; that the dissolving of it were their ruin; that for the keeping of it on foot and all our bygone losses, what would they not do!' Nor did this dependence lessen as the months passed. In April Baillie said the Commons feared the King and Lords would keep the Scots no longer, 'and so they were undone'.[1] But not all members of Parliament were so dependent on the Scots that they were sensitive to their demands.

Holles was prominent in supporting the Scots' interests. Much of his committee and conference work concerned their treaty negotiations with the English commissioners, in which he showed himself a sympathetic friend to the Scots. Early in November 1640 he made his support plain, when he and Glyn pounced on one member, Sir William Widdrington, who referred to the Scots as rebels. 'Those words 'rebels' the King had sweetened' he declared, and both he and Glyn pressed for a satisfactory explanation from Widdrington or a punishment for his offence. Nicholas says Holles moved that the Scots be called 'Brethren'.[2] Holles also supported the Scots in their treaty negotiations, particularly in one of the most difficult points, their demand for the punishment of the King's advisers in the recent wars.[3] Charles claimed this would dishonour the pardon he had already granted, and he was 'very earnest that the act of oblivion may be general', but the Scots persisted in their demand, although in June the Earl of Bristol pointed out it was 'hard and cannot be honourable to the King to leave three-score men that have adhered to him, to prosecution when an Act of Oblivion is passed for all others that have been [in] arms'.[4] In the Commons John Selden argued that it was contrary to the law of nations to agree to the Scots' demand for the return of persons who had fled to England for protection, but Holles argued that the law of nations did not apply between England and Scotland, who were one kingdom.

---

1 *The Letters and Journals of Robert Baillie, A.M. 1637-1672*, ed. D. Laing (Bannatyne Club, 3 vols., Edinburgh, 1841-2), i. 280-1 (12 Dec. [1640]); p. 346 (7 May [1641]).

2 *D'Ewes*, ed. Notestein, p. 20 & n. 4 (Palmer); Transcript of extracts, made by Thomas Birch, from an MS of Sir Edward Nicholas concerning a History of the Long Parliament, BL, Add. 31954, f. 183.

3 The letters of the Scots commissioners reveal behind the scenes collusion with the opposition over the Scots' treaty demands. For example, when their English friends objected to the demand that the Estates should have a voice in the marriages of the King's children, the Scots declined to persist in this; N.L. Scot., Wodrow MSS. Fol. xxii, n.f., Scots commissioners in London to the committee at Newcastle, 12 Mar. 1641.

4 N.L. Scot., Wodrow MSS. Fol. lxxiii, f. 92v., Scots commissioners in London to the committee at Newcastle, 19 May 1641; Burroughes, BL, Harl. 457, ff. 95-95v.

> Mr Holles answered Mr Selden in much he said showing that several states were governed by several Princes and treason committed in one state was no offence against the other, but here was one King over both kingdoms . . .

In the final debate on the clause relating to the Act of Oblivion on 19 June, Pym and Holles succeeded in pressing through the Scots' demands.

> My Pym spoke very effectually for the affirmative, showing that the addition of this clause stood with the justice, safety, honour, and laws of both nations. Mr Denzil Holles also showed the same, very largely.[1]

Again, it was Pym and Holles together who manipulated the Commons in May so that the offer of the customs farmers to provide enough money to send the Scots home was shelved.[2] A final piece of evidence showing Holles's relationship to the Scots is in a letter of John, Lord Maitland, to his 'much honoured friend Mr Denzell Holles' in September 1641 when the treaty was concluded.[3] As the Scots lacked enough money to complete the disbanding of their army, Maitland asked Holles to make sure that the money was sent, lest the Scots be blamed for a breach of the treaty and so the English army kept afoot. The implication — that the interests of the opposition and the Scots were the same — would not have pleased Charles.

In supporting these demands of the Scots in the treaty the English leaders may have overlooked considerations of natural justice and honour, but they went against no deeply rooted convictions. The Scots' demand for uniformity in religion was a different matter, for it raised the embarrasingly difficult question of episcopacy, on which the majority of members held strong and diverse beliefs. The opposition leaders appreciated the divisiveness of the religious issue, and had tried to avoid it. The Commons had discussed general religious grievances, such as innovations in ceremonies, the recent canons and oaths, the church courts, the secular power of the clergy, but when the Londoners presented their petition for the abolition of episcopacy 'root and branch' in December 1640, the House deferred its consideration.[4] When

1 D'Ewes's diary, BL, Harl. 163, f. 228-9; C. Russell, *The Crisis of Parliaments* was with Holles and Marten *against* the addition of a qualifying clause, which would have made the English Parliament the final arbiter of delinquency; *ibid.*, f. 334v. *CJ*, ii. 181, has the tellers the other way around, and says Holles and Marten supported the addition of this clause, but lost the division.

2 D'Ewes's diary, BL, Harl. 163, f. 228-9; C. Russell, *The Crisis of Parliaments. English History 1509-1660*, (London, 1971), p. 335.

3 Bodl., Tanner 1xvi, f. 176, J. Maitland to D. Holles, 3 Sept. 1641. He also wrote to Mandeville; *ibid.*, f.174, 3 Sept. 1641.

4 *CJ*, ii. 49 (11 Dec. 1641).

the ministers presented a moderate petition in January 1641 and the House agreed to commit this, there was a demand for committing the London 'root and branch' petition likewise. The Commons' debate on the commitment of the 'root and branch' petition on 8 and 9 February developed into one on the merits of episcopacy, but although the petition was committed, the Commons reserved to themselves the vexed question of episcopacy. In these debates it was observed that strong feelings were aroused: 'more passion appeared now than heretofore'.[1] Shelving the question of episcopacy seemed the simplest solution, but the Scots' publication of their demand for uniformity in religion made this impossible.

Holles, like Pym and other members of the opposition leadership, had not made his religious views plain before the Scots published their demand for uniformity in religion. He had participated in the Commons' general campaign for the reform of the church and the punishment of offenders, carried the impeachment against the Archbishop to the Lords, and headed the committee preparing the charge against the Bishop of Ely. He was on various committees preparing bills for the reform of religion, such as those against pluralities, abolishing super-stition, for free passage of the gospel, and preparating for a fast.[2] On 19 November 1640 he and Sir John Wray moved that the communion table at St. Margaret's Westminster 'might be brought down into the church'.[3] But he had not made clear his attitude to episcopacy. He did not contribute to the initial debate on the 'root and branch' petition in December, although when the Commons decided on 2 February that they would refer the ministers' petition to a committee, he moved that they should refer some of the points from the 'root and branch' petition also. In the debates on 8 and 9 February on the committal of the 'root and branch' petition, 'Mr Holles spoke very pathetically in defence of the London petition and against bishops'. He wanted the committee to discuss the whole question of episcopacy, but the House

---

1 Ibid., 81; D'Ewes; ed. Notestein, pp. 335-43; p. 315 n.13 (Coke).

2 CJ, ii. 54 (18 Dec. 1640); 56 (22 Dec. 1640); 101, 84, 122.

3 D'Ewes, ed. Notestein, p. 46. It seems that Holles lodged with Aquila Weekes near the Gatehouse at this date, as he had done in 1638, and as the King's Sergeant thought he did in January 1642; Sheff. C.L., Wentworth MSS. 18 (17a), Holles to Wentworth, 'From my lodging at Mr Weekes his house near the Gatehouse in Westminster', 16 April 1638; and see also ch.4, p.65. Weekes paid poor rates to St. Margaret's Westminster, so Holles probably worshipped at St. Margaret's; West. P.L., St. Margaret's Westminster, Overseers' Accounts, 1641, 1642, E.155, 156. Despite the motion of Holles and Wray, the communion table cannot have been moved, for the Lower House refused to receive communion there on 22 Nov. 1640 because the table stood altarwise: 'Diurnal occurrences, or the Heads of Proceedings of the House of Parliament houlden at Westminster [7 November 1640-10 September 1641] written in a contemporary hand'; BL, Add. 6521, f.9.

would not permit this. He was among the six members added to the committee of twenty four to consider the petition.[1] However, although these actions placed Holles among the more radical in religion, they do not show he wanted the abolition of episcopacy root and branch, but simply that he was not averse to considering the question. He was opposed to the bishops' exercise of secular power. On 5 February he was a member of the Commons' delegation to the Lord Keeper requesting that when the commissions for the peace were renewed, all the clergy should be omitted. In the debate he had been more extreme than the majority, arguing that not only the clergy but also all the laymen who had taken the oath enjoined by the recent canons should be excluded from the commission because they were 'thereby a party with the bishops against the common law and are the bishops' bondmen'. The Lord Keeper parried the Commons' thrust, saying that on so weighty a matter the Commons must refer to the King.[2] On 2 March the Commons read a bill to disable the clergy from holding any lay employment, and at the second reading on 8 March 'Mr Holles would have had their voices taken away also in the Lords House'.[3] It was the addition of this clause removing the bishops' votes which later in May induced the Lords to reject the whole bill.

Thus the Scots stirred up a dangerously contentious issue by demanding uniformity in church government. Not only was the King incensed, which was hardly surprising, but their English friends were displeased: 'diverse of our true friends did think us too rash' wrote Baillie. The debate in the Commons on 27 February was long and vehement and D'Ewes considered the Scots' paper 'raised one of the greatest distempers in the House that ever I saw in it'. Baillie, with the blindness he occasionally showed to the English political situation, did not perceive how embarrassing their demand for religious uniformity was, and attributed the hostility to English national pride.[4] To justify themselves, the Scots drew up several more careful documents arguing that once the demand for religious uniformity between England and Scotland had been accepted, the sole issue was to decide which form of church

---

1 On 2 Feb. Digby attacked the authenticity of the ministers' petition, and Holles and Pym 'desired to uphold the credit of the petition'; *ibid.*, p.315 n.13 (Coke); *ibid.*, p.336 and n.15; p.337; 'Mr Holles said that the question must be put of the whole petition'; *CJ*, ii. 81.

2 *Ibid.*, 79; *D'Ewes*, ed. Notestein, p.329 n.9 (Peyton) 5 Feb. 1641; p.422, Holles's report, 1 Mar. 1641.

3 *CJ*, ii. 95, 99. Holles was named second to the committee for the bill. *D'Ewes*, ed. Notestein, p.452.

4 *Ibid.*, p. 418; Baillie, *Letters and Journals*, i. 306; 'though they loved not the bishops, yet, for the honour of their nation, they would keep them up rather than that we strangers should pull them down'.

government should be adopted: since the bishops had recently been found so dangerous and destructive, the Scots concluded that church government without them was obviously preferable.[1] They pressed the English commissioners to refer their demands for uniformity to Parliament, but the Earl of Bristol threatened that if their paper went to Parliament, so too would the King send reasons against it. The Earl of Essex saved the Parliament from having to choose between the Scots and the King by asking the Scots to defer their demand for the present, since the Parliament was deeply engaged in the prosecution of the Earl of Strafford and the religious issue 'may breed distractions among the two Houses'.[2] Privately, their 'best friends' told the Scots that should they insist on their demand being presented to Parliament at that time, 'it would make a division in Lower House and would lose at least *100* who were set to oppose the earl of Strafford and now are in a fair way for public weal'.[3] To these arguments the Scots yielded for the time, but their demand for uniformity could not be stifled for ever. On 14 April the House of Lords considered it and voted to agree with the English commissioners 'that alterations of things settled in a church and kingdom by law is dangerous' — a reply which amounted to a sharp refusal.[4] The Commons considered the Scots' demand on 17 May after Holles unsuccessfully attempted to divert the debate to other business. A newswriter commented 'the party which would have that of uniformity in doctrine and discipline with them to be first set abroad was too weak' and were unable to carry the House.[5] The defenders of the Anglican church were critical of the Scots' church government, and Hyde proposed that the Commons return the same sharp reply as the Lords commissioners — that any alteration to the religion established by law was dangerous. D'Ewes marvelled at this motion 'by which we

---

1 N.L. Scot., Wodrow MSS. Fol. xxii, Scots commissioners in London to committee at Newcastle, 6 Mar. 1641; Gardiner, *History of England*, ix. 299; *Arguments given in by the Commissioners of Scotland unto the Lords of the Treaty, persuading Conformity of Church Government*, (10 March), [May] 1641, TT E. 157.2. Gardiner says Henderson drew this up.

2 Burroughes, BL, Harl. 457, ff. 75, 78.

3 N.L. Scot., Wodrow MSS. Fol. xxii, n.f., Scots commissioners in London to the committee at Newcastle; See also Baillie, *Letters and Journals*, i. 314: 'any division among them till Strafford's process were closed, might prove unhappy'.

4 Private diary of a Bishop, BL, Harl. 6424, f.55. C.S.R. Russell, 'The authorship of the bishop's diary of the House of Lords in1641', *BIHR* 61 (1968), 229-36, has suggested that the author of the diary was John Warner.

5 Parliamentary diary of John Moore, BL, Harl. 477, f.74v.: 'Mr Holles stood up and told us of some evident danger . . . against this house by the papist, and desired that we would put off the debate'. D'Ewes's diary, BL, Harl. 163, f.191: Holles drew attention to 'the danger of the papists' design upon this house and kingdom'. Notes of proceedings in the House of Commons from 12-18 May 1641, BL, Sloane 3317, f.22.

should not only slight the Scottish nation and their affection but utterly lay aside, as it were, the work of reforming religion' while a majority in the House, being sympathetic both to the Scots alliance and reformation, agreed 'that a civil answer should be returned', and the Scots thanked for their aid. Even so, some objected, 'not thinking their too busy care worth thanks'.[1]

Meanwhile on 1 May the Commons had sent their bill debarring the clergy from secular employments, including their sitting in the House of Lords, to the Upper House. The Lords did not immediately consider it, but on 24 May after three days' debate they voted against excluding the bishops from Parliament.[2] On this vote much was to turn in the Commons, for had the Lords acquiesced in paring away the bishops' secular power, the moderate majority in the Commons might have been satisfied.[3] Dissatisfied, some moderates joined the extremists, and on 27 May 1641 Sir Edward Dering introduced a momentous bill in the Commons for the abolition of episcopacy 'root and branch'. 'Mere necessity' he said had driven him to propose that episcopacy should be abolished completely. In later years he was more specific in explaining his action, claiming that 'the chief end then was to expedite the progress of another bill against the secular jurisdiction of the bishops (at that very time) labouring in the House of Lords'.[4] Furthermore, although the motives for members' support of the bill are impossible to determine, Culpepper sneered at Hampden in one debate on the bishops for his 'reverence to the Scotch Commissioners'.[5]

Holles supported the second reading of Dering's bill:

others spoke directly against the government of the Church by

1 D'Ewes's diary, BL, Harl. 163, f.192; *CJ*, ii. 148; Notes of proceedings, BL, Sloane 3317, f.22.

2 D'Ewes's diary, BL, Harl. 163, f. 121; *LJ*, iv. 256; diary of a bishop, BL, Harl. 6424, ff. 70-70v. says that there were 25 voices against bishops sitting in Parliament, but that 30 or 40 temporal Lords favoured the bishops' sitting, as well as the 16 Bishops present who voted in support of their own cause.

3 Falkland said Hampden assured him that if the Lords would exclude the bishops from their House, nothing further would be asked; Clarendon, *History* (Bk. III, 152), Macray, i. 312.

4 D'Ewes's diary, BL, Harl. 163, f. 237; Moore's diary, BL, Harl. 477, f.103 v.; *A Collection of Speeches made by Sir Edward Dering in Matter of Religion*, 1642, TT E.197.1, p. 3. D. Hirst, 'The defection of Sir Edward Dering, 1640-1641', *Historical Journal* 15 (1972), 193-208, explains Dering's later abandonment of 'root and branch in terms of the pressure of opinion in his county. But in addition, Dering may, like Holles, have seen 'root and branch' as a means to a more moderate end.

5 Unsigned notes of Parliament, BL, Sloane 1467, ff.96v.-97. Hampden said that the bishops' votes in the Lords were not simply inconvenient, but inconsistent with their function.

bishops and especially Mr Denzell Holles, Mr John Pym and Mr William Cage who showed that our bishops had well near ruined all religion amongst us and were not willing to yield to any the least reformation and the said Mr Holles showed that whereas we had lately passed a bill to debar them from having voice in the Lords house and that the said bill was not likely in respect of that part of it to be assented unto there, some of the said Bishops have since boasted that they would now sit in the upper house in despite of the house of Commons . . .[1]

Although Holles spoke against episcopacy, it is interesting to note that the reasons he offered were based on the refusal of the bishops to yield to moderate reform, and there is a spark of anger in his reaction to the bishops' defiance. He and Sir John Evelyn were tellers of a majority in favour of a second reading of the 'root and branch' bill.[2]

How did the Commons' threat to abolish episcopacy 'root and branch' affect the Lords? On 8 June they reconsidered the bill relating to the secular employments of the bishops and clergy, and although they still refused to exclude the bishops from their seats in the Lords, they were prepared to pass the other clauses in the bill. At this point those Lords who supported 'root and branch' abolition 'professed that the former manner of voting the bill by branches was unparliamentary and illegal and therefore moved the House that they should vote all together, either to take the bill in wholly or cast all out . . . The whole bill was utterly cast out by many voices'.[3] Sir Symonds D'Ewes, and doubtless others of the Commons who wanted sweeping changes in the episcopate, regarded this as the work of providence, for whereas the Commons had done their work by halves before, now they would proceed wholeheartedly.[4] Immediately, after the Lords rejected the moderate bill debarring the clergy from secular employments, D'Ewes says that Pym, Hampden, Sir Robert Harley, Stephen Marshall and others met together,[5] and on 11 and 12 June in the House of Commons they pressed on with the bill for 'root and branch' abolition. Holles

---

1 D'Ewes's diary, BL, Harl. 163, f. 239.

2 Both the printed version of the Commons' Journal and the original manuscript in the Victoria Tower of the House of Lords have the tellers incorrectly noted; *CJ*, ii. 159, Manuscript, p. 701. D'Ewes's diary, BL, Harl. 163, f. 237v. says that Holles and Sir John Evelyn told the Ayes – 139, and Kirton and Charles Price the Noes – 108. Moore's diary, BL, Harl. 477, f. 107 says 'Sir John Evelyn and Mr Denzil Holles were tellers for the Ayes, and Mr Kirton and Mr Charles Price for the Noes'.

3 Diary of a bishop, BL, Harl. 6424, ff. 71-71v.

4 D'Ewes's diary, BL, Harl. 163, f.308v. Some observers thought this more than providential, and believed the 'root and branchers' deliberately staved off discussion of the more moderate bill in the hope of 'a greater party' if the Lords should not remove the Bishops from Parialment; notes of Parliament, BL, Sloane 1467, f.98.

5 D'Ewes's diary, BL, Harl. 163, f. 306v.

alleged 'that the bishops are anti-monarchical, that they have ever laboured to introduce a power above the king',[1] which is again more a political than a theological objection. In committee, the Commons abolished episcopacy and debated their scheme of church government, until the King's projected journey to Scotland diverted their thoughts.

These debates on episcopacy have been discussed at some length because of the importance of knowing whether the majority in the Commons really wanted to abolish episcopacy, 'root and branch', or whether they would have been satisfied with a moderate, reformed episcopacy. Shaw believed that by mid 1641 the time for moderate reform had passed, and that the votes were the first step in the Puritan programme, but this was not necessarily so. Some members were using the bill for political and tactical advantage. 'Root and branch' policies kept the friendship of the Scots and the opposition were later able to persuade them to enter the war on their side against the King. In 1643 Parliament was forced to accept presbyterianism as the price of the alliance, which Shaw believed diverted the direction of Parliament's puritanism. If my suggestion is correct, the price Parliament paid for the Scots' alliance was greater than Shaw believed, for the Commons were forced to abolish episcopacy altogether, whereas in 1640-1 they may have only wished for its reform.[2]

Holles's speeches and votes during 1641 show he supported the abolition of episcopacy 'root and branch', but Clarendon did not think he was a 'root and brancher'.

> In the House of Commons, though, of the chief leaders, Nathaniel Fiennes and young Sir H. Vane, and shortly after Mr Hampden . . . , were believed to be for 'root and branch' . . . yet Mr Pym was not of that mind, nor Mr Holles, nor any of the northern men, or those lawyers who drove on most furiously with them: all who were pleased with the government itself of the Church.[3]

Clearly, Holles did not like the bishops, but he may have been satisfied with a godly, primitive episcopate. His later comments suggest it was not so much the institution of episcopacy as the conduct of the recent incumbents which he disliked. In June 1642, when speaking in support

---

1 Sir John Holland's Diary of the Long Parliament, May-August 1641, Bodl., Rawlinson D.1099, 11 June 1641. Oliver St. John employed the same argument, that bishops were anti-monarchical, for claiming their authority of another right, and not from the King; D'Ewes's diary, BL Harl. 164, ff. 217-217v. (11 June 1641).

2 W.A. Shaw, *A History of the English Church During the Civil War and under the Commonwealth 1640-1660* (2 vols., London, 1900), i. ch. 1, esp. pp. 76-7, 97-9.

3 Clarendon, *History* (Bk.III, 147), Macray, i. 309.

52

of Parliament's duty to defend religion, he maintained Parliament must
ensure that religion

> be not supplanted and changed by superstitious innovations; the
> truth and substance of it eaten up with formality, vain pomp, and
> unnecessary ceremonies; the gross errors of popery and Arminianism
> imposed upon us, as the doctrine of our church; a way opened to all
> licentiousness;[1]

He supported the 'root and branch' bill in 1641 but he knew that the
Lords would never pass it, and even if they should, the King's support
of episcopacy was well known. Meanwhile, he and his allies had shown
themselves friends to the Scots, and had shifted the onus of offending
them to the Lords and the King. Holles's propensity for taking up an
extreme position, only to climb down afterwards, taken in conjunction
with his conduct in later years, all suggest he advocated 'root and branch'
for tactical reasons.

If Holles did not make his real attitude to episcopacy clear he was
explicit in his dislike of religious anarchy. On 5 June he informed the
House, on the information of John White of Dorchester, of 'mechanical
men that preached now up and down in the town some publicly and
some privately', and asked the Commons to prevent 'this great disorder
before it came to a higher pitch and degree'. The House responded
promptly. 'Divers spake to it', said D'Ewes, 'and all disliked the practice
of these men'. The offenders were summoned for the Speaker to give
them 'a sharp reprehension, and a general distaste of this House,
of their proceedings'.[2]

v.

In these first months of the Long Parliament Holles was an active
member of the opposition leadership. His attitude to the remedy
of grievances was as tough as that of any one else. He warned of the
'danger by giving of subsidies before relief of grievances'.[3] He wanted to
demonstrate to Charles that co-operation in their reforming programme
would bring rewards, and after the King assented to the bill for triennial
Parliaments, Holles told the Commons that they 'had great cause to
rejoice in this day's work', and therefore they might express some

1 *The Speech of Denzil Holles at the Lords Barr Wednesday the 15th of June
Upon the Impeachment of the Earles . . . and of the Lords*, 22 June 1642, TT
E.200.48, p.1.

2 D'Ewes's diary, BL, Harl. 163, f.276; Holland's diary, Bodl., Rawl. D.1099,
f.42v. refers to 'shopkeepers and others', *CJ*, ii. 170 (7 June 1641).

3 *D'Ewes*, ed. Notestein, p. 535 (13 Nov. 1640). This appended diary was
subsequently identified as that of Sir John Holland.

of their thanks by reading the bill for the Queen's jointure a second time: this was agreed to. In March some members wanted to spare the King the embarrassment of reading his answer to the Commons' petition of 1625 about the employment of recusants in his service, but 'Mr Holles desired that the articles presented to his Majesty in the first years of his reign, with the answer he made to the House of Commons, might be read'.[1] (In his answer Charles had undertaken to employ no Papists in his service.) Many of Holles's contributions to debate were practical ones designed to expedite business and to prevent the House enmeshing itself in a long and tedious debate.[2] He could cite the rules of the House to bridle an opponent, or to assist a friend.[3]

Holles also participated in the House's committee work. Keeler, who examined the membership of the key committees active in the first three months of the Long Parliament, found that a group of seventy odd men manned these committees, and she tentatively suggested that those who attended five or more played a significant role in the leadership of the House. In this group, two men attended eight committees. Holles was one of the seven men who attended seven committees.[4]

The management and reportage of conferences with the House of Lords has received less attention from historians than has committee membership. A good relationship with the Lords was essential for the Commons, who needed the co-operation and assent of the Lords if they were to achieve anything. Consequently they took care to choose suitable personnel to manage the formal discussions. There were basically three types of conferences: those requested by the Lords, to which the Commons sent reporters; those requested by the Commons, to which the Commons sent managers; and free conferences, to which the Commons sent members as both managers and reporters to argue out the issue with the Lords' representatives. Predictably, the

---

1 *Ibid.*, p. 365 (16 Feb. 1641); p. 494 n. 13.

2 For example, in April 1641 he directed the House from particular business to general, beseeching the members 'not to spend so much time about one man's safety when the safety of the whole kingdom was in question'; *CSPD 1640-1*, 12 April 1641.

3 For example, he was against Sir Thomas Roe speaking twice without the specific leave of the House; *D'Ewes*, ed. Notestein, p. 121 (8 Dec. 1640). He and Pym urged the orders of the House in defence of Cromwell who offended on 9 February 1641; *ibid.*, p. 340.

4 M.F. Keeler, ' "There are No Remedies for Many Things but by a Parliament" Some Opposition Committees, 1640', in W.A. Aiken and B.D. Henning (eds.), *Conflict in Stuart England* (London, 1960), pp. 129-46. These key committees were selected as those a committee of the Commons, chaired by Sir Jon Hotham, decided should be continued because they were concerned with essential business. Keeler excluded those concerned with particular persons and religious issues.

qualities demanded of those representing the Commons varied according to the type of conference. Reporters noted the Lords' arguments and brought these to the Commons: to such conferences 'we only carry our ears' Pym said. Reporting could be difficult, and on one occasion Holles and others were unable to report because, they said, 'the conference was very long and the report intricate and that therefore they could not yet make it ready'. Similarly, the manager of a conference requested by the Commons had to present his material clearly, and generally the conference managers had already served on a committee to prepare the arguments. The duties of a manager and reporter of a free conference were more exacting, for as they had to argue and persuade, they were not so strictly briefed: 'In a free conference', said Pym, 'we carry not only our ears but all must go prepared to maintain what we have delivered up upon the message to the Lords', and, added Sir Thomas Roe, 'any of them may speak and and none hath other limits than his own discretion'.[1] At the beginning of the first session of the Long Parliament the Houses held few conferences — only five in November 1640 — but the number increased to a steady fourteen for some months in 1641, and reached the maximum of forty-six in August 1641 on the eve of the King's journey to Scotland. The increasing frequency of conferences indicates the importance of maintaining communications between the two Houses in the growing uncertainty of the political situation. An analysis of those members appointed to manage and report conferences reveals Holles to have been one of the three men who attended a significantly greater number of conferences than any others.[2] His talents as an orator must have been generally recognised.[3]

1 *D'Ewes,* ed. Notestein, p. 543; D'Ewes's diary, BL, Harl. 163, f.63 (17 April 1641).

2 There were at least 170 conferences in the first session. Sixteen of these were attended by very large groups from the Commons, and have not been included in the following analysis. The remaining 154 conferences were managed and reported by a group of 88 members, but 52 of these members attended only once or twice. The bulk of conference work thus fell on a group of 36 members whose attendance ranged from 3 to 73 conferences. 28 members attended between 3 and 10 conferences, 12 members attended between 10 and 20, 10 members as follows attended between 25 and 36 conferences apiece:

26 St. John, Fiennes, Sir John Hotham	34 Sir Henry Vane senior
27 Hyde, Barrington	36 Glyn.
28 Sir Walter Erle	

Three men attended over a third of the total number of conferences: Pym 66, Holles 72 and Culpepper 73.

These figures are a general guide. Some members' attendance figures are unreliable because they were absent from the House at various times; Holles, for example, left Westminster ten days before the end of the session. He was also dissociated from the trial of Strafford, which was the subject of at least seventeen conferences. However, there were clearly different degrees of activity among members.

3 Collins, who rightly observed Holles's acceptability as an orator 'on the most

The duty of carrying messages to the House of Lords demanded some skill, but was mainly a ceremonial duty.[1] Holles carried at least seven messages to the Lords. The delivery of messages to outside bodies, such as the City, or to individuals, such as the Lord General or the Lord Keeper, was a more responsible task since the procedure was not formally defined, and the House relied on the judgment and discretion of its messenger. The House sent Holles on several messages to outside bodies during the first session.[2] Holles also performed other procedural tasks in the Commons, such as acting as a teller,[3] and he and the Treasurer escorted the Speaker to the House of Lords to hear the King's answer to the bills for the subsidy and triennial Parliaments. In March 1641 Holles was one of the joint committee of Lords and Commons who went to the City to borrow £120,000, and in May he was one of a committee of four who negotiated with the Customs Farmers.[4]

During the first session, Holles was in the vanguard of the opposition. His impetuous nature may have carried him further than, on reflection, he would have wished, but like the other opposition leaders, he was animated by very real fears of the King's intentions. There was no guarantee that the King had accepted the Long Parliament's work of reform, and in his projected journey to Scotland the opposition sensed danger. Their previous security against a premature dissolution had depended upon the friendly co-operation of the Scots, but if the King should win the Scots as friends, he would have an armed force to back his will. Despite strenuous efforts to replace evil counsellors with 'good men' the Parliamentarians were no nearer their objective. Yet Holles was not irrevocably committed to opposition. His support of the Scots and his generally tough attitude to the King were necessary if he were to be vindicated for his role in 1629 and secure for the future. He depended on the House of Commons for his power and influence, but as he had seen that men who were formidable in

important occasions' is nevertheless mistaken in dissociating Holles from the proceedings against the bishops; Collins, *Historical Collections*, p. 115.

1 On 1 February 1641 ten members accompanied the messenger, but D'Ewes observed 'I never saw before but the number ordinarily of thirty or more went'; *D'Ewes*, ed. Notestein, p. 308.

2· The House sent Holles and Hampden to thank the Earl of Essex and the Admiral on 9 June 1641; *CJ*, ii. 172. On 7 July the House sent him with Strode to the Earl of Essex; *ibid.*, 201. On 5 February 1641 Holles and three others went to the Lord Keeper and the Chancellor of the Duchy to request that all clergy might be omitted from the commission of the peace, and Holles later reminded the House of the Lord Keeper's reply; *ibid.*, 79; *D'Ewes*, ed. Notestein, p. 422 (1 Mar. 1641).

3 He acted as teller six times in the first session.

4 *CJ*, ii. 113, 161.

Parliament could be taken into the King's service, so he had no incentive to moderate his behaviour. A contemporary ballad mocked his ulterior motive:

> Farewell Denzil Holles, with hey, with hey;
> Farewell Denzil Holles, with hoe.
> Twas his ambition or his need,
> Not his religion did the deed,
> With hey trolly, lolly, loe.[1]

---

[1] London's Farewell to Parliament, quoted in J. Forster, *Arrest of the Five Members by Charles the First* (London, 1860), p. 199.

4

THE ATTEMPTED ARREST OF THE FIVE MEMBERS, AND HOLLES'S COMMITMENT TO PARLIAMENT, OCTOBER 1641 – AUGUST 1642

The truth is, it cannot be expressed how great a change there appeared to be in the countenance and minds of all sorts of people, in town and country, upon these late proceedings of the King.[1]

Parliament adjourned on 9 September 1641, full of fears after the King had gone to Scotland. The Commons named a committee to sit during the recess, but Holles was not a member, for he had been granted leave on 31 August 'to go into the country upon his own earnest motion for the preservation of his health'. Although it is surprising that he should have withdrawn from Westminster at such a crucial time, contemporaries made no comment which might explain this action. [2] Holles was back at Westminster for the second session in October. He was, although he did not know it, at the turning of the ways.

In the House of Commons tempers were sharper. The opposition leaders were in a weaker position since their fears of Charles remained, but the justification for making further demands of him was less obvious. The outbreak of the rebellion in Ireland assisted Pym and his allies, since it revived the Parliamentarians' fears and strengthened their case for controlling the appointment of officers. The King's attempt to bring the Parliament to heel by accusing five of the Commons and one of the Lords of treason, and attempting unsuccessfully to arrest the five Commoners, was a complete disaster, and thereafter the two sides polarised and prepared for war.

A party emerged in the Commons to support the King.[3] Moderate men, such as Hyde, favoured a policy of constitutional royalism. He was unwilling to see Parliament divided between supporters of the King and his enemies, as Holles too would later oppose those whom he thought to be the King's enemies in Parliament. Hyde sought a settlement in the second session by resisting further changes, but the opposition leaders were so mistrustful of the King that a settlement without further security seemed impossible.

Gardiner believed that the division in the House of Commons was

---

1 Clarendon, *History* (Bk.IV, 191), Macray, i. 505.
2 D'Ewes's diary, BL, Harl. 164, f.81v.; *CJ*, ii. 286-9.
3 For a discussion, see B. Wormald, *Clarendon, Politics, Historiography and Religion 1640-1660* (Cambridge, 1964).

based on ecclesiastical differences. From an attack on the Book of Common Prayer in September 1641 he dates the formation of parties.[1] But the division cannot be so simply explained, for although religion contributed, the two 'parties' cannot be defined in religious terms alone. The situation was still fluid, and new events precipitated new alliances. Pym's supporters on the ecclesiastical issue did not necessarily follow him on constitutional issues: D'Ewes, for example, was among the most fervent supporters of ecclesiastical reform, but cold-hearted towards Pym's political programme.[2] Furthermore, Pym and his supporters were not necessarily committed to the abolition of episcopacy root and branch.

The immediate division in the Long Parliament relates much more to the political differences which centred on the appointment and control of the great officers of state. On his visit to Scotland Charles granted the Scots' request to make no appointments of officers without the approval of his Parliament. The significance of this was not lost on the opposition at Westminster, who developed a similar demand after the recess, confident that the King would consent. Others, known as constitutional royalists, believed that this demand trenched too far upon the King's prerogative. They urged the King to take his stand upon the law, and to grant nothing but that which by law he was obliged to grant.[3]

In addition to differences over religion and political appointments, members were divided in their attitudes to popular disturbances. Dr. Manning argues that future Royalists were not so much alarmed at the petitions against episcopacy as they were at the mobs which presented them, and at the prospect of social disorder.[4] The difference was that although Pym and his supporters did not intend any social dislocation by countenancing the tumults, they were prepared to use them for their own purposes. As Barnardiston wrote later in 1642,

> though the Parliament do utterly dislike the rude and barbarous carriage and behaviour of the tumultuous people, yet hold it fit to forbear to trouble and execute justice upon them until the kingdom be settled and at quiet again, lest it make the cure the more dangerous.[5]

1 Gardiner, *History of England*, x. 15.

2 For example, he left the House when the debate on the Grand Remonstrance began; *D'Ewes*, ed. Coates, p. 185.

3 Gardiner, *History of England*, x. 19-20; Stevenson, *Scottish Revolution*, pp. 235-6. At the Grocers' Hall committee in January 1642 it was resolved that 'such prime counsellors may be made as both houses of Parliament shall advise...' Portland Deposit, BL Loan 29/46, Bundle 8. See Wormald, *Clarendon*, p. 4 ff.

4 B. Manning, 'The nobles, the people and the constitution', *Past & Present* 9 (1956), 60-1.

5 Bodl., Tanner 63, f. 146, Barnardiston to Will Castleton, 1 Sept. 1642.

As the Commons polarised into parties, Holles remained with the opposition. He wanted further security for Parliament, especially by some parliamentary control over the King's advisers.

The question of the King's advisers was crucial in the second session. The attack on 'evil counsellors' was revived on 28 October 1641 when Robert Goodwin moved that if they did not control the King's counsellors 'all we had done this Parliament would come to nothing'; Strode seconded this view 'with great violence, saying all we had done this Parliament was nothing unless we had a negative voice in the placing of the great officers of the King and of his counsellors'. On 7 November Pym, using the Irish emergency as justification, argued that any assistance voted to the King should be subject to the proviso that 'unless the King would remove his evil counsellors and take such counsellors as might be approved by Parliament we should account ourselves absolved from this engagement'.[1] Holles's comments were less radical than Pym's, for he merely reiterated the need for good counsellors, and attempted to revive the process of impeachment against evil counsellors. In the debate on the Grand Remonstrance he said

> All the necessary truth must be told. If kings are misled by their counsellors, we may, we must, tell him of it. . . . we only beseech the King to choose good counsellors, for against such this house will never except.[2]

When the debate on Ireland resumed on 29 December, Strode and others named the Earl of Bristol as an evil counsellor,

> and Mr Denzil Holles did vehemently press the same and added further that the Lord Digby his son as he understood by common fame, had said openly at one time in the Lords house that the House of Commons had entrenched upon the privileges of the Lords House and upon the liberties of the subject and at another time (viz. yesternight) that this was no free Parliament, both which he said were the most dangerous and pernicious speeches that ever were spoken by a subject, and so he desired we might desire to have the said Earl of Bristol removed from the King's Council and Court; and that we might desire justice of the Lords against the said Lord Digby.[3]

However, as Sir John Holland pointed out, since the King would meet these demands for justice with a request for proofs, the House would do better to admit the King's right to choose his own counsellors, but to ask him for the present to choose only those in whom Parliament could trust. The House, doubtless perceiving the futility of the lengthy process of impeachment involved in Holles's proposal, committed the

1   *D'Ewes*, ed. Coates, pp. 44-5; p. 94.

2   Verney, *Notes*, pp. 124-5.

3   *D'Ewes*, ed. Coates, p. 361.

issue of the Earl, and asked the Lords to do them right if indeed Digby had spoken such words.[1] Thus the real attack on the King's freedom of choosing his counsellors was not made by Holles naming the Earl of Bristol, but by Pym, who proposed that the Commons' assistance against the Irish revolt should be conditional upon the King's removal of his evil counsellors. Opposition in the House persuaded Pym to alter his statement to one which, in the event, was even more radical, that if the King would not remove his evil counsellors, then 'we should take such a course for the securing of Ireland as might likewise secure ourselves'.[2] To this the Commons agreed, but the Lords refused to consent.[3]

Holles shared the opposition's view that Parliament should appeal to the nation against the King. From his speech on the publication of Grand Remonstrance, it is clear he did not intend it for the King's eyes alone: 'The kingdom consists of three sorts of men, the bad, the good, and the indifferent, and these we hope to satisfy. They can turn the scales'.[4] He was not alarmed, as were other M.P.s, at the public disturbances towards the end of December. On 28 December the Lords suggested Parliament should declare against the tumults but this the opposition leaders in the Commons refused. 'The greater part of the house', D'Ewes reported, 'thought it unseasonable to make any such declaration at this time to discontent the citizens of London, our surest friends'. Holles carried to the Lords the Commons' resolution that, while they would join in suppressing any tumults which threatened the safety or privileges of Parliament, they refused to declare against tumults altogether.[5]

Holles's attitude to episcopacy is no clearer in this period than earlier. He was still opposed to the secular power of the clergy. In October he seconded a motion by Cornelius Holland that the House should proceed on a bill 'to prevent the intermeddling of persons in holy orders with secular affairs', and he pressed Commons to name the crime of the bishops in their impeachment and call it treason. 'Mr Denzil Holles made a long speech to move us to give a name to our impeachment of the 13 Bishops and call it treason. He showed how they had been enemies to Parliaments and to the liberty'.[6] But although the House wanted to reduce the secular power of the clergy, they were not yet prepared to accuse the bishops of treason, and simply asked the Lords

1   *Ibid.*, 362 n.15 (speech of Sir John Holland); *CJ*, ii. 361.
2   *D'Ewes*, ed. Coates, pp. 94,99 (6 Nov. 1641); 104   (8 Nov. 1641)
3   *CJ*, ii. 307; *L.J.*, iv. 434; *D'Ewes*, ed. Coates, p. 125.
4   Verney, *Notes*, p. 124.
5   *CJ*, ii. 359; *D'Ewes*, ed. Coates, p. 356 & n.4, p. 358.
6   *Ibid.*, p. 30 (23 Oct. 1641); *ibid.*, p. 39 (26 Oct. 1641).

to sequester them from sitting.[1] This the Lords refused, so the bishops continued to sit until the tumults outside Westminster late in December prevented them from attending, whereupon, under the leadership of John Williams, they protested at the validity of the Lords' proceedings in their absence.[2] Since this attacked the very being of the Parliament — for the bishops could invalidate all proceedings by simply absenting themselves — the commons voted on 30 December that they were guilty of treason. Holles declared their petition treacherous, for it increased the divisions between Lords and Commons, under cover of which the Romish faction flourished. Besides it might cause violence in the City, where the citizens 'are altogether set against the bishops'.[3]

During this period Holles was clearly identified with Pym and the opposition, and it is possible to see their partnership in the debates. For example, Holles moved that the Scots' offer to assist the Parliament of England in reducing the Irish rebels be accepted. After debate the House agreed and named a committee, from which Pym reported the instructions to go to Scotland. When several members objected to the Scots being paid for their assistance, Holles and others suggested 'that at least we might offer to pay the Scots', so Pym's clause concerning payment remained unaltered.[4]

The debates in the House in the second session were increasingly acrimonious, but Holles was no peacemaker, and actively forwarded opposition business. On 23 October when Hyde opposed the consideration of the bill to reduce the secular power of the clergy, 'by reason of the thinness of the house', Holles smartly replied that just because other men neglected their duties, there was no reason why the business of the commonwealth should perish for want of their company.[5] He launched aggressive attacks against those who threatened opposition plans. In a debate in December on a bill to settle the militia and to name officers for places, Thomas Coke cited a troublesome precedent from a previous Parliament which condemned a member as guilty of high treason for introducing a bill against the King's prerogative. After it was established that Coke had cited the precedent incorrectly, Holles wanted him examined to see if he had read or remembered the whole precedent. When Chillingworth, a minister, was in trouble for remarks

1 *CJ*, ii. 362-3; *D'Ewes*, ed. Coates, pp. 40, 41 (27 Oct. 1641).

2 *LJ*, iv. 496-7 (30 Dec. 1641).

3 *Denzil Holles, Esquire, His worthy and learned Speech in Parliament, on Thursay the Thirteenth of December 1641*, 1641, TT E. 199.48, pp. 2, 4.

4 *D'Ewes*, ed. Coates, pp. 84-5 & n.25 (4 Nov. 1641); p. 93 (5 Nov. 1641); pp. 93-4.

5 *Ibid.*, p. 30 n.7 (MSS. diurnal).

supporting Palmer's right to protest against the printing of the Grand Remonstrance, it was on Holles's motion that he was examined to discover which members of Parliament he had conversed with. The opposition leaders were furious with Chillingworth, whose remarks implied that there were parties in the House and he was sent to the Tower. Towards the Lords, who were proving uncooperative over the Commons' plans for the relief of Ireland, Holles advocated firmness: the Commons should tell them 'that if the kingdom of Ireland were lost, it should be in their default, we having done what in us lay'. The Commons agreed and sent Holles with the message to the Lords. A later conference on the subject, D'Ewes noted (in cipher), Holles managed 'a little *too sharply* '.[1]

Thus from October 1641 to January 1642 Holles continued in his earlier course of opposition. He showed no sympathy for the ideas of the constitutional Royalists, but worked closely with Pym and the other opposition leaders.

ii.

By November 1641 the Commons were obviously divided. The length and heat of the debate on the Grand Remonstrance showed the strength of the party supporting the King. But although the King was gaining support in the House of Commons, outside Parliament he suffered several reverses. His hopes of support in the City of London vanished when Pym's supporters secured a majority at the elections for the Common Council in December.[2] Charles sought other means for his security, which aroused fears of armed force. He tried to control the Tower of London by appointing the unpopular Lunsford as governor. On 31 December the Commons sent a deputation to Charles requesting a guard for their security against the tumults. Holles spoke to the King of their danger from the malignant party coming to Parliament, but Charles refused their request, assuring them 'on the word of a King, that the security of all, and every one of you from violence is, and shall ever be as much our care as the preservation of us and our children'.[3] It was, in the circumstances, an unfortunate message: by the time the Commons received it, on 3 January, Charles had decided to impeach five of their members of treason and on the following day he attempted to seize them by armed force.

1 *Ibid.*, pp. 244-8, especially p. 247n.24 (Holland's diary); pp, 232-4; p. 315 (18 Dec.1641); p. 332 (21 Dec. 1641) (words *underlined* in cipher); *(CJ*, ii. 349; *LJ*, iv. 482, 485-6.
2 V. Pearl, *London and the Outbreak of the Puritan Revolution, City Government and National Politics, 1625-43* (Oxford, 1964), pp. 132-9.
3 Rushworth, *Historical Collections*, iv. 471-2.

On 3 January 1642, the Attorney General Sir Edward Herbert appeared in the House of Lords and charged Pym, Hampden, Holles, Haselrig and Strode and Kimbolton with high treason. The chief of the seven articles were that they had attempted to subvert the law and fundamental government, alienated the people from the King, and invited a foreign power to invade.[1] The Attorney General asked the Lords to commit the members but they refused. Before the information officially reached the Commons,

> the whole house, or at least the most of us, were much amazed with Mr Pym's information who showed us that his trunks, his study, and his chamber, as also the trunks, study, and chamber of Mr Denzil Holles were sealed up by some sent from his Majesty.[2]

Privately, the members had heard of Herbert's accusation against the five in the House of Lords, but the first official information came from a Sergeant-at-Arms who asked for the delivery of five members, read their names, and accused them of treason. The House refused to deliver their members but ordered them to attend from day to day.[3]

On Tuesday 4 January the five members attended the Commons and Pym informed the House of the articles which had been preferred against them. All protested their innocence.[4] When news was given of a great gathering of armed men around Whitehall, Pym moved that they inform the Lord Mayor and Common Council of Parliament's danger. The Commons then took the unusual step of adjourning until 1 p.m.[5] At their reassembly they learnt, in answer to their enquiries from the Inns of Court, that these societies would be neutral; they would defend Parliament as well as the King's person so the M.P.s had nothing to fear from that quarter. The unofficial news from Whitehall was less reassur-

1 Gardiner, *Documents*, pp. 236-7.

2 *D'Ewes*, ed. Coates, p. 377. The following account of the attempted arrest is based on Coates's edition of D'Ewes which collates the additional detail in unpublished manuscript accounts. Forster, *Arrest of the Five Members*, is unreliable.

3 *CJ*, ii. 367; *D'Ewes*, ed. Coates, p. 378 n.22 (Peyton).

4 *D'Ewes*, ed. Coates, p. 379. Various speeches were printed as those of the accused members, but Gardiner had 'no doubt that they are all forgeries'; *History of England*, x. 135 n.2. However, although the speech of Holles, *Master Holles his Speech in Parliament, Concerning the Articles of high Treason*, 5 Jan. 1641 [2], TT E.199.55, cannot have been spoken on Wednesday 5 January — for the five members did not appear on that day — there is no internal evidence, as there is in the speech of Pym's, which precludes its being spoken at this point in the proceedings on Tuesday the 4th. There are various touches which give the speech an authentic ring: an equation between a true Christian and a legal subject, an appeal to the House to consider his former record and insistence upon evil counsellors. Conversely, there is nothing in the speech contrary to Holles's known beliefs.

5 *D'Ewes*, ed. Coates, pp. 279-80. The House had sat without a mid-day recess during the second session.

ing: Nathaniel Fiennes reported that the officers told him they were simply commanded to obey Sir William Fleming in all things. The accused members were noted as present. Then, after 3 p.m., came the news 'that his Majesty was coming from Whitehall to Westminster with a great company of armed men'.[1]

It was news to the five members that the King was actually on his way, but as they had received three warnings that he would come, they were not unprepared. The House gave them liberty to stay or withdraw as they saw fit, and Pym, Hampden, Holles and Haselrig left speedily. Strode 'being a young man and unmarried' took some persuading, for he vowed he would seal his innocence with his blood, but Sir Walter Erle 'his entire friend' pulled him out by the cloak just as the first of the King's men marched into Westminster Hall.[2]

Charles, attended by the Elector Palatine, came into the House of Commons a little after three o'clock.[3] There ensued a memorable scene, described with a breathtaking sense of drama by D'Ewes, as Charles took the Speaker's chair and asked for Pym, 'and when there followed a general silence that nobody would answer him he then asked for Mr. Holles whether he were present and when nobody answered him he pressed the Speaker to tell him'.[4] Kneeling, the Speaker declared that 'he could neither see nor speak but by command of the house' and so Charles, declaring his eyes were as good as another's, searched the rows of bare-headed members. Finding that 'all the birds' had flown, he left the House 'in a more discontented and angry passion than he

1 *Ibid.*, pp. 380-1; *CJ*, ii. 368; W.R. Prest, *The Inns of Court Under Elizabeth I and the Early Stuarts 1590-1640* (London, 1972), pp. 232-7.

2 *D'Ewes*, ed. Coates, p. 384 & n. 21.

3 The question of timing is interesting. D'Ewes says that the House resumed between one and two o'clock, that they had notice of the King's coming 'about 3 of the clock' and that the members fled only just in time to escape; *ibid.*, pp. 380-1. This agrees with La Ferté who says that his servant gave the members a quarter of an hour's warning; *ibid.*, p. 383 n. 19. Peyton gives a different time schedule. He says that 'this day about 2 o'clock the King came from Whitehall', the members were given leave to withdraw, 'and the King coming half an hour after was disappointed of his purpose'; *ibid.*, p. 382 n. 18. Clarendon also suggests that the members withdrew half an hour before the King arrived; Clarendon, *History* (Bk.IV, 152), Macray, i. 384. However, if the King were actually on his way when the news was brought to the House, and some time was required for the Commons to vote the five members leave to absent themselves, then it was unlikely they had half an hour to spare, and the tighter timing of D'Ewes seems more probable. Sir Arthur Haselrig's account to the Parliament in 1659 confirms this. He says that the debate on the members' presence was shortened, and that he and Hampden withdrew: 'Away we went. The King immediately came in, and was in the House before we got to the water'; *Diary of Thomas Burton . . . 1656 to 1659*, ed. J.T. Rutt (4 vols., London, 1828), iii. 92.

4 *D'Ewes*, ed. Coates, p. 381. Peyton says that Charles asked 'if Mr Holles were there, and named no others but him'; *ibid.*, p. 382 n.18.

came in'. The doors were shut, and the members adjourned immediately until 1 p.m. the following day.[1]

As Charles left he told the Commons that he expected them to hand the members to him, 'otherwise I must take my own course to find them'. Charles meant what he said. On leaving Westminster he 'gave orders to the Sergeant-at-Arms to find out and attach them'. Sergeant Dendy, the Commons later learnt, went to Mr Weekes's house at the Gatehouse, where Holles had lodged in the past, and demanded that Holles be handed to him 'for he is a traitor. How dares Mr Weeks lodge a traitor in his house'.[2] An account in the commonplace book of a London turner may refer to the same incident:

> there went up some men to Mr Holles's study, thinking to have had them [him?] with two or three more, and there to have destroyed them . . . And that night also there was observed two men that dogged Mr Pym, and another that went with him. . .[3]

On 6 January Sergeant Dendy 'went into London to seek the accused men to apprehend them, where he was much abused by the worse sort of people'.[4]

Contemporaries knew that the members were in the City with friends; Baxter says they were 'together at an inner house in Red Lion Court in Watling Street, near Bread St. London'.[5] The City would not have surrendered the members without a struggle: 'Tis believed the City is resolved to protect them'.[6] Although Digby offered to seize them, 'and bring them away alive or leave them dead in the place', Charles did not care for such an attempt.[7] The King was wise, for it is probable that civil war would have broken out in the City streets had he attempted violence. On the night of 6 January when there was an alarm in the City, 'in the dead time of the night there was great bouncing at every man's door to be up in their arms presently. . . And women and children did then arise, and fear and trembling entered on all'.[8]

1   *Ibid.*, p. 381-2; Rushworth, *Historical Collections*, iv. 477-8; *CJ*, ii. 368.

2   Rushworth, *Historical Collections*, iv. 478; *CSPD 1641-43*, p. 242; *CJ*, ii. 386 (17 Jan. 1642.) For Holles's residence at Weekes's house see above, p. 46 n.3

3   Nehemiah Wallington, *Historical Notices of Events Occuring chiefly in the Reign of Charles I*, ed. R. Webb (2 vols., London, 1869), i. 279-80.

4   *CSPD 1641-43*, p. 241.

5   Baxter, *Reliquiae Baxterianae*, p. 28. Clarendon says 'it was well known that they were altogether in a house in the city, without any fear of their security'; *History* (Bk. IV, 155), Macray, i. 485.

6   *CSPD 1641-43*, p. 245 (7 Jan. 1642).

7   Clarendon, *History* (Bk.IV, 155), Macray, i. 485.

8   Wallington, *Historical Notices*, i. 289.

The public reaction to the attempted arrest could not have been more hostile, and Charles was regarded as a breaker of his word, one who would try to destroy Parliament by force. Legal niceties meant little in this context: that he had entered the House of Commons with armed men waiting outside was enough. The five members had done nothing to prevent the King's blunder. In fact, they gave Charles every reason to believe that he would find them all sitting in their places. The five attended on Tuesday the 4th, although they had been warned the night before that Charles would come. At the dinner recess they received a second warning, but they still returned to the House. One observer says that the King set out 'upon notice that the 5 persons were in the house'.[1] Only when they heard the King was actually on his way did their organisation swing into action; the Commons resolved that they might go or stay as they thought fit. The speed with which this was done suggests definite pre-arrangement,[2] which Peyton's account confirms: 'although the House of Commons in the generality knew nothing of the King's coming and the suddenness of it amazed most of them, yet among some few it was known which caused a motion to be made'.[3] As later writer observed, 'the King in this surprising visit was no doubt most welcome to his greatest enemies, because they knew their advantage in it'.[4] D'Ewes thought Providence alone had averted the disaster, but careful planning had played a part.

When the Commons reassembled on 5 January, there are again signs of preparation. They appointed a committee to draw up a declaration about the events of the previous day, which returned in a quarter of an hour with a long declaration 'ready penned', announcing that as the members were no longer safe at Westminster, they would adjourn as a committee to sit at Guildhall.[5] After two days' proceedings at Guildhall and the Grocers' Hall, the committee called for the five members to attend, but they probably did not attend until the 10th.[6] A triumphant

1 Bodl., Tanner 1xvi, f.234, J. Berners to J. Hobart, 10 Jan. 1642.

2 See above p.64 n. 3 concerning timing. The Commons were rarely able to cope with the unexpected in a quick, efficient manner. After the King's visit, the House could do nothing but adjourn: 'The House not being versed in such rare matters as the day afforded, rose presently'; D'Ewes, ed. Coates, p. 382 n. 18 (Peyton). Clarendon also comments that many members did not appear surprised; Clarendon, History (Bk.IV, 154), Macray, i. 484.

3 D'Ewes, ed. Coates, p. 382 n.18 (Peyton).

4 [W. Kennet], A Complete History of England (vol. iii. 2nd edn. London, 1719), p. 123.

5 D'Ewes, ed. Coates, p. 385. Clarendon says that although none of the accused members appeared on 5 Jan. 'they had friends enough, who [were] well enough instructed'; Clarendon, History (Bk.IV, 158), Macray, i. 486. The decision to adjourn to the City was carried after a division; CJ, ii. 368.

6 D'Ewes, ed. Coates, p. 396. n.12; ibid., p. 399 n.9.

return to Westminster was planned for the 11th, at which prospect Charles was so alarmed that he fled from London with his family, not to return until his trial in 1649. At one o'clock on the afternoon of the 11th, the accused members and the members of the committee embarked at the Three Cranes, 'attended with thirty or forty long-Boats with Guns, Flags, &c' and returned to Westminster.[1] Holles was at the summit of his career as a popular victim of arbitrary government.

Why did Charles choose these five men? There are two kinds of explanation which are not altogether compatible. The first is either that Charles had seen or heard of treasonable correspondence with the Scots from the previous year, and these were the men involved,[2] or that he believed they were about to impeach the Queen.[3] The second explanation is that the men were singled out for their pre-eminence in the House of Commons.[4] Clarendon believed that Digby chose them and, disliking Digby, contended that he chose the wrong men.[5] Strode and Haselrig, Clarendon believed, lacked the influence to do much mischief, so their reputations were enhanced by the King's action and Kimbolton was one 'against whom less could be said than against many others, and who was more generally beloved'. But as for Pym, Hampden and Holles, Clarendon rightly recognized that they 'had indeed a great influence'.[6]

iii

Clarendon considered that the attempted arrest of the five members was a complete disaster, as indeed it was for him personally and for the constitutional Royalists. After the attempt, all the members accused became fiercer than before: Pym 'never entertained thoughts of moderation', Manchester was made desperate, Hampden's 'nature and carriage

1 Rushworth, *Historical Collections*, iv. 484.

2 This view is held by Forster, *Arrest of the Five Members*, p. 12. G.N.T. Grenville (Lord Nugent), *Some Memorials of John Hampden, his Party and his Times* (2 vols., London, 1832), ii. 125 states a variant of this, that Charles was 'relying on information, more or less authentic, which he had received in Scotland, respecting the English leaders, and assuming as probable what does not appear to have existed, some correspondence between them and Richelieu'.

3 *HMC Montague MSS.*, p. 141.

4 Gardiner, *History of England*, x. 129. The five were the main offenders in the attempt to reduce the royal authority to a cipher. J.H. Hexter, *The Reign of King Pym* (Harvard, 1941), p. 9 implies a similar view.

5 Digby may have resented the attack Holles had made upon him on 29 Dec. 1641. See part i of this chapter.

6 Clarendon, *History* (Bk.IV, 154, 192), Macray, i. 484, 506. Russell, *Crisis of Parliaments*, p. 338 suggests that the selection of Strode and Holles probably reflected Charles's view of a long-standing conspiracy.

seeming much fiercer than it did before'.[1] The effect upon Holles of
the attempted arrest is of particular interest because before the year
was out he was among the leaders of a party in the Commons which
sought peace with the King.

Immediately after the attempt, Holles's attitude toward the King
was unconciliatory. He opposed the suggestion that the Houses should
desire the King to return until he and his fellows were cleared of the
charge of high treason. When a letter did arrive from the King at the
end of January concerning the five members, a letter D'Ewes considered
was *'very graciously penned'*, Holles, Strode and others *'spoke vehemently against it'*.[2] Holles continued to take a tough line with the House
of Lords. On 25 January the Duke of Richmond proposed the Lords
should adjourn for six months. The Lords reprimanded Richmond,
but after twenty peers protested against the inadequacy of the punishment, Sir John Clotworthy brought these proceedings to the Commons'
notice on 27 January. A great attack was launched on the Duke. Pym
said they should ask the Lords to 'desire he may be removed from the
King and that his person may be restrained and that he may be banished
the kingdom'.[3] Some objected that to take notice of proceedings in
the House of Lords was contrary to their privilege, but Holles disposed
of this speedily: he who 'shall not freely deliver his voice here is not fit
to sit within these walls, and I am sure will never enter into the kingdom of heaven'. The Lords' privileges weighed lightly with him against
the many years 'we have groaned under ill counsels'.[4] After a lengthy
debate the House divided on whether they had sufficient cause to accuse
the Duke of Richmond as one of the malignant party and 'an ill counsellor': Holles and Stapleton were tellers of the majority against
Richmond, and on 29 January Glyn laid the information against
Richmond before the Lords. Holles, speaking after him, declared that
it was the Commons' duty 'to prevent the evils that hang over our
heads'. He left the matter with their Lordships: the Commons, he
said, 'see the stone that hit them, but could not discover the arm that
threw it, they say they wash their hands of the ill consequences of
these things, and lay it at their Lordships doors'.[5] However, the Lords
refused to proceed any further against Richmond.

1 Clarendon *History*, (Bk.VII, 413; Bk. VI, 408; Bk. VII, 84), Macray, iii. 323,
ii. 546, iii. 63.
2 D'Ewes's diary, BL, Harl. 162, f. 322v. (13 Jan. 1641); *ibid.*, f. 322v. (29
Jan. 1642), words *underlined* in cipher.
3 Notes of the Long Parliament by Sir Framlingham Gawdy, BL, Add. 14827,
ff. 17v.-18. Holles spoke in support of Pym's proposals; *ibid.*, f. 18.
4 Parliamentary diary of John Moore, BL, Harl. 480, f. 1002.
5 *CJ*, ii. 400, Holles & Stapleton — 223; Culpepper & H. Price — 123; D'Ewes's

Furthermore, Holles justified the petition of the poor tradesmen presented on 31 January 1642, which also touched on the Lords' privileges. The tradesmen, complaining of the decay of trade and of their utter impoverishment, suggested that Parliament should separate out the peers who supported the Commons so that all might vote 'as one entire body', and the obstructions made by the bishops and other malignants would be removed.[1] Instead of censuring this direct advice, which was contrary to the privileges of Parliament, the Commons sent Holles with it to the Lords where on 1 February Holles 'very boldly' told them that 'there were some things in the petition extraordinary, which at another time the Parliament should be tender of: but now, considering the necessity of a multitude, the House of Commons thinks it not good to waken a sleepy lion'. He spoke of the dangers threatening the land, announced that the Commons had done their part and that 'therefore they must declare and protest for their own safeties, lest they should be involved, that they are not guilty of these mischiefs'.[2] After this conference, Holles delivered the Commons' message to the Lords who were refusing to join in asking the King to entrust the Tower and the militia to those in whom Parliament could confide. Holles announced that the Commons could take no responsibility for the ensuing troubles if the Lords should fail in their duties, and that 'they must not expect this House to come to them again, in this business'. This plain speaking seemed to work, for Holles was able to report to the grateful Commons that the Lords had agreed to join with them, and on Reynolds' motion, the House thanked him.[3]

Holles was enjoying a time of great influence in Parliament. His prestige was high from surviving the attempted arrest, and his unyielding stance towards the King won him the approbation of the House. It remained to be seen to what purpose he could deploy his prestige as the danger of war increased. However, at the same time as he enjoyed influence in Parliament, his own freedom of action was circumscribed, for the King's accusation meant that Holles had no option but to support Parliament. He could hardly emulate his brother John, who had followed Charles to York.[4]

diary, BL, Harl. 162, f. 355; *LJ*, iv. 550.

1 Printed in Clarendon, *History* (Bk. IV, 264-268), Macray, i. 549-50.

2 *CJ, ii. 404-5; LJ*, iv. 559; D'Ewes's diary, BL, Harl. 162, f. 362v. There are printed versions of Holles's speech which differ in details. *The True Diurnal, 31 Jan. - 7 Feb. 1642*, TT E201. 13, referred to this as 'a learned speech'.

3 *CJ*, ii. 408; D'Ewes's diary, BL, Harl. 162, f. 365v. Charles later mentioned this speech as one of Holles's further crimes; *His Majesties Declaration to all His loving Subjects of August 12 1642*, [York, 2 Sept.] 1642, TT E. 115. 11, p. 56.

4 *DNB;* Clarendon, *History* (Bk. V, 346), Macray, ii. 186.

When civil war seemed inevitable, many of those who remained at Westminster were so appalled at the prospect they sought immediate peace with the King. In the months from May to August 1642 the well known political groupings which Professor Hexter described for the months after the outbreak of the war, the middle, the war and the peace groups, were taking shape in the House of Commons.[1] Although D'Ewes saw only two groups, the fiery spirits and the peace lovers, Pym, whom D'Ewes considered a fiery spirit, pursued a middle group policy of preparing for war while allowing the possibility of conciliation, steering his policy through the House in combination with one or other of the extreme groups. On 20 May, for example, the warlike spirits wanted to declare that the King intended to make war against Parliament: Pym inserted a saving clause, that the King, 'seduced by evil counsel', intended to make war. On 4 June Sir Robert Harley moved that the House should publish the names of all the Merchant Adventurers who refused to lend money, but Pym suggested that a committee consider this first.[2] Nevertheless, there was a limit to Pym's conciliatoriness. In June some M.P.s proposed sending terms for accommodation to the King, and on receipt of his reply, Tomkins and Rudyard moved 'that we should embrace an accommodation of peace'.[3] The House agreed to reconsider the propositions, despite opposition from the war party, but Pym would not permit the discussion of peace propositions to interfere with measures for Parliament's defence.[4] On 1 July, according to their former order, the House proceeded to revise the peace propositions,

> that so some means might be thought upon for an accommodation but Mr Pym diverted the business and said we must look to our present safeties and thereupon delivered in a letter newly come out of Leicestershire. . . .[5]

On 2 July, the modified propositions were finally dispatched to the King, but while the Commons were waiting for his reply, they considered a commission for the Earl of Essex to command the parliamentary forces. Objections were overruled and Holles carried the

---

1 Hexter, *King Pym.*
2 D'Ewes's diary, BL, Harl. 163, f.128v., f. 146.
3 The King's reply arrived on 21 June 1642; *CJ,* ii. 635. D'Ewes's diary, BL, Harl. 163, f. 207v. (23 June 1642).
4 Gawdy's notes, BL, Add. 14827, f.147 (30 June 1642). The presence of war, middle and peace groups explains the apparent contradictions in the Commons' policy around this date.
5 D'Ewes's diary, BL, Harl. 163, f. 252v. See also Gawdy's notes, BL, Add. 14827, f. 148; Pym suggested that they should 'declare to the kingdom in what state we stand. That we should provide for our safety'.

commission to the House of Lords.[1] When the Commons considered the King's reply to the modified propositions, Holles was with the majority of the House who believed they could not agree with the King's demands: 'Mr Waller, Sir John Potts and others speaking for an accommodation to be had with his Majesty and that a civil war might be avoided: but Mr Denzil Holles, Mr Strode and other fiery spirits would not hear of it. . . .'[2]

Holles was actively associated with all the preparations for war. In February the Commons appointed him lieutenant of the town of Bristol, and in July named him one of the commissioners to execute the militia ordinance in Dorset. He served on committees for raising and borrowing money, and was a teller in favour of raising 10,000 men.[3] He personally subscribed £300, and offered to maintain four horse 'and set them forth in buff coats'.[4] On 30 July he justified the Defence of the Militia Ordinance to the House of Lords: 'Master Holles made an excellent speech, showing the great danger wherein the kingdom now standeth'.[5]

In all this there appears no sign of the future leader of the peace party, and yet on 24 April, Sir John Coke remarked to a correspondent 'I hear that Mr Holles since he hath married a bitch wife is not so violent in the House as he was'. Holles's second wife, Jane was the eldest daughter of Sir John Shirley of Ifield in Sussex and the widow of Sir Walter Covert of Slougham, Sussex and of John Freke of Cerne, Dorset.[6] Holles left Westminster for Pepperharrow in Surrey on 9 March in the company of Roger Hill, a fellow Dorset member who acted as his legal adviser on the occasion, and the marriage was celebrated on Saturday the 12th. Hill considered 'he hath an extraordinary good, great and rich match for which I do not a little rejoice'.[7]

---

1 *CJ*, ii. 673, 15 July 1642. Holles supported Essex's commission: 'A court may appoint a guard'; D'Ewes's diary, BL, Harl. 163, f. 272v.

2 *CJ*, ii. 690; D'Ewes's diary, BL, Harl. 163, f. 293 v. (25 July 1642).

3 *CJ*, ii. 426, 694, 534, 570, 586, 598, 602, 663; Holles & Evelyn – 125; Sir John Strangways & Selden – 45.

4 K.F. Lenthall, *Notes and Queries* 12 (1855), 338. The cost of maintaining a horse is difficult to estimate; Hodges offered two horse, or one horse and £50, which suggests that the contribution of four horse may have been worth another £200. There were contributions more generous than Holles's – for example Barrington gave £500 and offered to maintain four horse, Rolle gave £600 and Ashe £500 – but the majority of contributions were smaller; *ibid.*, pp. 338-59.

5 *CJ*, ii. 697; *A Perfect Diurnal*, 25 July – 1 Aug. 1642, TT E202.26, p. 7.

6 *HMC COWPER MSS.*, ii. 314. Thomas Fuller, a divine who deserted Parliament's side in 1643 for that of the King, dedicated a book of sermons to her in 1640; [Thomas Fuller] *Joseph's Party-Coloured Coat* (London, 1640).

7 Papers of Roger Hill (1605-1667), BL, Add. 46500, f.21, f.23, Roger Hill to

The match excited some contemporary comment. One parliamentary supporter, Henry Parker, in answer to the royalist jibe that the Parliamentarians' factiousness was designed to secure them offices, made a heavy handed jest that he knew of none who had gained promotion in the service of Parliament, 'except Master Holles his rich widow'. Digges, in all seriousness, questioned in return what Holles's parliamentary record had to do with his marital good fortune.[1]

It is possible that Holles's conduct moderated after his marriage in March although there are no signs of this prior to Sir John Coke's statement in April which might substantiate such a view. On 26 April the Commons considered the security of the town of Hull and Strode proposed they should tell Sir John Hotham, the governor there, that he 'should not admit the King in person. Mr Holles modified it'. In June Holles suggested that members who wished might contribute money to the parliamentary cause anonymously, which the Commons overruled as 'very derogatory to the work'.[2] But the evidence does not really amount to a view of Holles as a changed man, as one of his fellow Dorset M.P.s Sir John Bankes, Chief Justice of Common Pleas, found when he wrote to Holles, warning him that much notice was taken in York of his saying in the Commons that he 'liked not the word accommodation'.[3] Holles wrote his reply in haste, on the clerk's desk in the House, thanking his friend for his concern but explaining he was misinformed about his views. When Parliament intended to send a committee to Yorkshire, Holles said that they should first address themselves to the King, and when some of the members glanced at him, 'as if I intended some underhand accommodation', he stood up and said

> that I knew not what they meant by such an accommodation, if it was a complying and a going less, and a departing from our grounds, as if we had done something that we could not justify, I abhorred the thought of it, but if it was a good understanding between the King and the Parliament, it was that which myself and every good man did desire more than his own life.

He continued that Bankes could see by the enclosure — perhaps the

---

his wife Abigail, 4 & 18 Mar. [1642].

1 [Henry Parker], *Observations upon some of his Majesties late Answers and Expresses*, [2 July] 1642, TT E. 153. 26 p.11. [Dudley Digges], *An Answer to a Printed Book entitled, Observations upon some of his Majesties late Answers and Expresses*, [Oxford, 1642], TT E1945.24, p. 28. This contemporary comment on Holles's 'rich' wife make one wonder whether Sir John Coke had heard correctly, or was correctly copied, for I have found no justifying evidence for his view, nor any other reference to Jane as a 'bitch'.

2 D'Ewes's diary, BL, Harl. 163, f.93; f. 157 v. (11 June 1642).

3 *HMC*, Report VIII, appendix i part i. 211b. (18 May 1642).

draft of the Nineteen Propositions which were passed ten days later — the terms upon which Parliament stood, 'how far from what you wish in your letter'. There is no hint that Holles was out of sympathy with Parliament's attitude. He told Bankes he was convinced that Parliament

> will most readily cast itself at the King's feet with all faithful and loyal submission, upon the first appearance of change in his Majesty, that he will forsake those counsels which carry him on to so high a dislike and opposition to their proceedings by mispossessing himself of them.

Parliament would continue in affection to the King's person, 'though we follow that dictate of nature which makes us provide for our safety, and of duty to take care of the commonwealth.. . .'[1] If Bankes were testing Holles, he would have been disappointed, for Holles's reply was completely orthodox in support of Parliament's official position and showed no attempt to secure his own interest with the Royalists.

iv

In looking for signs of the future leader of the peace party, there is one further body of material which may be considered: Holles's speeches. While his contributions to the debates and general business of the Long Parliament reveal him as one of the opposition leaders, his formal speeches suggest he was less of a fiery spirit. Most of these speeches were delivered at conferences with the House of Lords, and were therefore prepared and quite possibly read. Subsequently they were published, sometimes at the order of the Commons, to win support outside Parliament or, as a hostile observer remarked, 'to busy the people with popular themes'.[2] Although rhetorical in form, and frequently platitudinous in content, the speeches reveal some of Holles's underlying attitudes and assumptions.

The chief concern of his speeches was with parliament. To parliament Holles assigns many specific functions, some of which had previously been thought of as those of the king, such as the defence of

---

1 Printed in G. Bankes, *The Story of Corfe Castle* (London, 1853), pp. 124-6 (21 May, 1642).

2 In normal debate in the Commons the reading of speeches was frowned upon. A hostile observer mocked the members who brought elaborately prepared speeches into the House and were forced to read them 'out of a hat perhaps, or behind a friend'; *A Letter from an Ejected Member of the House of Commons, to Sir John Evelyn* by G.S., [14 Sept.] 1648, TT E.463.18, p. 3. [John Vicars], *God on the Mount, or a Continuation of Englands Parliamentary Chronicle*, [27 Oct. 1643], TT E.73.4, p. 383 quoted one of Holles's published speeches with approbation.

the law, religion and the kingdom. He describes these functions in various metaphors. Parliament is 'the balm of Gilead which healed our wounds, restored our spirits, and made up all the breaches of the land'; the members are 'as so many sentinels to watch for the [people], to give them notice of the good or the evil, friends or enemies. . . '.[1] Parliament alone gives a man the security to call his wife and his property his own, and upon it depends 'the safety of peace of the whole kingdom'.[2] A parliament whose sittings are interrupted, whose members are threatened, a parliament without power is useless, 'a mere shadow, without substance, without efficacy'.[3] Nothing should interrupt its proceedings but the natural termination of its business.

> [Parliaments] should be like that blessed old man, who dyeth *(plenus dierum)* in a full age, after he hath fought a good fight, and overcome all his enemies; as the shock of wheat which cometh in due season, to fill our granaries with corn, uphold our lives with the staff of bread. For, Parliaments are our *panis quotidianus,* our true bread; all other ways are but *Quelques choses,* which yield no true nourishment, breed no good blood.[4]

Such metaphorical writing is an effective way of referring to several complex ideas within the space of a few short sentences. Holles claims that parliaments are always well intentioned, fighting against evil; they are productive of good, and as necessary and healthful as ripe wheat which is transformed to bread. He sketches out a world picture in which parliaments are part of the natural order, as necessary to man as his basic food. Any attempt to sow differences between the two Houses is a threat, for as each link depends on others, so the harmony between the Lords and the Commons

> is the golden Chain which binds up in one Gordian knot the strength, the beauty, the happiness of this kingdom, which so knit together is not to be broken in sunder by the fiercest violence. Therefore, who desires to unlink this Chain, and dissolve this knot, or fails of his part, to the preserving and continuing it fast, and firm, and entire, let the sin of it lie at his door [5]

His auditors would know that to break this chain was to unleash disorder.[6]Holles's most moving speech on the importance of parliament

---

1   Holles, *Speech . . . Concerning the Protestation,* p. 3; *The Speech of Denzil Holles Esquire, at a conference with the Lords on Tuesday the third of August, 1641,* 1641, p. 4.

2   Holles, *Speech, . . . 15th June, 1642,* p. 4; An Address to his Majesty in the name of the Commons, Rushworth,*Historical Collections,* iv. 471 (31 Dec. 1641).

3   Holles, *Speech . . . 15th June, 1642,* p. 3.

4   Holles, *Speech . . . Concerning the Protestation,* p. 3.

5   Holles, *Speech . . . the third of August, 1641,* pp. 1-2.

6   E.W.M. Tillyard, *The Elizabethan World Picture* (London, 1943).

to the kingdom he delivered on 21 June 1642 on the desertion of nine of the Lords.

> The parliament is the foundation and basis of government, and consequently of the peace and happiness of the kingdom . . . Therefor those who would destroy the building, apply themselves to undermine the foundation. If they can take away parliaments, or but weaken the power and authority of parliament, which is all one (for if it once have no power, it will soon have no being) they know then all will be at their mercy, nothing will stand in their way to oppose them, but a flood of violence will run over, and cover the whole surface of the kingdom, and carry away all, both present enjoyment, and future hope of religion, liberty and whatsoever else is precious and dear unto us.[1]

Interestingly enough, none of Holles's speeches are concerned with the role of the king nor with Holles's expectations of him. This is a significant omission. Holles redefines parliament's role in society, appropriating to it many of the functions, such as care of the people, (previously believed to be the king's), but he does not review the king's position, nor consider how king and parliament were tó function together. He assumes that the king is good, but misled by evil counsellors, implying that once the land is cleared of 'these vipers', all will be well. It is an orthodox, not a realistic approach, for Holles ignores the much more complex problem which really existed, that Charles had views of his own, and denied that evil counsellors misled him.

Contemporary parliamentary political theory was that there were three estates: king, Lords and Commons.[2] This the royalist theorists denied, arguing that the three estates were the Lords spiritual and temporal and Commons, with the king a sovereign power over all. Holles could not have supported the exclusion of the bishops from the House of Lords in 1641 had he believed them to be one of the three estates. He was a member of the committee which considered the King's reply to the Nineteen Propositions in June 1642, in which Charles conceded that the king was one of the three estates. In 1648 Holles wrote of the Army trying to make itself 'an absolute third estate' and later in the 1670s was again trying to exclude the bishops from the House of Lords.[3] However, in his writing, the mutual

1 Holles, *Speech . . . 15th June, 1642,* pp. 1-2. The Commons thanked Holles for this a 'worthy Performance' and requested him to print it; *CJ,* ii. 625-6, 636; D'Ewes's diary, BL, Harl. 163, f. 162v.

2 C.C. Weston, *English Constitutional Theory and the House of Lords 1556-1832* (London, 1965), Introduction and Ch. 1, discusses the importance of mixed monarchy theory.

3 Holles, *Memoirs,* p. 142. An anonymous work of 1679, which is almost certainly Holles's (see appendix 1), *A Letter of a Gentleman to his Friend,* p. 100, cites the reply of Charles I to the Nineteen Propositions as a justification of a mixed monarchy theory.

dependence of king and parliament is a theme he discusses frequently, while the details of a mixed monarchy theory are not mentioned. Furthermore, his metaphor of parliament as the foundation of the building makes clear his view of the necessity of parliament.

Holles's view of justice is a limited one, and in his formal speeches he refers to it in homely, proprietary terms as 'the bars of our gates, to protect us', 'props to support us' and 'our landmarks . . . the bound stone of the property of the subject'.[1] It is not a very exalted ideal he depicts, but few of the seventeenth-century propertied classes saw justice in wider terms. He refers to the broader concepts of the laws of nature and reason in justification of parliament's self defence,[2] and also appeals to a law of necessity. Referring to those suffering from decay of trade, he claims

> necessity hath no law. There is no delaying of present necessity. it is not to be thought that millions of men, women and children will starve and perish, so long as there is corn in the land of Goshen, or in the custody of Joseph.[3]

But despite these bold words Holles was a firm believer in private property.

In his speeches on religion, Holles stressed Parliament's role in its preservation. He attacked the bishops, arguing that their recent practices put them on a par with Pope and the bishops of the Roman Catholic church whose departures from 'true religion' unleashed all the 'bloody and long wars' of the Christian world. Parliament should prevent God's wrath falling upon the nation by enacting laws to restrict vice and maintain virtue so that the government of church and state 'shall be congruent to the word of God'.[4] Such views have their roots in his conception of 'true and real faith . . . without which we are nothing'. That faith, as 'we now profess in the Church of England', stands only on Christ. Like Luther, Holles believes that 'no grounds of salvation can be had, but by and through those extraordinary merits and sufferings, which we are partakers of in Christ'.[5]

---

[1] *A Speech made by the Honourable Denzil Holles Esquire . . . Concerning Sir Randel Crew,* [July] 1641, TT E.198.34, pp. 3-4.

[2] The Commons requested permission from the King to provide for their own safety 'which the very law of nature and reason doth allow unto them'; Rushworth, *Historical Collections,* iv. 471.

[3] *Mr Holles, His Speech in Parliament; On Monday the 31st of January . . . Concerning the Poore Tradesmens Petition* 1642, TT E.200.25, p. [6].

[4] Holles, *Speech Concerning the Poore Tradesmens Petition,* pp. 2-4.

[5] *Master Holles His Speech in Parliament, the 21 of March. 1642. Wherein is contained his Declaration concerning the Kings Attorney General . . .* TT E.200. 42, p. 4.

Holles's speeches thus reveal his ideals about religion and Parliament, but not how these might be translated into practice. Nowhere does he suggest how the differences between crown and parliament should be resolved peaceably. Nevertheless, if he did not think very deeply or very well about consititutional difficulties, he believed that an independent parliament should occupy an important position in national life, a belief he never abandoned so long as he lived.

5

HOLLES'S MILITARY CAREER AND HIS LEADERSHIP OF THE PEACE PARTY

> [Holles] had gone in with great heat into the beginnings of the war: but he soon saw the ill consequences it already had, and the worse that were like to grow with the progress of the war.[1]

As the war drew nearer, Holles threw himself into military preparations. Although he pursued an active military career for three months, by the end of November 1642 he was leading a peace party at Westminster, and by August of the following year he was so disenchanted with Parliament and its cause that he sought to retire abroad. His contemporaries believed that the fiery spirit had become a moderate.

i.

In the months before the outbreak of war, Holles enjoyed prominence as a popular politician. While other Dorset members returned to their county to keep an eye on the local scene,[2] Holles remained at Westminster. He enlisted a regiment of foot soldiers which left London with the Earl of Essex's army in August, while their colonel's other military duties took him to the west of England. Although Holles, like the majority of the Parliamentarians, had no prior military experience, Parliament appointed him deputy-lieutenant for Bristol, the largest, richest and most strategically significant town in the west. According to Clarendon, he played an important part in securing the city against the Royalists. Although the gentry of Somerset had advised the Marquis of Hertford to seize Bristol as his strong-point, Holles's activity with the militia there had so strengthened the supporters of Parliament that the Marquis was forced to look elsewhere.[3] It is not clear when Holles actually went to Bristol, or if he was there long enough to do anything useful. The Minute Books of the Corporation reveal that the town admitted him to review the trained bands, but they did not offer him the hospitality usually extended to the reviewing officer, for only 33 shillings were expended on his entertain-

1 Burnet, *Own Time*, i. 64.
2 D'Ewes's diary, BL, Harl. 163, f. 273v. (16 July 1642).
3 Clarendon, *History* (Bk. VI, 3) Macray, ii. 294-5.

ment so perhaps he did not stay long.[1] Early in August, thwarted in his plans for Bristol, Hertford fortified himself in Sherborne castle. From Dorset, Holles's fellow-member, Dennis Bond, reported that Hertford could be subdued if Parliament sent forces.[2] Parliament directed the Earl of Bedford to besiege the castle, and on 30 August Holles left Westminster to join him, boasting openly that he would bring up the marquis, alive or dead.[3] His boast betrays the false optimism which characterised many Parliamentarians at the outbreak of war, and Bedford later bemoaned his misfortune in being 'engaged in a business that the world thinks so easy to be effected'.[4]

Holles's first direct experience of war was a sobering one. On 6 September 1642, from their quarters at the siege of Sherborne Castle, Bedford, Holles and Colonel Essex described the affray with somewhat wry humour. Their efforts, they concluded, had occasioned much suffering to themselves and little hurt to the enemy. Their raw untrained officers were of poor quality: 'If a bullet come over their heads, they fall flat upon their bellies'.[5] Of 3,100 of their men, not 1,200 were left. By 7 September their commanders found that so many had stolen away during the night that they were forced to raise the siege and to march away to Dorchester to await assistance. Bedford, Holles and Essex concluded their letter with the assertion that while they would gladly lay down their lives in Parliament's service, 'truly we would die like men and with men and not like fools in the company of heartless beasts'.[6] Before reinforcements arrived to complete the siege successfully, Holles returned to Westminster.[7]

Although the parliamentary commanders wrote scathingly of their soldiers as heartless beasts, other observers were more sympathetic to the soldiers' difficulties. By taking up arms for Parliament these local men were called upon to injure their landlords. Many of them were tenants for life to the Marquis of Hertford and Sir Ralph Hopton, so that when they saw their landlords against them, they realised that

1   J. Latimer, *The Annals of Bristol in the Seventeenth Century* (Bristol, 1900), pp.158-9. No date given. Clarendon's account would necessitate Holles's presence in Bristol before mid-August, but he was not absent from Westminster for any length of time prior to the outbreak of war.

2   D'Ewes's diary, BL, Harl. 163, f. 297v. (letter dated 18 Aug. 1642, read in the Commons 20 Aug. 1642).

3   *Ibid.*, f. 372v.

4   *A Letter from the Earle of Bedford of the passages about Sherborn Castle, 6-8 Sept.*, [15 Sept.] 1642, TT E.117.6. n.p.

5   *HMC Braye MSS.*, p. 147.

6   *Ibid.*, p. 148.

7   D'Ewes's diary, BL, Harl. 163, f. 372 v. (21 Sept. 1642).

they might not be able to renew their leases, and retreated.[1] To overcome their justifiable fears, a newsletter writer tried to arouse hostility to the upper landlord class by claiming that Lord Paulet stated it was not fit for any country yeomen to have more than ten pounds a year.[2] The Royalists retaliated by saying that Holles had tried to engage the soldiers in the parliamentary cause by suggesting that they fire Sherborne Castle and allow the soldiers to pillage.[3] Apart from the social and economic difficulties in fighting a civil war, the physical discomforts of soldiering drove many home. Besides, it was harvest time.[4] As one newsbook writer pointed out, soldiers raised in London and sent down to the country 'will more terrify the Cavaliers than a thousand volunteers of the country trained bands in harvest time'.[5]

After a brief stay in London, Holles left again at the end of September presumably to join his regiment of foot, which had marched out of London in August.[6] While he had been in the west, his soldiers were coping cheerfully with the physical discomforts of military life. Camped in the rain, they ate fruit, drank water, and kept warm with some good fires kindled from hedges, fencing and gates. They enlivened their marches with burning altar rails from churches, sly plunder of Papists, and some enjoyable sermons.[7] The men were said to be 'butchers and dyers', most of the officers were civilians and inexperienced, and the chaplain of the regiment was Obadiah Sedgewick.[8] Holles was with these men in the Earl of Essex's army at

1 Rushworth, *Historical Collections*, iv. 685; *A Perfect Diurnall*, 26 Sept. – 6 Oct. 1642. TT E.202-45.

2 *A True Relation of divers passages in Somersetshire between the Country and the Cavaliers concerning the Militia and the Commission of Array*, 5 Aug. 1642, TT E.109.34, p. 3. Clarendon later commented on the success of this deception upon the substantial yeomen and freeholders; *History* (Bk. VI, 4), Macray, i. 295-6.

3 *A Most Exact Relation of the proceedings of his Majesties Armie at Sherbourne, 2-7 Sept.*, [15 Sept.] 1642, TT E.117.12, n.p.

4 *Newest Relation*, p. 2; Rushworth, *Historical Collections*, iv. 685.

5 *Speciall Passages*, 6-13 Sept. 1642, TT E.116.41, p. 37.

6 G. Davies, 'The parliamentary army under the Earl of Essex, 1642-5', *EHR* 49 (1934), appendix iii. 51, claimed that Holles stayed at Westminster for three months, but there is no evidence to support this. His activity at Sherborne castle in early September has been discussed. There is no record of his presence at Westminster from 28 September until early November. The regiment probably marched with those of Brooke, Hampden, Fiennes and Goodwin to Warwick; *A Perfect Diurnall*, 15-22 Aug. 1642, TT E.239.9.

7 These details are derived from a fascinating series of letters from one of the non-commissioned officers; Nehemiah Wharton, 'Letters of a subaltern officer of the Earl of Essex's army written . . . in 1642', ed. Sir H. Ellis, *Archaeologia* 25 (1853), 310-34.

8 P. Young, *Edgehill 1642. The Campaign and the Battle* (1967), p. 254. Holles's

the first serious battle of the Civil War. On the morning of 23 October the Parliamentarians lined up against the Royalists on Kineton field. Holles's regiment of foot was at the rear of the left wing.[1] The Royalists had the advantage of high ground and when their charge began, the Parliamentarians were discomforted by the desertion of one of their cavalry commanders and his troop. Routed, the left wing of Parliament's cavalry turned back through their infantry, and infected six hundred musketeers with panic. As the musketeers abandoned their weapons and turned to run through Holles's regiment with the royalist cavalry at their heels, Holles himself stood in the breach, and succeeded in persuading some of the troops to hold their ground. Although four regiments fled, Holles's own regiment stood firm, and as he himself proudly declared, fought most gallantly. Holles's part in averting defeat in the battle was praised by Strode in an address to the City. All the credit, he said, went to four regiments, of which Holles's was one.[2]

But soon afterwards Holles's regiment was smashed. Essex had successfully brought his army back to London from Edgehill and was moving out again to meet the King. Holles's regiment, together with Lord Brooke's, was quartered at Brentford on Friday 11 November. Next morning, when a thick mist covered the ground, Prince Rupert launched a surprise attack.

> Suddenly they fell upon Colonel Holles his regiment that were quartered at Brainford (being the red regiment, those honest religious soldiers, that to their great honour and fame, had fought so courageously and valiantly in the late battle at Kineton), and cut off divers of them, who fought with all that force of the King's from 12 o'clock, until half an hour past 3 in the afternoon . . .[3]

Sergeant Major Quarles had rallied Holles's regiment, John Lilburne, in the absence of any other superior officers, rallied Brooke's, but although the two fought bravely, they were saved only by the timely arrival of Hampden with his troops. Brentford was a disaster: the

brother had corresponded with a minister, Mr. Sedgewick, in 1629, so possibly there was a family connection. Nott. U.L., PW V. 5, p. 303. Sedgewick was minister at St. Paul's Covent Garden in 1645 where Holles attended.

1   The following account of the battle is based on the report of the parliamentary commanders to Parliament, 23 Oct. 1642; Rushworth, *Historical Collections*, v. 37; N. Fiennes, *A Most True and Exact Relation of Both Battles* . . . , 9 Nov. 1642, TT E.126.38, p. 5.

2   *Eight Speeches Spoken in Guild-Hall* . . . *27 October 1642*, [29 Oct.] 1642, TT E.124.32, p. 11; see also *England's Memorable Accidents* 24-31 Oct. 1642, TT E.240.49, p. 62: Lord Wharton and Strode declared that 'through the valour of Colonel Holles's regiment and the Lord General's they obtained a victory'.

3   *Special Passages*, 8-15 Nov. 1642, TT E.127, p. 119.

Royalists captured 500 prisoners, 15 guns and 11 colours. So many of Holles's men were lost that the regiment was disbanded and the survivors paid off by warrant on 22 November 1642.[1] It was said that Holles was absent at the time of the attack; indeed, it was alleged that most of the Parliamentary commanders had gone to London for the weekend.[2]

Thereafter Holles was without military duties, although the debacle evidently had not shaken the Commons' faith in his military prowess. In those early days most of the Parliamentary commanders were inexperienced; besides, what Essex and the committee of safety really wanted was 'to interest persons of estate and relations (though not bred soldiers) in that employment'.[3] When the Earl of Pembroke excused himself from the western command, pleading his age and military inexperience, it was proposed on 3 December that Holles should be General of the West.[4] Prompted by Pym on 13 December, the Commons asked Holles to undertake the western command, to which he willingly agreed. In response to his request, the House proposed that he should have 1,000 men and a regiment of horse.[5] The Commons directed two members to ask the Lord General Essex for a commission, and the *Perfect Diurnal* reported that men and money

---

1   John Lilburne, *Innocency and Truth Justified,* [6 Jan. 1646], TT E.314.21, pp. 40-1; A.H. Burne & P. Young, *The Great Civil War* (London, 1959), p. 32; Davies, 'Parliamentary army', p. 54. The account of events presented to Parliament, *A True and Perfect Relation of the Barbarous and Cruel Passages of the Kings Army, At Old Brainford,* 25 Nov. 1642, TT E.128.17 describes the inhumanity of the Royalists who shot at Holles's men who had fled into the River Thames for safety. Among those taken prisoner was William Allen, later to be a prominent 'agitator' in 1647; *Clarke Papers,* ii. 431.

2   *HMC Cowper MSS.,* ii. 326. One account, *The Valiant Resolution of The Sea-Men under the Earle of Warwick who slew many of the Cavaliers . . . ,* 16 Nov. 1642, TT E.127.19, mentions that Hampden and Holles came in with their forces in the afternoon. When news of the attack reached the Commons on 12 November between 1 & 2 p.m. they ordered the Lord General to take the field with his commanders; L. Whitacre, House of Commons proceedings 1642-1647, BL, Add. 31116, f. 8v. In 1647 Amon Wilbee commented that 'the Earl of Essex, and his chief commanders, Merrick, (one of the traitorous crew) and the rest, came to London, to laze, smoke tobacco, and drink sack, court, compliment, vaunt and vapour of that they never did, and a potent enemy at hand in the field, who came up to Brainford . . . and no chief officer there'; A. Wilbee, *Plain Truth, without Feare or Flattery,* [2 July] 1647, TT E.516.7, p. 16.

3   *A full Vindication and Answer of the XI Accused Members,* [15 July] 1647, TT E.398.

4   Parliament had appointed Pembroke on 19 Oct. 1642; *CJ,* ii. 814. Prideaux moved they ask him to set out on 26 Nov.; Journal of proceedings in the House of Commons, and of public events, from 19 Sept. 1642 . . . kept by Walter Yonge, of Colyton, Devon, BL, Add. 18777, f. 78; *CJ,* ii. 874. *A Continuation Of Certain Speciall and Remarkable Passages,* 3-8 Dec. 1642, TT E.244.4, p. 2.

5   *CJ,* ii. 886; Yonge's diary, BL, Add. 18777, ff. 91v., 93 (13 Dec. 1642).

would be raised in the City.[1] On 13 December Bristol was also anxious for Holles's services, claiming that if Parliament would order Holles to join them, they would fear no attempts by the Cavaliers.[2]

Holles never set out as general of the west, nor on any other military duties. A week later the House of Lords directed that Lord Robartes should serve as General, but finally it was the Earl of Stamford who took the post.[3] Holles later claimed that he was the poorer for his military activity, for he had lost £300 from his wagon at Edgehill, lent £300 to Guildhall, and had spent £1,000 in Parliament's service before he laid down his commission.[4] There was a rumour that Holles had excused himself from the western command,[5] but whether he was supplanted by his social superiors or had chosen to abandon military life for Westminster politics is not clear. Certainly by mid December 1642 Holles was among the foremost of a group of Parliamentarians who favoured negotiations for peace with the King. His retirement from the army was probably no great loss to the Parliamentary cause. Unlike Cromwell, he despised and scorned the common soldier, and this lack of sympathy for his troops would have made it difficult for him to be a successful military leader.

ii.

Gardiner believed that in late November 1642 there were again two parties at Westminster. These he described as the peace and war parties, and he wrote of Holles and Pym as their respective leaders. While Holles and the peace party were prepared to trust the King, Pym and the war party were not. But Hexter, in his brilliant analysis of parliamentary politics after the outbreak of war, showed that the division was not a simple one between peace and war parties.[6] There was a third party, the middle group led by Pym, which generally held the balance between the other two. Although at the two extremes the peace party and war party consisted of leaders and a hard core of devoted adherents who rarely changed sides, their supporters were a fluctuating body. The middle group was even less stable in composition. In all the groups, personal or sectional interests could cut across other allegiances to

1   *CJ*, ii. 886; *A Perfect Diurnal*, 12-19 Dec. 1642, TT E.244.15.
2   *A Continuation of Certaine Speciall and Remarkable Passages*, 8-12 Dec. 1642, TT E.244.10, p. 5.
3   Gardiner, *Civil War*, i. 85.
4   Holles's account to the Speaker, 1646, Bodl., Tanner 59, f. 507.
5   *HMC Cowper MSS.*, ii. 328 (19 Dec. 1642).
6   Gardiner, *Civil War*, i. 61; Hexter, *King Pym, passim*.

influence an individual's vote. Hexter's reassessment of Pym and his position also led to a reconsideration of the war party leadership, whom he saw to be Henry Marten and Sir Henry Vane junior. However, like Gardiner, he saw Holles as the leader of the peace party. Nor did his view of Holles and the peace party's policies differ from that of Gardiner: both saw Holles as the leader of a party bent on complete capitulation to the King.[1] But was Holles really so changed that he wanted to abandon all Parliament's demands?

On 21 November 1642 when the House of Commons was discussing propositions for peace, D'Ewes noted with surprise that Holles was speaking earnestly for peace. Mr. Holles, he explained, 'was much cooled in his fierceness by the great slaughter made in his regiment at Brentford'.[2] D'Ewes had forgotten his earlier observation of Holles's restraint, for in September, before the loss of his regiment, when Holles had pleaded for moderate treatment of the Royalists in the peace terms, D'Ewes had remarked upon 'such a violent and fiery spirit' making such a plea.[3] On a third occasion, in February 1643, D'Ewes again commented on Holles's changed behaviour, and this time he attributed Holles's altered conduct to the effect of the war. 'Perceiving that both church and kingdom must in all human reason be ruined', Holles sought peace.[4] But Holles's alteration was neither so sudden nor so dramatic as D'Ewes observed.

Some had thought Holles less fiery even before the war broke out. His behaviour at that time shows clearly the ambivalence many Parliamentarians felt about the approaching conflict. They had not sought war. They did not want to fight against their King, but to advise him. What future was there in war? Earlier Holles may have seen his activity in Parliament as a means of recommending himself to Charles's attention, and it is possible that in supporting peace negotiations after war had broken out he was still trying to recommend himself to the King. Certainly the Royalists noticed his efforts. Captain Hotham told the Earl of Newcastle in January 1643 that Holles and Pierrepont were 'two converts' to peace.[5] In February the parliamentary diarist, Walter Yonge, noted in bold capitals amidst his miniscule shorthand 'SOME SAY MR HOLLES WILL BE SECRETARY OF STATE'.[6] Even the King, who had consistently included Holles

1   Gardiner, *Civil War,* i. 62, 184; Hexter, *King Pym,* pp. 8-9.
2   D'Ewes's diary, BL, Harl. 164, f. 99. (21 Nov. 1642).
3   D'Ewes's diary, BL, Harl. 163, f. 372 v. (21 Sept. 1642).
4   *Ibid.,* f. 303 (18 Feb. 1643).
5   *HMC Portland MSS.,* i. 89.
6   Yonge's diary, BL, Add. 18777, f. 155 (15 Feb. 1643).

among the factious troublemakers he refused to pardon during 1642, finally omitted Holles's name from the list of unpardonables later in 1643.[1] Holles was not the only member of Parliament in whom the war appeared to cause an alteration. D'Ewes thought Whitelock and Glyn had also changed, and favoured peace.[2] There is no obvious explanation of Holles's change, and he himself offers no clues in his writings. Several factors may have influenced him. Firstly, there were his military experiences. The difficulty of warfare, his personal experience of the poor quality of the soldiers and the unfortunate loss of his regiment may have chastened his spirit, as D'Ewes thought. Secondly, his family was divided by the war. His brother John returned to Parliament in August, (though he would waver between the two sides),[3] cousin Gervase fought for the King, and when Denzil asked his uncle Thomas to fight fot the cause of religion, Thomas declined, saying he had a hearty respect for religion, but as for the religion of rebellion, he understood it not.[4] Thirdly, there may have been the influence of his 'bitch wife', or at least of her wealth, inclining him to end the war and the destruction of property as speedily as possible. Although Denzil was not so dedicated as his brother John to worldly goods, he was not indifferent to material advantages, and died a wealthy man.

Furthermore, although his contemporaries and later historians viewed Holles as a changed man after the outbreak of the war, he was probably little altered. While other Parliamentarians became sterner in their attitude to the King, Holles was still trying to return to the 'old known ways'. It would be interesting to know whether he chose a conservative device for the cornet of his regiment as this may be a guide to his war aims, but unfortunately no details of this have survived.[5] There are signs that he was still firm in support of Parliament. Early in November 1642 he responded aggressively when the King sent an unsatisfactory reply to a parliamentary request, and suggested that they

1 *His Majesties Declaration*, pp. 78, 56.

2 D'Ewes's diary, BL, Harl. 164, f. 99 (21 Nov. 1642).

3 After excusing his absence 'about some of his domestic affairs' in 1642, Clare was permitted to sit in the Lords; *LJ*, v.282, 284. Charles subsequently stayed at the Earl's house in Nottingham, but whether this was with the owner's permission is doubtful; J. Nalson, *A True Copy of the Journal of the High Court of Justice, for the Trial of King Charles I* (London, 1684), pp. 68-9. A.C. Wood, *Nottinghamshire in the Civil War* (Oxford, 1937), pp. 15-16 argues that Clare's absence left the Parliamentarians in Nottingham without a recognized leader.

4 G. Holles, *Memorials*, p. 86.

5 The details were left blank or not included; Dr. Williams's Library, Modern MS 12.7, f.20; Cornets or Flags of the Several Companies, BL, Add. 5247. I am grateful to Dr N. Tyacke for these references.

should send into the City immediately to tell them that the King's ears were shut against his Parliament.[1] In December 1642 he was willing to undertake further military duties, and he joined with Pym in negotiations for a loan of £20,000 from the Customs Farmers.[2] In the debates on peace in February 1643 he agreed with Pym that they should not treat with the King by commissioners, but should satisfy him only on doubtful points.[3]

Nevertheless, in the debates on peace negotiations from November 1642 onwards, Holles was in favour of moderating the peace terms and opposed angering the King unnecessarily. An analysis of his conduct shows that in none of this was he selling out the parliamentary cause. On 21 November, despite a petition from the City against peace, the Commons debated whether they should send any propositions to the King. Vane junior spoke against it, as being unwise given Parliament's present weakness, but in reply Holles skilfully argued that they should send the propositions as a means of gaining public support to carry on the war. 'The King says he is in a condition of strength to give us a battle. If we can make such proposition as may set us in a course of satisfaction [this] may enable us for war'. Parliament would thus satisfy the kingdom of its peaceful intent, Holles continued, whereas if we sent no propositions, 'and say we will fight with him, will not that sound in the world that we will have no peace?'[4] In two speeches on 21 and 22 November, he reiterated his earlier ideas about a settlement.[5] While Gardiner thought these speeches showed Holles's willingness to make political concessions, but demonstrated his religious intransigence,[6] in fact Holles was not uncompromising, for his plans to redistribute the wealth of the church need not have touched the existence of the office of bishop. Clarendon believed that most M.P's at this date were prepared to use concessions over the church to bargain with the King over the militia, and partly for this reason they had pushed through their bill for the abolition of episcopacy in November 1642.[7] Shaw discounted Clarendon's view completely, as a mere

---

1 Yonge's diary, BL, Add. 18777, f. 52 (7 Nov. 1642).

2 The Commons asked several persons to lend money, but they declined. Holles reported that the Customs Farmers could not advance £20,000 because they had promised to lend this amount for the Navy. Nevertheless, they thought that if they could meet together they would be able to find enough money to keep the army afoot during the time of the treaty; *CJ*, ii. 901.

3 Yonge's diary, BL, Add. 18777, ff. 146v.-147 (8 Feb. 1642).

4 *Ibid.*, ff. 64-64v.

5 *Ibid.*, f. 65v., f.66.

6 Gardiner, *Civil War*, i. 62.

7 Clarendon, *History* (Bk. VI, 229), Macray, i. 438-9.

perversion of fact,[1] but while it may be exaggerated — Clarendon never saw a genuine religious impulse in anything the Parliamentarians did — Parliament's caution and delay in actually abolishing bishops suggests the unwillingness of the majority to proceed to such radical lengths. Thus although Holles perhaps assisted the passage of the bill for the abolition of episcopacy in January 1643, by suggesting that Sir Robert Harley should defer taking it up to the Lords until they had finished a conference lest the Lords lay it aside,[2] he was not necessarily committed to the abolition of episcopacy. He may well have seen the whole issue as a means of giving Parliament additional bargaining power in the coming treaty negotiations.

There are many examples of Holles's attempts to forward peace after November 1642. For example, St. John wanted to place a justification of Parliament in the preamble to the propositions for peace to be sent to Charles, but Holles, D'Ewes and others argued against this 'ripping up of old sores, which ought rather to be skinned and healed'. [3] Holles thought Parliament should promise to proceed against no more than two named Royalists,[4] and he considered Parliament need not adhere to the proposition enshrining the militia ordinance.[5] In addition, Holles consistently supported peace negotiations with the King before the vexed questions of a complete disbanding or a truce should be settled. When on 1 February Charles refused to agree to disband all forces, and proposed instead a truce, the Lords accepted his suggestion, but the Commons were divided.[6] Holles and the peace party finally gained a majority in the House on 17 February in favour of some treaty before the forces were disbanded, although the negotiations were to begin on the question of the armed forces and forts.[7] On 18 February the Commons agreed to a truce, but with the qualification that the Lord General must advise Parliament of the details.[8] After Essex replied, Rous and Armine suggested on 21 February that they ask him for further advice.[9] Holles immediately opposed their suggestion as

1 Shaw, *History of the English Church*, i. 138.

2 D'Ewes's diary, BL, Harl. 164, f.280 (23 Jan. 1643).

3 Yonge's diary, BL, Add. 18777, f.104 (26 Dec. 1642); D'Ewes's diary, BL, Harl. 164, f. 275 (26 Dec. 1642).

4 *CJ*, ii. 906 (29 Dec. 1642).

5 *Ibid.*, 928 (14 Jan. 1643).

6 *Ibid.*, 959: Holles & Evelyn — 102; Stapleton & Moore — 92.

7 *Ibid.*, 966: Holles & Clotworthy — 86; Hampden & Marten — 83.

8 *Ibid.*, 970. (18 Feb. 1643. The division was actually on whether the question should be put). D'Ewes's diary, BL, Harl. 164, f. 302, says that Pym, Hampden, Marten and Strode insisted upon this qualification, although Holles argued against them.

9 Yonge's diary, BL, Add. 18777, f. 160 (21 Feb. 1643).

delaying peace. He appealed to the notion of blood guilt, that whoever delayed peace was responsible for any blood shed in war. If Parliament should refuse the King's request for a truce, on it would fall the guilt of any subsequent blood shed. A committee should consider what was 'fit to be done' then send to the Lord General, and on Whitelocke's supportive motion, that the committee should sit that afternoon, then advise with the Lord General, the House agreed to proceed as Holles and Whitelocke suggested.[1]

During March 1643 Parliament's commissioners negotiated with the King at Oxford about the truce. In the House of Commons the supporters of peace were able to command such a majority that there were no divisions. D'Ewes thought that about three-quarters of the House favoured peace, but it is clear from later voting that the peace party at this date depended on middle group support. The cause of peace was also supported strongly by the House of Lords. D'Ewes thought·many of the Lords who had earlier favoured the war now saw it as the way to speedy ruin. He named the Earls of Northumberland, Rutland, Bedford, Pembroke and Holland as the most prominent converts to peace.[2]

Holles did all he could during the negotiations to support the cause of peace. For example, on 23 March, when the Commons learnt of the King's objections to the terms of the truce proposed by Parliament, D'Ewes half feared that the whole negotiation would break down, but Holles 'very seasonably and fortunately' moved that they should treat on the propositions notwithstanding.[3] On 30 March he smoothed over a censure of the committees with the King at Oxford, and tried to delay the return of the commissioners from Oxford on 3 April.[4] But the negotiations foundered, so on 8 April Parliament reverted to its demand for a disbanding.[5] The middle group would no longer support the treaty when the King seemed unwilling. Charles's response to the request for the forces to disband was so unsatisfactory that the Commons voted on 14 April to recall their commissioners. There was not even a division on the issue.[6]

Pym used the peace negotiations to demonstrate the King's intransigence, and so persuaded the House to create machinery for

1 *Ibid.*, ff. 160v. – 161.
2 D'Ewes's diary, BL, Harl. 164, f. 334 (18 Mar. 1643).
3 *Ibid.*, f. 341 v.
4 *Ibid.*, ff. 348, 352-352v.; *CJ*, iii. 28.
5 Rushworth, *Historical Collections*, v. 191-2.
6 *CJ*, iii. 45.

fighting the war. Holles and the peace party gained no countervailing advantage. Holles later wrote that the treaty had failed solely because the majority in Parliament had insisted upon unreasonable conditions, 'as the Devil did to our Saviour, to have him fall down and worship them, lay his honour at their feet, his life at their mercy'.[1] The remedy, Holles believed, was to offer the King even more moderate terms, and this he would try to do later in 1643. But Holles took no account of the King's attitude. Charles would not agree to Parliament's demand so long as he was in a position of military strength. Holles's persistent belief in the King's willingness to compromise weakened the peace party and deprived it of influence and a viable policy.

The only policy Holles could pursue after the failure of the peace negotiations was to try to prevent the breach between the King and Parliament from growing wider, especially to stop Parliament antagonising the King further. For example, he resisted the making of a new Great Seal. Parliament had found their want of the symbol of royal authority more hampering to the execution of government than their want of the King himself, so in May 1643 it was proposed Parliament make a new Seal. Despite the opposition of the lawyers, the division was carried against Holles and Sir John Evelyn.[2] Holles also opposed interference with the King's property. On 2 June he was at the Earl of Holland's house in Charing Cross together with D'Ewes and some other members of the Commons when they heard that Henry Marten was breaking open the locks on the King's regalia in Westminster Abbey. They hurried to the scene, where Marten, 'as pale as ashes' desisted on the persuasion of Holland and Holles. The next day Marten formally moved that the Commons should order the locks be opened. Many, including Holles, objected, fearing a scandal 'as if this were done in contempt of Majesty itself', but were overruled.[3] Holles was more successful on the question of the customary firing of guns to mark the King's accession. Initially the Commons had ordered that no guns should be fired because powder was scarce — a decision which some members considered would dishonour Parliament through all Christendom — but Holles was a teller in favour of rescinding this.[4] He unavailingly opposed entering the Queen of Bohemia's indiscreet letter to Prince Rupert in the *Journals*.[5]

1 Holles, *Memoirs*, p. 7.

2 *CJ*, iii. 86: Clotworthy & A. Goodwin — 86; Holles & Evelyn — 74 (15 May 1643).

3 D'Ewes's diary, BL, Harl. 165, f. 97; *CJ*, iii, 112.

4 *Ibid.*, 18; D'Ewes's diary, BL, Harl. 164, f. 342 v. (25 Mar. 1643).

5 *CJ*, ii. 989: Holles & Sir C. Yelverton, — 46; Lord Grey of Ruthin & Sir J. Corbett — 54 (4 Mar. 1643).

Holles also tried to defend traditional property rights against the exigencies of war. At the end of March 1643 some residents of Surrey complained of a Lord General's warrant for raising £1,000. Holles 'very honestly and boldly' said that Essex was a servant of Parliament employed to reserve property, not to destroy it by imposing unreasonable taxes on any part of the kingdom. Pym, Strode and others excused the action as necessary.[1] Holles also cited parliamentary privilege in defence of an M.P. against those who wanted to seize his contribution by force.[2] At the end of June Holles again defended traditional rights. There was a discussion of forthcoming trials of conspirators by council of war: a dangerous business, as D'Ewes observed. Holles questioned whether the commission for the trials was according to martial law and the practice of other armies, and desired the House to be 'very wary how we proceeded in taking away the lives of men and to go upon sure ground'. Glyn's assurance that the judge advocate of the Army, Dr. Dorislaus, justified the proceedings disturbed the members even further, for they were unhappy about taking away men's lives according to the opinion of a Dutchman.[3]

Some of the peace party supporters chafed at this ineffectual policy of not-widening-the-breach between King and Parliament, and sought a more active course to end the war. One of the Commons, the poet Edmund Waller, plotted with the Royalists. His plot implicated many members of the peace party including Holles. On the morning of Wednesday 6 June, the members of Parliament were dramatically summoned from Church and Pym told them of a plot to seize the City's military power and a group of leading Parliamentarians, after which a royalist force would enter the city.[4] There were in fact two strands to Waller's so-called plot. Waller worked in Westminster, with the King's approval, to keep the peace party coherent and solid in London so they might secure the reopening of peace negotiations. Meanwhile, Charles issued a commission of array to Nicholas Crispe and others for an armed uprising in the City. Pym took the two plots and wove them into one, which made the peace party look very sinister. Pym made much of the fact that this plot had been fostered under the cover of those who came to London ostensibly as messengers of peace, and others were quick to take up the association between the peace party and Royalists in the City, saying that the plot had grown from

1   D'Ewes's diary, BL, Harl. 164, f. 342 v. (31 Mar. 1643).

2   *Ibid.*, f. 356v. (5 Apr. 1643). Sir Edward Hales had incurred distrust by Feb. 1643 because of his absences; Keeler, *Long Parliament*, pp. 200-1.

3   D'Ewes's diary, BL, Harl. 165, f. 103 (29 June 1643).

4   *CJ*, iii. 117; *The Kingdomes Weekly Intelligencer*, 30 May – 6 June 1643, TT E.105.8, p. 174.

the ashes of the London petition for peace of the previous December. [1] Waller and his associate Tomkins had told the citizens that many of the Lords and Commons would join them — the Earls of Clare, Portland and Bath — and they had negotiated with the Earls of Northumberland, Pembroke, Holland and Salisbury, and Holles, Pierrepont, Sir John Holland and Maynard. The conspirators had planned to seize several members whom they feared. These were the Lords Saye and Wharton, and the Lord Mayor, Stapleton, Hampden, Strode and Pym.[2] The Commons resolved to publish the details of the plot, but there was long debate in the House whether to mention the names of the four members of the Commons — Holles, Pierrepont, Holland and Maynard — whom the plotters had described as friendly to their design. Finally it was resolved to name the men but declare that they had cleared themselves.[3] A special day was set aside for thanksgiving, when the details should be read. The effect of the news of this plot was electric. D'Ewes, not always susceptible to Pym's interpretation of events, considered that

> the discovery of this plot did more work upon most men than anything that had happened during these miserable calamities because it seemed now that there was a fixed resolution in the popish party utterly to extirpate the Protestant religion. . .[4]

Waller's plot confirmed earlier suspicions of the peace party as crypto-Royalists, and the reputations of the party leaders were severely tarnished. There was an attempt in the Commons at the end of June to have Northumberland imprisoned. Not even the members' willingness to take the covenant vowing adherence to Parliament was acceptable, because two Lords, Conway and Portland, had taken the covenant and yet were involved in the plot.[5] Holles was publicly mentioned as sympathetic to royalist designs. His contemporaries would also have noted that the King was willing to pardon Holles's offences in June. He was the only one of the five members so distinguished.[6]

1 *A Discovery of the Plot for the Ruine of the City of London and the Parliament as it was made known by John Pym. Esq.,* [8 June] 1643, TT E.105.21, n.p.; *A Brief Narrative of the Late Treacherous and Horrid Designe which hath been Lately Discovered,* [15 June] 1643, TT E.106.10, p. 2; *A Perfect Diurnall of the Passages in Parliament,* 5-12 June 1643, TT E.249.16. Gardiner, *Civil War,* i. 74-5.

2 Whitacre's diary, BL, Add. 31116, ff. 55-55v. (6 June 1643).

3 *Ibid.,* f. 56; D'Ewes's diary, BL, Harl. 165, f. 98 (8 June 1643).

4 D'Ewes's diary, BL, Harl; 164, f.400 (7 June 1643).

5 D'Ewes's diary, BL, Harl. 165, f.103v. On 29 June Marten moved that Northumberland be committed to safe custody, and this was supported by St. John and Strode. *A Perfect Diurnall of the Passages in Parliament,* 12-19 June 1643, TT E.249.17.

6 The King proclaimed the Parliament at Westminster was not free, and there-

iii

As the war intensified during 1643, so Holles's hopes of effecting a speedy settlement with the King receded. Parliament's military position deteriorated so seriously that the majority in the Commons was prepared to consider Pym's proposal for an alliance with Scotland. Since the outbreak of the war Pym had nurtured a plan for an alliance, but the Commons had been unenthusiastic. Holles, for example, spoke against precipitating a quarrel with the Scots in March 1643,[1] but he did not want the Scots to enter the war. But when Parliament faced military disaster in mid 1643, a majority in the Commons agreed that at least messengers might go to Scotland to discuss their situation, and finally on 5 July the Commons resolved that they would ask the Scots for help.[2] There was no directly expressed opposition in the Commons to asking the Scots' aid, but the delay in the dispatch of the English commissioners was probably due to Pym's difficulties with the peace party.[3] Furthermore, the peace party's attempts during July and August to renew negotiations with the King were a direct attempt to avert the Scots' entry into the war, since once the Scots had entered the war, peace would obviously be harder to negotiate. Parliament would be unable to make peace with the King without the Scots assent and the price of the alliance would be religious Presbyterianism.[4] Holles was still sympathetic to moderate Anglicanism at this date. On 11 July he and Glyn were tellers in support of Dr. Daniel Featley, a moderate Anglican who, like Archbishop Ussher, envisaged further reform of the church, and whom some sought to expel from his Lambeth living.[5]

fore offered to pardon all the members, with some exceptions, who would join him at Oxford; *CJ*, iii. 145; D'Ewes's diary, BL, Harl. 164, f. 278v.

1 *Ibid.*, f. 339. (21 Mar. 1643).

2 *CJ*, iii. 146, 155; Whitacre's diary, BL, Add. 31116, f.61.

3 L. Kaplan, 'Steps to war: the Scots and the Parliament, 1642-1643', *Journal of British Studies* 9 (1970), 61.

4 D'Ewes's diary, BL, Harl. 165, f. 126v.

5 Featley was said to have opposed Arminianism 'when it was in its fullest ruffle', and in June 1643 Parliament named both Ussher and Featley to sit in the Assembly of Divines; *The Gentle Lash; or, The Vindication of Dr. Featley, a known Champion of the Protestant Religion*, Oxford [2 Jan. 1644], TT E.80.4; An Ordinance for the calling of an Assembly of learned and godly divines, [12 June 1643], *Acts and Ordinances of the Interregnum, 1642-1660*, ed. C.H. Firth & R.S. Rait (3 vols., London, 1911), i. 182. Whitacre says that Featley's good conduct in the past, together with his being chosen for the Assembly, persuaded the House not to eject him; *CJ*, iii. 161: Holles & Glyn – 69; Sir R. Harley & R. Goodwin – 60. Whitacre's diary, BL, Add. 31116, f. 62. Featley was one of the few Anglicans who actually attended the Assembly; Baxter, *Reliquiae Baxterianae*, p. 73; Richard Parr, *The Life of the Most Reverend Father in God, James Usher, Late Lord Arch-Bishop of Armagh, . . .* (London, 1686), p. 80. However, he was expelled from his living in the following year, ostensibly on the charge of corres-

Holles did not directly oppose the Scottish alliance, as this would have been futile, but he supported the House of Lords in their plans for further negotiations with the King which, if they had led to peace, would have obviated the need for Scottish participation in the war. On 10 July the Earl of Essex suggested that either Parliament offer propositions to the King, or else decide the Civil War by a set battle between the two armies, the King being withdrawn from the field. (At the reading of his letter in the Commons the 'violent spirits were observed to pluck their hats over their eyes').[1] The Lord General's support of peace negotiations was awkward for the Commons, because they knew that he was discontented at their neglect of his army. Consequently Pym set to work to conciliate him with votes of support, and before the Commons debated his letter, Pym and Lord Saye talked round two of Essex's friends in the House of Commons, Sir Philip Stapleton and Colonel Arthur Goodwin, so that when a treaty was discussed on 11 July, Stapleton spoke against it.[2] Goodwin did not speak for the treaty, and neither, to D'Ewes's surprise, did Pierrepont, Evelyn nor Holles. Afterwards D'Ewes learnt that the peace party had miscalculated their tactics. They had been waiting for the Lords to send down a second letter from the Lord General supporting a treaty but the Lords were so annoyed with the King for declaring that Parliament was not free that they voted against the General's suggestion.[3]

It is symptomatic of the weakness of the peace party in the Commons that they could initiate nothing: they depended on leadership from the Lords.[4] The Lords drew up peace propositions and sent these to the

ponding with Ussher at Oxford, but he had offended in other ways. His nephew says he spoke against the Solemn League and Covenant in the Assembly; John Featley, *Doctor Daniel Featley Revered . . . With a Succinct Account of his Life and Death,* [20 Dec.] 1660, TT E.1927.2, p. 47. Yonge adds that Featley had crept into Henry VII's chapel to spy on the members, he had opposed the abolition of episcopacy, refused to administer the sacrament to those who would not kneel, and said 'that the parliament have sat long and did nothing'; Yonge's diary, BL, Add. 18778, ff.58v., 75 (30 Sept. & 26 Oct. 1643). Featley was imprisoned but was admitted to compound in 1644; *DNB*. When he died in April 1645, the newsbook writers remembered points in his favour. He had written against Anabaptists, and looked to Parliament for reformation. 'For some of his works', wrote *The Weekly Account*, 16-23 Apr. 1645, TT E.278. 23, p. 8, he 'deserves great commendations'.

1   Whitacre's diary, BL, Add. 31116, f.61v.; D'Ewes's diary, BL Harl. 165, ff. 122-122v.

2   On the previous day, both in public and private, Stapleton had supported a treaty; *ibid.,* ff. 123v.–124.

3   *Ibid.,* f. 125. This information came from Holles's brother, the Earl of Clare.

4   The connection between the two groups awaits study in this period; for the later period, M.P. Mahony, 'The presbyterian party in the Long Parliament, 2 July 1644 – 3 June 1647' (Oxford D. Phil. thesis, 1974).

Commons on 4 August. So far as Pym and his allies were concerned, the propositions could not have been worse timed, for the great military danger in the west following the loss of Bristol demanded that Parliament should concentrate on military affairs. Pym wrote to his friend Sir Thomas Barrington on 2 August, 'we use all the means we can, to raise a considerable army to send into those parts',[1] but negotiations for peace cut across these plans. Besides, it was no time to talk of peace when the Scots were on the point of entering the war, as the opponents of peace pointed out, chorusing that they were not averse to accommodation, only to accommodation at that inconvenient time.[2]

On Saturday 5 August the Lords informed the Commons of their propositions. Although Gardiner suggested that the Lords' terms were no compromise but a capitulation, Laurence Whitacre, the parliamentary diarist, thought the terms were much to the same purpose as those formerly presented to the King.[3] Parliament insisted upon its privileges and its right to call the King's officers to account.[4] The war party did not want the propositions considered at all. Their first tactic was to raise a red herring — that there were men in the House who had not taken the May covenant. Maynard successfully averted a lengthy debate by urging the orders of the House. The members argued about peace terms for three hours after which Pym moved 'with much violence' that they should tell the Lords they could not send to the King for peace. When the question was put Holles and Evelyn had a majority in favour of further considering the propositions.[5] Because many of the peace supporters went home after this, there seemed some danger that their opponents might be able to reject the propositions individually. Holles, as an experienced parliamentarian, countered with a procedural device, so that what his supporters lacked in numbers they might make good with eloquence. He proposed that the House adjourn into committee where men could speak oftener than once, perhaps hoping that at the prospect of an all-night sitting, the House would adjourn — as it did.[6]

1   Barrington Papers, BL, Egerton 2643, f. 13.

2   For example, *The Parliament Scout*, 3-10 Aug. 1643, TT E.64.13, p. 51: *A Perfect Diurnall of some Passages in Parliament*, 31 July — 7 Aug. 1643, TT E.249.31, p. [48].

3   Whitacre's diary, BL, Add. 31116, f. 68.; Gardiner, *Civil War*, i. 184.

4   HMC, Report V. 98-9.

5   *CJ*, iii. 196: Holles & Evelyn — 94; Marten & Strode — 65. D'Ewes's diary, BL, Harl. 165, ff. 141-141v.

6   *Ibid.*, ff. 142v.-143. The Commons customarily met early in the morning, and adjourned at dinner time, leaving the afternoon for committees. Late sittings thus indicate important or unexpected debate.

Although Pym's middle group together with the war party could out vote any peace party proposals, these debates showed that he could not always rely upon his supporters to oppose peace. Defeated in the House on Saturday, he turned to the City to organise opposition. D'Ewes believed opponents of peace met together on Saturday night and drew up a paper which they handed to the City ministers. On Sunday 6 August the pulpits rang with denunciations of the peace proposals and appeals to the well-affected to assemble at Westminster on Monday.[1] The City drew up a petition — which *Mercurius Aulicus* claimed to be the work of Pym — stating their objections to peace negotiations: the propositions, they feared, would destroy 'our religion, laws, and liberties', and even the mere discussion of them would deject the spirits of the well affected and retard the expected brotherly assistance from Scotland.[2] 'These firebrands' wrote Holles later, 'set the City in a flame'. Possibly this City agitation and petition influenced some of the members of the Commons, for by Monday several had changed their minds: Sir Christopher Yelverton, Sir William Waller, John Glyn and William Jephson had supported peace earlier, but on Monday opposed it.[3] Glyn made a long speech about the inadequacy of the propositions: no concern for religion, none for security, nothing about payment of debts, and nothing about Ireland. He argued that by considering the propositions Parliament earned the reproach of the kingdom and disheartened the Scots.[4] There was a crowd outside Parliament to endorse this view. The division was a tense one. Holles and Sir John Holland were tellers in favour, and counted 81 supporters; Sir Robert Harley, one of the tellers for the noes, 'being in years' missed nine of his men and reported only 79 against. After an uproar, there was a recount and the hopes of peace were dashed — 88 opposed the terms.[5]

As the Lords who supported peace drew away from Westminster in

---

1   *Ibid.*, ff. 145-145v.

2   *Mercurius Aulicus*, [Oxford], 32nd week, TT E.65.26*, p. 437; *Mercurius Civicus*, 3-11 Aug. 1643, TT E.65.4, p. 85.

3   Holles, *Memoirs*, p. 10; Yelverton was a middle grouper, and had earlier tried in vain to promote a peace treaty; Hexter, *King Pym*, pp. 39-40. Like Holles, he applied for leave to travel in August 1643; *CJ*, iii. 205. Sir William Waller, at this date, was an active military leader. Glyn, the Recorder of London, later pursued a middle group attitude to peace negotiations; Valerie Pearl, 'Oliver St. John and the "middle group" in the Long Parliament: August 1643-May 1644', *EHR*, 71 (1966), 510 n.2. Jephson had been in Ireland at the outbreak of the revolt there, but Inchiquin had sent him to England in March 1643 to solicit aid from Parliament; *DNB*.

4   Yonge's diary, BL, Add. 18778, ff. 9v.-10.

5   *CJ*, iii. 197; D'Ewes's diary, BL, Harl. 165, ff. 148-148v.; Whitacre's diary, BL, Add. 31116, f.68.

their coaches, they were assaulted by the crowd, but the Lord Mayor eventually dispersed the mob.[1] Hexter does not think the mob influenced the decision, and that Pym triumphed because he had been able to neutralise the Lord General's support for peace by voting supplies and support for his army.[2] Undoubtedly Essex's neutrality was of decisive advantage to Pym, but even so there was a majority in support of the negotiations on Saturday the 5th. The City's opposition may well have swung the balance.

On Tuesday and Wednesday 8 and 9 August, there were counter-demonstrations for peace. Some hundreds of women appeared with yards of silk ribbon shouting in favour of peace and against Lord Saye and Pym. It was generally thought that the demonstrations had been instigated by wealthy titled men. Various names were mentioned. St. John later said that the Earl of Holland, a prominent supporter of the peace party, had been blamed for the disturbances.[3]

Holles was not named as an instigator of the counter-demonstrations. Indeed while the women shouted for peace outside the House on Wednesday 9 August, John Glyn moved inside that Holles might have the Speaker's warrant to go overseas with his wife, children, servants and household goods. The House granted leave to Holles and also to Sir Christopher Yelverton, Lord Wenman and Winwood, provided they took no plate nor children over sixteen.[4] (Holles's only son Francis was 13 at the time). Disillusioned and defeated Holles was now evidently trying to escape from the war. D'Ewes thought Holles's decision reflected the failure of the peace overtures and his general ineffectiveness in Parliament.[5] Many of the peace party supporters in the Lords and Commons suffered similar feelings of impotence. Holles may also have been influenced by the loss of Dorset to the Royalists, news of which arrived in the Commons on 7 August.[6] The war in the west had been going badly for some time. The Royalists surrounded Dorchester

1 Yonge's diary, BL, Add. 18778, F. 12: Whitacre's diary, BL, Add. 31116, f.68v.

2 Hexter, *King Pym*, p. 145.

3 Yonge's diary, BL, Add. 18778, f.88v. (11 Nov. 1643). For further discussion of the women petitioners, see Patricia Higgins, 'The reactions of women, with special reference to women petitioners', in Manning, *Politics, Religion and the English Civil War*, pp. 189-98.

4 *CJ*, iii. 198-9; D'Ewes's diary, BL, Harl. 165, f. 151v.; Yonge's diary, Add. 18778, f.13. Holles's mother and sister had been granted passes to travel on 19 May 1643; *CJ*, iii. 93. His mother was still in France in 1646.

5 D'Ewes's diary, BL, Harl. 165, f.151v. (11 Aug. 1643).

6 *CJ*, iii. 197. In 1645 John Bond said 'the West is now become a kind of Turkey . . . to all that are Christians indeed'; John Bond, *Occasus Occidentalis; or, Job in the West. Two sermons at two Public Fasts, for the five associated Western Counties*, [25 Jan. 1645], TT E.25.22, p. 48.

on 3 August and the town was soon lost. Some blamed Sir Walter Erle the governor of Dorchester, for panicking needlessly, but he claimed that the defenders of the town were demoralised because the wealthier men, of whom Holles was probably one, had sent their goods out of Dorchester.[1] Holles might still have retired to his wife's estates in Surrey, safe from royalist attacks. But neutralism was very difficult to sustain in the counties, so it is not surprising that he now decided to leave England altogether.

Yet Holles was not allowed to leave. The day after his pass was granted, it was revoked, on Pym's motion.[2] On the 19 August Millington moved, at Pym's behest, that the House should be called, which D'Ewes thought was out of spite to Holles, Sir William Lewis and some others who had retired into the country.[3] Not spite but suspicion of desertion influenced Pym. In the ten days since Holles had applied for permission to go abroad, several of the peace Lords had fled to the King. Holles's brother, the Earl of Clare, was among them.[4] These lords had tried to enlist the Earl of Essex's support for peace negotiations, but Pym's promises of men and money kept the Earl loyal to Parliament, so the Earls of Bedford, Holland, Clare and Portland, together with Lords Lovelace and Conway, fled to Oxford. The Earl of Northumberland retired to Petworth, his house in Surrey, to see what reception his fellows received from the Royalists before venturing himself. Some members of the Commons joined him there, including Sir John Evelyn who had been associated with Holles as an enthusiastic supporter of peace. It was generally believed that these men all intended to desert to the King, so Pym posted Colonel Herbert Morley to keep watch on their activities.[5] Not surprisingly, the Commons ordered that any member who left the House without leave should have his estate sequestered. Holles was granted leave to settle his wife in the Isle of Wight and to return. The House was more lenient towards non M.P.s: Sir John Conyers, the Lieutenant of the Tower, was allowed to transfer his family into Holland, and Sir Theodore Mayerne was still permitted

1 John Lilburne, *Rash Oaths unwarrantable*, 31 May [25 June] 1647, TT E. 393. 39, p. 39, abuses Erle for 'base cowardice' in deserting Dorchester.; Bodl., Tanner 62, f. 160-160v.; f.217, copy of summons to Dorchester; f. 218 [Sir Walter Erle to Lenthall], 6 Aug. 1643. One of Holles's servants, Ezekias Lambe, said he had moved all Holles's goods from Dorset to the Isle of Wight; Papers in the suit of Denzil Holles against Ezekias Lambe, his servant, Nott. U.L., Ne L 506, p.2.
2 *CJ*, iii. 201; D'Ewes's diary, BL, Harl. 165, f. 151v. Yonge was absent at the time so there is no mention of the incident in his diary (10 Aug. 1643).
3 *Ibid.*, f. 152v.
4 *Mercurius Aulicus*, 32nd week, TT E.65.26, p. 432.
5 D'Ewes's diary, BL, Harl. 165, ff. 152v.-156.

to depart from England.[1] But Parliament would not tolerate neutralism in its own members.

The division on whether or not to proceed with the peace propositions on Monday 6 August was crucial for the peace party as well as for Holles. It was really a division about the future of the war, and whether or not Parliament would persist in calling in the Scots and intensifying the struggle. Interestingly enough, a pamphlet published in 1650 commented on it in these terms. There was, said the anonymous author,

> a mystery heretofore not known to everybody, but yet a very great truth: that when the commissioners of Parliament were in Scotland, and the Covenant agreed upon . . . the Lords House here in England, and a party of the Commons, apprehending that by the coming in of the Scots, matters would become irreconcilable towards the King, they made an underhand agreement with the King, and in the House of Commons matters were brought so far, that it was debated and put to the question, whether they should enter in Covenant with the Scots yea or no?[2]

After this vote Holles was not alone in trying to withdraw from the war. His alteration was conspicuous because of his earlier prominence in the parliamentary cause. Since the war broke out, Holles had pinned his faith on a negotiated settlement with the King, although the Royalists had used peace discussions as a cover for their attack on Brentford in November 1642, and Holles and the peace party gained nothing from the Oxford treaty. Nevertheless, Holles persisted in his view that only by negotiation between the King and Parliament could the nation return to the old, known ways. To his contemporaries, he appeared to be a changed man, but perhaps it was they who had changed, not Holles.

---

[1] *CJ*, iii. 211, 212, 187, 202.

[2] *Memorandums of the Conferences held between the Brethren scrupled at the Engagement; and others who were satisfied with it. On Feb. 15 and 22, and March 1. 1649* [1650], TT E.610. 2, p. 5.

6

1643 — 1645 : DIFFICULTIES AT WESTMINSTER

> Those creatures of theirs whom they sent commissioners into
> Scotland . . . represented the state of affairs to the Parliament
> clear otherwise than it was, endearing their own party to them as
> the only sincere public spirited men, . . . giving characters of all
> others as malignants, . . . With which prejudice of us the Scots
> were strongly possessed at their coming in about January [1644],
> and were in England some time before they were disabused.[1]

i.

For more than twelve months after Holles's attempted withdrawal
from England following the failure of the August 1643 peace bid, his
influence in the House of Commons was greatly reduced. This was
partly due to the weakening of the old peace party, but more
significantly, his relative powerlessness was a consequence of his
opposition to the Scots' entry into the war.

The peace party's position in Parliament was weakened by desertions.
Despite the fact that three of the peace party lords, Holland, Bedford
and Conway, returned to Westminster after the Royalists gave them
such a cool reception, their actions tainted the peace party with disloyalty. Holles's brother had a sojourn in Nottingham but was
permitted to rejoin his fellows in the Lords in 1644. Eventually, the
truants were all excluded from the Lords at the insistence of the
Commons,[2] and although over the next three years there were attempts
to readmit them, none was successful. In the House of Commons many
former supporters of the peace party found both the intensification of
the war and the alliance with the Scots unpalatable. Sir John Holland
withdrew from Parliament with limited leave to visit his wife in the
Low Countries.[3] He did not return for some time. The two Sir John
Evelyns, uncle and nephew, seemed to be trying to join the Royalists,
so the House imprisoned them at the end of August.[4] In both William
Pierrepont and Sir Ralph Verney the Covenant precipitated a crisis of

---

1 Holles, *Memoirs,* pp. 13-14.

2 C.H. Firth, *The House of Lords During the Civil War* (London, 1910), p. 136.

3 There was an attack on Holland for his absence on 13 Sept. 1643; D'Ewes's
diary, BL, Harl. 165, f.190. The leave was granted on 22 Sept. 1643; *CJ*, iii. 251.

4 *Ibid.,* 217; D'Ewes's diary, BL, Harl. 165, ff. 156-156v; Whitacre's diary,
BL, Add. 31116, ff. 74-74v., Yonge's diary, BL, Add. 18778, f. 22.

conscience. Pierrepont tried unsuccessfully to retire into the country or to go abroad, but even though he offered to leave his estates worth over £7,000 *per annum* to Parliament's management, the Commons refused him permission.[1] Verney left England.[2] Both men were, like Holles, members of families which had been divided by the war. As many of the old leaders of the peace party deserted, others were disheartened. D'Ewes stayed away from the House after September 1643 when he found 'the violent spirits' had the numbers to carry what they wanted.[3]

Far more than the loss of numbers and credit, the peace party's hostility to the Scots weakened their position. After their unsuccessful attempt to initiate further negotiations for peace, the Solemn League and Covenant was accepted by the English Parliament and Holles had no choice but to swear to it, together with his fellow M.P.s, in September 1643.[4] Baillie thought that the peace party, 'the powerful faction', finally acquiesced in the Covenant because they believed the Scots would not come, or would be unable to enter the war before the following spring, by which time they might have concluded a peace. None of the English Parliamentarians perceived the Scots' desperate anxiety to join the war. The peace party's hopes were foiled by the Scots' herculean efforts, setting forth in the depth of winter and arriving in England in January 1644: 'now seeing we are ready, they are at a non-plus' wrote Baillie happily. On their arrival the Scots found friends in Parliament among those who had summoned them — Northumberland, Saye and Wharton in the Lords, Vane and St. John ('the sweet man, Mr Pym's successor') in the Commons, and in military affairs, 'none so panting for us as brave Waller'. As for Holles, the Scots numbered him among 'the strong lurking party' which gave them so much trouble, a party comprising two peers with west country influence, Pembroke and Salisbury, in the Lords, Reynolds, Stapleton and Clotworthy in the Commons, all men wedded to the interests of the Lord General Essex.[5]

What terminology should be used for the political parties in 1644?

---

1 *Ibid.*, f. 84; *CJ*, iii. 304: Solicitor & Vane — 55; Sir W. Erle & Sir T. Walsingham — 56; D'Ewes's diary, BL, Harl. 165, f. 224v. D'Ewes says Sam Browne asked for leave on Pierrepont's behalf, but Yonge, BL, Add. 18778, f. 84, and Whitacre, BL, Add. 31116, f. 90v. say St. John moved it.

2 *DNB.*

3 D'Ewes's diary, BL, Harl. 165, f. 164 (1 Sept. 1643).

4 Rushworth, *Historical Collections*, v. 481.

5 Baillie, *Letters and Journals*, ii. 125-6, 115, 132, 155, 136, 138, 155; Kaplan, 'Steps to War', p. 61.

Rowe suggests that the period can be discussed in terms of 'Vane's group' and 'Holles's group', but she points out that it takes time for a group to coalesce around Holles.[1] Towards the end May 1644 Sabran observed Holles and Vane to be leaders in the House of Commons.[2] However, Professor Pearl has argued that the middle group did not disintegrate, as Hexter thought, on the death of Pym, but that from the time of his illness and withdrawal from politics in October 1643, Oliver St. John stepped into his place as its leader.[3] Since the peace and war parties likewise continued in an attenuated form, the terminology of middle, peace and war party remains the most useful for 1644. The respective strengths of these parties alter. The middle group was weaker and less influential than when controlled by Pym, but then Pym was unique, and no-one ever replaced him. (As Baillie observed of the Commons in 1644, there were 'many very good able spirits, but not any of so great and comprehensive a brain').[4] Under St. John, the middle group followed Pym's old policy, compromising on issues which aroused major opposition and supporting the Earl of Essex while strengthening the association armies.[5] The peace party still continued after August 1643, although it was weaker than before. There were still attempts at initiating peace negotiations, but these were prompted chiefly by foreign ambassadors — by the French and the Dutch — and although Holles and his friends supported these, they had little success.[6] Nevertheless, Holles's policy during 1644 was directed towards ending the war and settling the kingdom. The war party continued also, although it was weaker after the expulsion of Marten in August 1643, and damaged by its association with the abortive scheme for a general uprising.[7]

By the end of 1644 the names 'Presbyterian' and 'Independent' come into contemporary use for the parties at Westminster. Although several religious issues had come before the Houses during the year — whether the church settlement was to be Erastian, was there to be any

1 Violet Rowe, *Sir Henry Vane the Younger. A Study in Political and Administrative History* (London, 1970), ch. 2.

2 'Negotiations de Monsr. de Sabran en Angleterre, aux années 1644-1645', BL, Add. 5460, f. 49, Sabran to Brienne, 23 May/3 June 1644.

3 Pearl, 'Oliver St. John'.

4 Baillie, *Letters and Journals,* ii. 216 (10 Aug. 1644).

5 Pearl, 'Oliver St. John', pp. 505-7.

6 For example, he supported the disucssion of peace 13 April – 3 May 1644; *CJ,* iii. 458-78; D'Ewes's diary, BL, Harl. 166, f. 55.

7 C.M. Williams, 'The political career of Henry Marten, with special reference to the origins of Republicanism in the Long Parliament' (Oxford D. Phil. thesis, 1954).

toleration — these did not dominate the politics of 1644.[1] Initially the English Parliamentarians were ignorant of how the Presbyterian system functioned in Scotland.[2] None of the Parliamentarians were very happy with the terms of the Solemn League and Covenant, but those who summoned the Scots realised they had no choice, as their speeches make clear. St. John, for example, justified presbytery on the grounds of expediency.[3] The contentious discussion of the religious settlement was referred to the Assembly of Divines and during most of 1644 the issues on which the Commons divided were those of peace, war, and the Scots. Even in the Assembly the discussion of religion was initially muted. Dr. Kaplan argues that this was the result of a definite peace made by the ministers of England in the autumn of 1641 to suppress their religious differences so long as they were threatened by a common enemy.[4] Nor were the Scots anxious for a break with the Independents, for they hoped to use the support of the Independents to destroy that 'great idol of England, the Service-Book'.[5]

Because Holles had not supported the Scots' entry they in turn viewed him with suspicion. For the first time Holles found himself excluded from the executive committee directing the war. He was a member of the previous executive, the committee of safety, and defended it against Marten's attacks during 1643. Marten had claimed that the committee was incapable of discharging its business, adding 'a pint pot would not hold a pottle of liquor'. 'Some', said Holles, 'were ever snarling and railing at it'. Holles was very bitter about the creation of a new committee: 'such juggling, as never was heard of before in Parliament, none but such hocus-pocus's could have the face to have done'.[6] It seems that Holles was mistaken, for the creation of the committee was not a war party manoeuvre at the expense of the pro-Essex, pro-peace group. Even the peace party saw the need for a new committee, and in composition it was not anti-Essex, for only six of its fourteen members were hostile to the Lord General.[7] Holles's bitterness is under-

1 Here my view agrees with that of David Underdown, *Pride's Purge: Politics in the Puritan Revolution* (Oxford, 1971), p. 16, and differs from that of George Yule, *The Independents in the English Civil War* (Cambridge, 1958), p. 42.

2 D'Ewes's diary, BL, Harl. 165, f. 158v. (26 Aug. 1643).

3 *Mercurius Aulicus*, [Oxford], 37th week, 10 Sept. 1643, TT E.68.4, pp. 504-5.

4 L. Kaplan, 'Presbyterians and independents in 1643', *EHR* 84 (1969), 244-56.

5 Baillie, *Letters and Journals*, ii. 117.

6 D'Ewes's diary, BL, Harl. 164, f. 254v.; Holles, *Memoirs*, p. 14.

7 W. Notestein, 'The establishment of the committee of both kingdoms', *American Historical Review* 17 (1912), 486-8; Pearl, 'Oliver St. John', pp. 512-3.

standable, because the committees absorbed some of the business of the House.[1] He was forced to rely on others for his information about current events, which was difficult because the committee had an oath of secrecy. His advocacy of peace was hampered because the propositions were prepared in the committee, so that all he could do was to rally his supporters to the House of Commons when peace was under discussion. Come to Westminster, he urged Sir John Potts, 'we shall shortly have more need of you than ever'.[2] When the ordinance for the committee's tenure lapsed in May, the 'lurking party' — that is, Holles and his allies — resumed their machinations to diminish the committee's power and the Scots' influence.[3] The Lords suggested new members for the committee, including Holles, but the Commons objected to the infringement of their privileges. Eventually, the old committee of February 1644 was renewed.[4]

One important development for Holles and the peace party during 1644 was the emergence of Stapleton as an ally. Previously Stapleton had been sympathetic to the cause of peace. He had shared the peace party's policy of supporting the Lord General Essex, since he was himself the captain of Essex's lifeguard, but Pym could persuade Stapleton to change his mind about peace negotiations, because Pym gave Essex more help than Holles was able to.[5] By February 1644 Baillie wrote of Holles and Stapleton as allies.[6] Unlike Holles, Stapleton was a member of the committee of both kingdoms. They were tellers together regularly in the House, and jointly worked to end the war.[7] Publicly and privately they supported the Earl of Essex. Both men reacted sharply in the House in May when Vane made derogatory reflections on the Earl.[8] Holles's one public speech during 1644 was to

1 *Mercurius Aulicus,* week ending 11 May 1644, Oxford, TT E.49.23, p. 975. Aulicus mocks the Commons' amazement when they learnt of letters coming to the committee, not to the House.

2 Bodl., Tanner 61, f. 14 (16 Apr. 1644).

3 Holles, Maynard, Whitelocke and Reynolds all spoke against the ordinance on 22 May 1644; D'Ewes's diary, BL, Harl. 166, f.64v.

4 Yonge's diary, BL, Add. 18779, f. 102v. (8 May 1644); Baillie, *Letters and Journals,* ii. 187. How this was done, Baillie was too rushed to explain in his letter, but it was by the revival of an earlier and more radical ordinance which the Lords had passed in January; Pearl, 'Oliver St. John', pp. 514-5.

5 See above, p. 93.

6 Baillie, *Letters and Journals,* ii. 136.

7 At 32 divisions during 1644, Holles was a teller 11 times; 7 with Stapleton, and twice with both Lewis and Reynolds. Whitelocke, Annals, BL, Add. 37343, f.297v. discusses behind-the-scenes activity.

8 D'Ewes's diary, BL, Harl. 166, f.56. (4 May 1644). Stapleton, as a fellow soldier, was probably closer to Essex than Holles. It was to Stapleton that Essex

persuade the Londoners to support the Earl of Essex's army.[1] Holles and Stapleton were, Whitelocke said, 'the two most secret counsellors and friends of the General'. Whitelocke was their go-between, and says they advised Essex 'for his good and the advantage of the Parliament'.[2] On 9 August Stapleton, Reynolds and Clotworthy wrote to Holles and Whitelocke urging them to hasten to Westminster where 'my lord General's condition requires his friends being here'.[3] As Holles, Stapleton and their friends were not the only group supporting Essex at this date, this may explain why Whitelocke found Essex 'was not well fixed' in affection to Holles's party.[4] Nevertheless, at the crisis of Manchester's quarrel with Cromwell at the end of 1644 and the consequent re-examination of the military structure of Parliament's armies, it was Holles and Stapleton who continued to support Essex and to oppose the New Model, and St. John and other middle groupers who abandoned the Earl.[5]

Local politics and national politics were also closely related, as Professor Underdown has shown, but Holles's relationship with the county of Dorset seems minimal, for unlike Erle, Bond and other Dorset M.P.s he seems little involved in county affairs.[6] Nor did he participate in Sussex politics, although his marriage may have linked him to some prominent families there, such as the Shirleys. D'Ewes learnt in December 1643 from Thomas Erle that the House had polarised into three factions on the basis of local issues and general army strategy, but Holles seems unaffected.[7]

wrote of his defeat in the west in Sept. 1644; Rushworth, *Historical Collections,* v. 701. (3 Sept. 1644).

1   *Six Speeches spoken in the Guild-Hall, London, by the Earle of Warwick, Sir Henry Vane, the Earle of Essex, the Earle of Pembroke, Col. Holles, and Master Recorder,* 9 Apr. 1644, TT E.42.18, p. 5. *The Parliament Scout,* 4-11 Apr. 1644, TT E.42.10, p. 355 reported that 'Master Holles excellent well spoke to the business'.

2   Bulstrode Whitelocke, Annals, BL, Add. 37343, f. 297v. There is a similar account in Whitelocke's 'Diary', in Lord Bute's possession, for the 39th year. I am grateful to Miss R. Spalding for allowing me to use her transcript of this manuscript.

3   Whitelocke Manuscripts, in the possession of the Marquis of Bath, Longleat, Whitelocke ix. f.27.

4   Whitelocke, Annals, BL, Add. 37343, f. 297v.

5   Division on whether to except Essex from the Self Denying Ordinance, 17 Dec. 1644; *CJ*, iii. 726.

6   Underdown, *Pride's Purge.*

7   Fletcher, *A County Community;* D'Ewes's diary, BL, Harl. 165, f. 233 (6 Dec. 1643).

During 1644 the Scots changed their friends from Vane and St. John's group to that of Holles and Stapleton. This vitally affected the political balance, and was for Holles another swing of the see-saw. Friendly with the Scots in 1640 and 1641, he had opposed inviting them into the war in 1643 and had been hostile to them during much of 1644. Now he would be allied with their interests again.

There were signs of strain between the Scots and their war party friends from the summer of 1644 onwards. By claiming all the credit for the joint victory at Marston Moor, Cromwell displeased the Scots. The victory itself reduced the Parliamentarians' sense of grateful dependence as the dark days of imminent defeat receded.[1] Furthermore, as the Scots gained familiarity with the English political scene, they probably appreciated that they had more in common with Holles and the peace party than with the war party. The Scots were politically conservative. Whether or not Sir Henry Vane junior sounded them out about the possibility of deposing Charles when he went north in June 1644, they probably realised that the war party was prepared to take a firm stand against Charles, and the war party in turn doubtless realised that the Scots were indifferent to English political issues.[2] Clarendon considered that political differences played a part in dividing the Scots from their first friends.[3]

Religious differences also played a major role: 'The first and main occasion of mistake betwixt those men and the Scots was the church government'.[4] The Scots had tolerated the Independents in the Assembly so that they might help destroy episcopacy, but with that work nearly completed by the autumn of 1644, differences emerged as the establishment of an alternative form of church government demanded attention. Baillie was shocked by the defection of Stephen Marshall, the minister

---

1 For Holles's comments on this, see *Memoirs*, pp. 17-18.

2 J.R. MacCormack, *Revolutionary Politics in the Long Parliament* (Cambridge, Mass., 1973) p. 33 and n. 51, argues that Vane made a bold proposal to overthrow the monarchy and establish a republic. The evidence for the subject of Vane's conversations with the Earl of Leven, Lord Fairfax and the Earl of Manchester rests on the uncorroborated testimony of two foreign observers and is not so conclusive as he suggests. Rowe, *Sir Henry Vane the Younger*, pp. 52-5, concluded that the incident was obscure, and L. Kaplan 'The 'Plot' to depose Charles I in 1644', *BIHR* 44 (1971), 216-23 doubts the ambassadors' reports.

3 Clarendon, *History* (Bk.VIII, 186), Macray, iii. 454.

4 [David Buchanan], *Truth its Manifest*, [12 Nov. 1645], TT E.1179.5, pp. 54-5. See also [Edward Bowles], *Manifest Truths, or an Inversion of Truths Manifest*, [4 July] 1646, TT E.343.1, pp. 44-5.

with whom they had been most friendly. He was not a supporter of the presbytery as they thought, but was for 'a middle way all of his own'.[1] Furthermore, the Scots discovered in September that the Independent ministers had supporters in the House of Commons who issued an accommodation order directing the Assembly to consider how far religious toleration might extend, even before the Assembly had determined the form of church government. What shocked the Scots was apparently the discovery that members of the Commons supported the Independent ministers.[2] Baillie was disgusted with their 'greatest friends, Sir Henry Vane and the Solicitor' who had procured the accommodation order, for it was with Scottish aid that these two had been raised 'to the height of the power now they enjoy'. No wonder he concluded that the English were 'a very fickle people'.[3] As Baillie's uneasiness about Vane and St. John increased, so his attitude towards 'the strong lurking party' changed. His comments about the Earl of Essex are a barometer of his feelings. Derision of the Lord General in his letters ceased, and by September 1644 Baillie was prepared to see Essex as an honourable man.[4]

It was at the time of the accommodation order in September that the Scots realised that they needed new allies. 'We must seek for new friends at last', Baillie wrote, 'when our old ones, without the least cause, have deserted and half betrayed us'. Around this time the Chancellor of Scotland, the Earl of Loudoun, arrived in London and it was not long before Baillie felt more comfortable. Overtures to the peace party probably began in October shortly after Loudoun's arrival. In that month, when 'the Independent party' sought to be rid of Manchester and then Essex, Baillie observed that 'God helped us to

1 Baillie, *Letters and Journals*, ii. 230 (16 Sept. 1644). Sabran said that the Scots were scandalised because Parliament was so far from agreement with them on uniformity in religion; BL, Add. 5460, f.374v., Sabran to Brienne, 24 Nov. 1644.

2 Buchanan claims that the Scots were shocked at the revelation of Independent views in the Assembly, but I have already shown that the Scots knew of these at the beginning of 1644; [Buchanan], *Truth its Manifest*, pp. 55-6. Buchanan was a supporter of the Scots' interests, one Baillie thought 'a most sincere and zealous gentleman'. Parliament voted Buchanan an incendiary for a publication in 1646, and Baillie told his friends that should he flee to Scotland he was 'worthy of great honour for many good services'; Baillie, *Letters and Journals*, ii. 367 (24 Apr. 1646).

3 *Ibid.*, ii. 230 (16 Sept. 1644).

4 For example, Essex's sending some royalist overtures straight to Parliament showed him to be honest; *ibid.*, 222 (18 Aug. 1644). Nathaniel Fiennes commented on how the Scots had at first cried up Waller, and looked at the Earl of Essex 'at a distance, with an evil eye'; [Nathaniel Fiennes], *Vindiciae Veritatis*, [12 Sept.] 1654, TT E.811.2, p. 97.

guard it so, that the General keeps his place and credit, and knows who are his friends and foes'.[1] On 10 November Sabran noted that the Scots and the peace party had drawn together.[2]

Although the new alliance was not at first general knowledge, the Scots and the peace party were soon to be observed in action together in the quarrel between Manchester and Cromwell and in opposition to the new modelling of the army. In both cases their interests were identical: to save Manchester, and to keep Essex in control of the parliamentary forces.[3] Early in December the Scots and their allies tried to attack Cromwell by accusing him of being an incendiary between the two nations of England and Scotland according to the fourth article of the Solemn League and Covenant. The Scots and their allies met at the Earl of Essex's house late one December night to hear the advice of the lawyers, Whitelocke and Maynard, about the prospects of making a charge stick.[4] Holles was less inclined than the Scots to accept the lawyers' cautious advice that very clear proofs would be needed for any accusation, because Cromwell was a man 'of quick and subtle parts' who did not lack friends in the two Houses.

> Mr Holles and Sir Phillip Stapleton and some others spoke smartly to the business, and mentioned some particular passages and words of Cromwell tending to prove him to be an incendiary, and they did not apprehen his interest in the house of Commons to be so much as was supposed; and they would willingly have been upon the accusation of him.

Holles never wanted for courage in a crisis, though he may have lacked caution and wisdom. In this case the lawyers prevailed, but Cromwell learnt of Holles's animus against him.[5] Holles's part in the quarrel

---

1 Baillie, *Letters and Journals*, ii. 230 (16 Sept. 1644); 231 (Oct. [1644]); 234, 235 (25 Oct. 1644).

2 Sabran, BL, Add. 5460, ff. 349-350. In November Holles told the Royalists that the Scots had made overtures to him and his party but that 'for a months space durst not comply with them'; Lord Savile's paper, Bodl., Nalson Papers, xiv, f.112 (2 July 1645).

3 C. Holmes, *The Eastern Association in The English Civil War* (Cambridge, 1974), p. 209, argues that the new alliance encouraged Essex to realise his own claims to supreme command.

4 A variant account in Lord Bute's manuscript suggests that the Scots were agents rather than initiators of the idea: 'Jealousies growing betwixt the Lord General & Cromwell, it was advised to rid Cromwell out of the way, and that the best course for it would be by the Scots Commissioners of whom he had spoken something distasteful'; Whitelocke, 'Diary' (Dec. 1644).

5 Whitelocke, Annals, BL, Add. 37343, ff.343v.–346. The date of the meeting is not clear from Whitelocke. Gardiner suggests 3 Dec. 1645; *Civil War*, ii. 86 n.4. Holmes, *Eastern Association*, follows Hexter in arguing that it was within 3 days of 28 Nov. 1644. Whitelocke says that the commissioners returned from Oxford to Westminster on 29 Nov. 1644; BL, Add. 37343, f. 342v.

between Manchester and Cromwell is obscure, although Godwin believed that he penned the Earl's reply.[1] Needless to say, he and his party met with no success in their opposition to the formation of the New Model and the Self-Denying Ordinance.

Less well known is an earlier instance of Holles's activity in association with the Scots. Parliament agreed to negotiate with the King. Peace propositions were drawn up under Scottish influence, with the approval of the middle and war party, and sent to the King at Oxford in November 1644.[2] Gardiner censures the peace party for offering Charles such distasteful terms,[3] but they had, of course, no option because they were powerless to alter the terms in Parliament. Realising this, Holles and Whitelocke, two of the parliamentary commissioners, used the occasion to make their own party's overtures to the King with the Scots' acquiescence. This was not known until a Royalist deserter Thomas Lord Savile, raised the charge the following year. Although his testimony was suspect, other sources confirm his account.

Holles and Whitelocke left London with Parliament's commissioners on 20 November 1644. The Royalists did not welcome them to Oxford, but forced them to wait outside the town 'in the wet and cold open field', and the townspeople reviled them as 'traitors' as they rode through the streets. When some officers of the King's army called the commissioners 'rogues' in their own lodgings, Holles did not hesitate, but seized one man, 'a tall big, black man', shook him and disarmed him. Whitelocke 'thought himself engaged in honour to do the like to another'. Thereafter they were no more insulted, and the Royalists commended them for behaving 'like gentlemen'.[4]

Holles and Whitelocke later admitted that when they went to Oxford the commissioners privately agreed to visit those Royalists who visited them, provided these were not persons Parliament had excepted from pardon. The Earl of Lindsey, a distant cousin of Holles's, was wounded, but he sent a message to greet Whitelocke and Holles and they decided it would be only courtesy to return the compliment with a visit. What they never admitted to the House, but Whitelocke later wrote in his Annals, was that when they were there the King came in, and asked them what answer he should return to the propositions.

---

1 Quoted in the *The Quarrel between the Earl of Manchester and Oliver Cromwell: an Episode of the English Civil War*, ed. D. Masson (Camden Society, n.s., 12 1875), p. 1xxiii.

2 Baillie, *Letters and Journals*, ii. 178.

3 Gardiner, *Civil War*, ii. 78.

4 Whitelocke, Annals, BL, Add. 37343, ff. 338-338v.

Both Holles and Whitelocke advised him to return to Parliament: 'the best answer would be your own coming amongst us'. At the King's request, they withdrew into an adjoining room and drew up a paper which Whitelocke wrote out in a disguised hand; the King came, took it up, and went away.[1]

The dispatches of the French agent, Sabran, show that this meeting with the King was no chance event, and the conduct of Holles takes on a more sinister air. At the beginning of November 1644 Holles and Stapleton met Sabran secretly — since it was contrary to the orders of the Commons for their members to visit foreign representatives — by the arrangement of the Countess of Carlisle and the Earl of Holland.[2] Holles and Stapleton, with the approval of Loudoun and Maitland, urged Sabran to use his influence so that the King would not reject the peace propositions absolutely, lest he ruin that party of Lords, Commons and Scots, which supported him. The King should use the propositions to propose a treaty at which there would be some chance of moderating Parliament's articles. They wanted Sabran to send his secretary to the King with this information and to engage the interests of the Queen to the scheme.[3]

Savile's account of the Royalists' conversations with Holles and Whitelocke at Oxford were never substantiated but are extremely interesting. Holles, Savile said, spoke to the Royalists of a 'violent and Independent party' which was opposed to peace. Nevertheless, Holles argued that the King should use his friends on Parliament's side who wanted peace. Charles should come to London, adding 'as an argument that there was nothing in the world the violent party did so much fear, as his coming to London . . . and bid us assure the king that if he

---

1   *Ibid.*, ff. 338-340. G. Holles, *Memorials*, p. 252 n.29.

2   When Sabran arrived in England in mid 1644 to offer French mediation, he brought letters to the Earl of Holland and the Countess of Carlisle, among others. The Earl of Holland was not permitted to sit in the House of Lords, but he supported the Scottish alliance and believed the King should make religious concessions. He did not find Sabran sympathetic to the Scots; Leopold von Ranke, *A History of England Principally in the Seventeenth Century* (5 vols., Oxford, 1875), ii. 407; v. 475, 479. Lucy Hay, Countess of Carlisle, once allied with Strafford, became the ally of the parliamentary leaders after his death. The Army, later in 1647, accused Holles of meeting at her house to correspond with the Queen and her party in France. This plotting Holles and others denied, alleging that they only paid her 'that respect which is due unto her (a person of so great honour and desert). . . ' *A full Vindication and Answer of the XI Accused Members*, p. 8. Sabran's design, which was to persuade the Scots to assist the King, is discussed in D.A. Bigby, *Anglo-French Relations 1641 to 1649* (London, 1933), pp. 57-80.

3   Sabran, BL, Add. 5460, ff. 349-350v.; Sabran to Brienne, 10 Nov. 1644. Maitland was a friend of Holles's from 1641.

knew as much as they did he would be there the next day'. The Independent party would, of course, oppose this, but Holles was confident they would be unsuccessful. There were friends in the City of London who would rise to support the King should he come to London.[1] Holles explained that he and his party were now allied with the Scots, so it was clear that with Essex still in command of the Army and the Scots as friends, the Independents had no military force at their disposal, while he and his friends controlled the armies of the parliamentary alliance.[2] How far Holles proposed to capitulate to the King he did not then make clear, or certainly not enough to make the King think seriously of throwing himself on London. Nevertheless, Holles's remarks appear to have made some impression on the King's plans.

As the official parliamentary delegation had no power to negotiate, Charles treated them as messengers and gave a sealed reply. Although the commissioners demurred at carrying a paper which bore no direction, they returned to Westminster where Holles reported on their activities.[3] Charles perceived the Parliamentarians were divided, so he saw some advantage in discussing peace. He requested that the Earls of Richmond and Southampton might come to London, where on arrival they proposed a peace treaty. Pressure for peace from Parliament's supporters was strong, so the Houses agreed to negotiate, but the majority was anxious for Richmond and Southampton to leave the City, for there was talk of underhand plots with the peace party.[4]

Negotiations for peace opened at Uxbridge at the end of January 1645, when both sides treated by commissioners of whom Holles was one. Holles showed himself anxious for agreement, and he followed the royalist Earl of Southampton in declining to hear Whitelocke and Hyde debate the respective rights of King and Parliament to the militia:

> though I should account the time very well spent to hear these worthy gentlemen, who I believe would very much enlighten our judgements in this matter, yet I doubt [i.e. anticipate] it may not tend so much to a composure of it; as may be by declining the debate.[5]

In private, the peace party Lords and Commons among the commis-

---

1 Savile's paper, Bodl., Nalson Papers, xiv, ff. 112-112v.

2 Because the implications of Holles's remarks were so clear and so dangerous, he later strenuously denied he had said the Scots had changed their friends; *ibid.*, f. 124.

3 Holles's narrative, Bodl., Tanner 61, f. 199.

4 *Perfect Passages of each days Proceedings*, 18-24 Dec. 1644, TT E.22.7, p. 80; *The Kingdoms Weekly Intelligencer*, 17-24 Dec. 1644, TT E.22.9, pp. 687-90.

5 Whitelocke, Annals, BL, Add. 37343, f. 362v.

sioners tried to persuade the Royalists to consent to Parliament's propositions. The Earls of Salisbury, Pembroke, and Denbigh expounded the vile designs of the Independents to the King's commissioners. Clarendon observed that the commissioners were mutually mistrustful. Three of them — Vane, St. John and Prideaux — did not really desire peace but were sent simply as 'spies upon the rest', Pierrepont and Crew seemed more reserved towards the Royalists than before, but Holles and Whitelocke were still as open towards the King's commissioners in supporting the cause of peace as they had been earlier at Oxford. Clarendon's comment on Holles at this date is worth quoting:

> Holles, who was the frankest amongst them in owning his animosity and indignation against all the Independent party, and was no otherwise affected to the Presbyterians than as they constituted a party upon which he depended to oppose the other, did foresee that many of those who appear[ed] most resolute to concur with him would by degrees fall from him purely for want of courage, in which he abounded.[1]

The Royalists also observed a coolness between the English and their Scottish allies. The Parliamentarians' attitude towards the Covenant was inconsistent, for they insisted that the King should take it, but at the same time waived it for the soldiers of the New Model.[2] The Scots were left alone to defend the demands for Presbyterian church government, while 'all the English sat still without speaking a word, as if they were not concerned'. The Earl of Loudoun privately told the Duke of Richmond and Edward Hyde that if the King would agree to their demands over church government, they would not insist on any other terms.[3] Sabran confirms that the Scots were willing to declare for the King at the time of the treaty if he agreed to their religious demands.[4]

In later years Holles's attitude to the failure of the treaty was unrealistic. He told Burnet that he had left Oxford in November 'not doubting a peace would have followed' but the success of Montrose in Scotland encouraged the King to hope for military victory and persuaded him to reject the peace proposals offered at Uxbridge. Charles's 'affairs declined totally in England that summer, and Holles

1 Clarendon, *History* (Bk. VIII, 243-6), Macray, iii. 494-6; (Bk. VIII, 241), Macray, iii. 492; (Bk. VIII, 248), Macray, iii. 497. Holles may have been using the term 'presbyterian' here to refer to the Scots.

2 *Mercurius Aulicus*, [Oxford], 2-9 Feb. [1645], TT E.271.4, p. 1366.

3 Clarendon, *History* (Bk. VIII, 324), Macray, iii. 478; (Bk. VIII, 223), Macray, iii. 477.

4 'Negotiations de Monsr. de Sabran en Angleterre, aux années 1644-1645'. vol. 2, BL, Add. 5461, f. 66, Sabran to Brienne, 9 Feb. 1645.

said to me, all was owing to Montrose's unhappy successes'.[1] There was some substance to Holles's contention, for the royalist commissioners *had* gained a concession over the militia from the King, but when they saw the negotiations would fail they did not offer it.[2] Even so, Holles was mistaken if he thought that military defeat would make Charles capitulate.

For a brief time at the end of 1644 before the parliamentary army was new modelled, Holles and the peace party were in a position of great strength outside Parliament, although they were weak within it. Their new alliance with the Scots had gained them allies in the City, and they had the friendship of the two parliamentary armies. Powerless to change the peace terms in Parliament, they made direct overtures to the King. On paper, there may have seemed much to recommend Holles's desperate gamble of inviting the King to London, but basically, the gamble was as unrealistic as it was dangerous. He took no account of the King's own position: what had he to gain by throwing himself on the mercy of Holles and his party? His military position was not so poor nor his hopes so low that he would leave the safety of his own side for such a scheme. For Holles himself the gamble was highly dangerous, for although he may have persuaded himself that he was acting in Parliament's interests, there is no doubt that Parliament would have viewed his unauthorised invitation as treason. Indeed, Holles's action was treacherous, for it boosted the Royalists' hopes that the parliamentary alliance would collapse in factional strife, and gave them inside information which they could use against the Parliamentarians to divide them further. Holles's underhand activity had serious repercussions for him personally later in 1645.

iii.

The new alliance between the Scots and the peace party was not generally known until February 1645 when *Mercurius Aulicus* published an intercepted letter from one of the Parliamentarians, John Pyne. Pyne was suspicious of the basis of the new alliance, for while he hoped the Scots had changed friends 'to advance the Presbyterial government with us' he found it hard to believe that they could be friends with 'those that they know to hate them, and are their

1 Burnet, *Own Time*, i. 64-7.

2 Clarendon, *History* (Bk. VIII, 249-50), Macray, iii. 498-9. C.V. Wedgwood, 'The Covenanters in the first civil war', *Scottish Historical Review* 39 (1960), 13, points out that Charles's attitude to the negotiations was determined before the news of Montrose's victory arrived.

enemies in heart'.[1] The new alliance distanced the Scots from some members of Parliament who were genuinely sympathetic to their religious aims, men who were 'like affected with them, for the main of Church-government', such as John Gurdon, a religious Presbyterian but an ally of St. John and the political Independent party, and Zouch Tate, likewise a religious Presbyterian, but the proposer of the self-denying ordinance. Furthermore, the old peace party probably included many who, as Buchanan put it, 'kept still a bit of a Bishop in their belly'.[2] This is not to underestimate the importance of Presbyterianism in the new alliance, but to stress that Holles and his friends did not ally with the Scots simply on the basis of mutual religious sympathy.

When Holles and Whitelocke discussed their alliance with the Scots with the Royalists at Oxford in November 1644, they claimed that the Scots had abandoned hopes of establishing a *jus divinum* presbytery, as in Scotland. Holles said 'We had discourse of the Scots [whether?] yet still earnest to bring in a rigid presbytery. . . . I say that they were fallen off from being so rigid for that presbytery'. Whitelocke offers an even clearer statement of the basis for the new alliance: 'It was said that the Scots were altered from rigid presytery and they would willingly have a good peace'.[3] But although in Holles's view the Scots had abandoned their claim to *jus divinum* presbytery, this was not in fact so, as the Scots had shown in their private overtures to the Royalists at Uxbridge. There may be two reasons for the mistake. Although both Loudoun and Maitland were of the covenanting party, they were not ministers, and inclined towards upholding the interest of the nobility.[4] Secondly, the Scots may have hoped to use the peace party to establish an imperfect presbytery, then later to abandon their allies and perfect the church government. There was political calculation on the English side also. Edward Bowles, who thought the alliance was partly religious, claimed that the peace party struck in with the Scots 'partly out of envy and opposition to the Independents'.[5] The peace party Lords had expressed to the French ambassador their need of allies.[6] Both

1 Pyne's letter dated 3 Feb [1645]; *Mercurius Aulicus*, [Oxford], 23 Feb. – 2 Mar. [1645], TT E.273.13, pp. 1392-3.

2 [Bowles], *Manifest Truths*, p. 45; [Buchanan], *Truth its Manifest*, p. 30.

3 Savile's paper, Bodl., Nalson Papers xiv, f.112; Holles's information, *ibid.*, f. 124; Whitelocke's information, *ibid.*, f. 125.

4 John Maitland, Earl of Lauderdale in 1645, made the Engagement with the King in 1647 with Loudoun and Lanark. Loudoun joined the Campbells in opposing the Engagement in 1648.

5 [Bowles], *Manifest Truths*, pp. 44-5.

6 Ranke, *History of England*, ii. 407.

had similar political aims, for the peace party Lords and Commons wanted a treaty with the King upon moderate terms, and the Scots were anxious to see the King restored to his throne. Together they may have had some chance of checking the power and policies of the war party and their Independent allies in the Army and the Assembly. The Scots, wrote Nathaniel Fiennes in disgust, fell off from the good patriots and took by the hand 'those, who both in the two Houses of Parliament and in the City, carried on the court designs'.[1] Although both Scots and peace party were sympathetic to the idea of offering the King the most moderate terms possible, as their religious aims were not identical the alliance was never a close one, and the Scots found their real friends and religious allies in the City.

Around the end of 1644 the terms 'Presbyterian' and 'Independent' have some meaning for the two parties at Westminster. It is useful to distinguish the parties at Westminster — as contemporaries did not always do — from the religious parties of these names, and to note that the political parties were not aligned on the basis of religious differences.

iv.

From early June till the end of August 1645 political scandals involving members of Parliament were the talk of London and the pre-occupation of the Houses.[2] Pearl has written of the effects of the attempts of an Independent sub-committee of the committee of both kingdoms to negotiate via a royalist deserter for the betrayal of Oxford.[3] The same royalist, Thomas Lord Savile, also made allegations to the sub-committee about Holles, claiming that he sent weekly information to Oxford. In the pursuit of evidence of substantiate this, Savile negotiated with Oxford, but a letter of Lord Digby's to Savile was intercepted in June, which put a halt to the scheme. The House of Commons, to whom the matters were reported, directed a joint committee of Lords and Commons of which Holles was a member, to investigate Digby's letter. But before they began, a tremendous scandal erupted in London, when James Cranford, a Presbyterian minister, announced on the

---

1 [Fiennes], *Vindiciae Veritatis*, p. 73.

2 The Venetian ambassador in France was informed that the leading men were objects of envy and suspicion to the common people and rivalry and party spirit were to be found in Parliament itself; *CSP Ven, 1643-1647*, XXVII. 195-6.

3 Valerie Pearl, 'London puritans and Scotch fifth columnists: a mid-seventeenth century phenomenon', in A.E.J. Hollaender & W. Kellaway (eds.), *Studies in London History Presented to Philip Jones* (London, 1969), pp. 318-9.

Exchange on 10 June that an Independent sub-committee was treating underhand with Oxford for their own peace. The horrified House of Commons referred the matter to the committee for Lord Digby's letter, and when Holles said that Savile had accused him of sending information to Lord Digby, they referred this to the committee likewise.[1] Whitelocke chaired the committee during June as it examined all these matters, but on the point of Holles's correspondence with Digby, Savile refused to substantiate the charge by naming his source of information. In danger of contempt of Parliament, Savile endeavoured to prove that Holles was disloyal to Parliament by offering an account of the secret dealings of Holles and Whitelocke with the Royalists at Oxford in the previous November.[2]

This was the most serious political scandal of Holles's whole career. He recognised the danger he had been in when he wrote in 1648 that in the charges of Savile his opponents had come closest to destroying him. His account of the affair was that the Independent party in the House had determined to be rid of the honest party who opposed their schemes. They began with a smear campaign, then enlisted Savile to accuse him of corresponding with Lord Digby and of underhand dealings at Oxford when he took the propositions there. His enemies' machinations were foiled only because they prosecuted him with such injustice and partiality that 'the eyes of many indifferent persons, members of the House, were opened, and their spirits raised to an indignation, in so much that in spite of the Solicitor and his party', he was acquitted by the House.[3] But the true story was rather different from that told by Holles in his *Memoirs.*

The evidence about the Savile affair is tangled, and in the end no clear or consistent picture of Savile's end or motives emerges. The two separate charges against Holles, that it was he who sent information weekly to Oxford and that he had attempted his own negotiations with the King in November 1644, were never proved but enough detail was given for his loyalty to be questioned.

Holles continued about his usual activities in June. He had little reason to worry about this story of royalist correspondence. When he voluntarily gave evidence to the joint committee, he admitted that he had received a letter one evening as he was walking in the Covent Garden

1   Whitacre's diary, BL, Add. 31116, f. 215.
2   For a fuller discussion of this, see my 'The Savile affair', *EHR* 354 (1975), 76-93.
3   Holles, *Memoirs,* pp. 37-41.

Piazza.[1] The letter lacked a direction or signature, and when he held it before the fire the invisible ink simply stated that the bearer could be trusted.[2] He thought he had burnt the letter, but as it was some time ago, he could not really remember more. He declared he had ripped his whole soul bare and stated his abhorrence of such treachery.[3] Doubtless he felt confident Savile would never be able to substantiate the charge. He and his friends were busy rescuing William Lilley, the astrologer, who had fallen foul of Miles Corbett. Holles, Stapleton, Sir Christopher Wray, Robert Reynolds, Sir Robert Pye and Francis Drake all turned up at the committee for examinations around the end of June to crush the charges against William Lilley.[4] Holles was interested enough in astrology to have received Lilley's *Starry Message* sheet by sheet as it came off the press in June, and Lilley cast his horoscope some time after 1647.[5] While Holles was among Lilley's friends, Lilley's 'mortal enemies' were the Presbyterians.[6]

Meanwhile, at the end of June Savile was lodged in the Tower for his contempt of Parliament in refusing to name the person who told him Holles sent weekly information to Lord Digby. Savile sought some other information to prove his contention that Holles was a traitor to the Parliament. He alleged in a paper to Samuel Browne that when Holles and Whitelocke had taken the parliamentary propositions for peace to Oxford the previous November they had discussed their own ideas for a settlement with the King.[7]

Surprised in the Commons with this information on 2 July, Holles

1   Holles was living at the Covent Garden Piazza after 1644; Poor rate ledgers, 1644 & 1645, accounts of collection for the poor, 1647, Westminster Public Library, F.1040, F.1044, H.433.   He wrote a letter in April 1644 from Covent Garden; Bodl., Tanner 61, f. 14.

2   Yonge's diary, BL, Add. 18780, f. 78 (17 July 1645); Whitacre's diary, BL, Add. 31116, f. 221v. (19 July 1645).

3   Holles's information, BL, Add. 32093, ff. 227-229.

4   Bodl., Ashmolean 421, ff. 200-220v. I am grateful to Dr M.P. Mahony for this reference.

5   Bodl., Ashmolean 243, f. 162v. The last event mentioned in the horoscope is Holles's flight from Parliament in Sept. 1647. Astrology was a respectable interest for educated men in the seventeenth century. A notebook among the Harleian MSS BL, Harl. 6633 which may have belonged to Holles contains detailed notes about the stars. The name on the flyleaf of the book is Arbella Holles, but the contents do not reflect the interests of a lady. The handwriting appears identical with that of a commonplace book in the Nottingham University Library which I have suggested was the work of Denzil, and also with that of the Parliamentary diaries for 1628, for which see appendix 1.

6   Lilley, Bodl., Ashmolean 421, ff. 200v., 205, 209, 214.   Lilley named Samuel Vassal as one Presbyterian, and wrote in general against the ministers who were more lordly than the bishops, and more tyrannical than the great Turk.

7   Lord Savile's letter and paper, Bodl., Nalson Papers, xiv. ff. 122, 112-112v.

'protested his innocency therein with much passion, even unto tears'. He admitted to some visits and to giving a paper, which he said concerned the King's refusal to acknowledge them to be a Parliament although he denied Savile's account of the conversations and the contents of the paper. Whitelocke thought Holles had been foolish to confess so much.[1]   In vain Sir William Lewis, seconded by Stapleton, reminded the members of Savile's untrustworthiness, and argued that as the information came from one already under imprisonment for unsupported allegations, it was a breach of privilege and should be ignored.[2]   The House refused to view Savile's paper as a charge of high treason, as Holles's opponents urged, but they ordered Whitelocke to attend to give an explanation, and subsequently ordered a committee to examine the business.[3]   Further investigations were serious for both men since much that Savile alleged was true, and they did not wish the Commons to learn what had passed on their visit to Oxford. For Holles the affair was far more serious than for Whitelocke, since Savile's information crowned previous intimations of his disloyalty.[4]   'Holles's friends', wrote Baillie, 'have been in great fear for his undoing by it' and one of his opponents observed 'his party thereupon made a great bustling'.[5] The chief of these friends were Stapleton, Maynard, Lewis, Clotworthy, Glyn, Wenman, Winwood and Sir John Holland.[6]   The committee may have suspected that Holles and Whitelocke were not telling the truth — as Whitelocke admitted in his Annals — but they could prove nothing. In the end it was only Savile's word against that of Holles and Whitelocke, whose friends pointed out that if Parliament were to believe every disloyal Royalist against the word of their own fellows, then Oxford would have enormous power over Parliament. The committee realised that Savile's mere word would convict nobody,

---

1   Whitelocke, Annals, BL, Add. 37343, f. 394.

2   *Ibid.*, ff. 394v.-395. See also a manuscript speech by Sir John Holland in Bodl., Tanner 321, f. 10v.

3   *CJ*, iv. 195; Whitelocke, Annals, BL., Add. 37 343, f. 394.

4   Whitelocke says his friend Osbaldiston found their opponents 'not so sharp against me'; Whitelocke, 'Diary', Lord Bute's MSS., 11 July 1645. See also Whitelocke, Annals, B.L. Add. MSS. 37343, f. 398.

5   Baillie, *Letters and Journals*, ii. 303, (15 July 1645); [Fiennes], *Vindiciae Veritatis*, p. 139.

6   Whitelocke, Annals, B.L., Add. MSS. 37343, ff. 397v. — 398v., f. 395; 'Diary', Lord Bute MSS. 7 July 1645. Whitelocke was surprised to find their friend Reynolds who had been working with them to save Lilley, looked coldly towards him, so perhaps this may be the point at which Reynolds changed sides. Whitelocke, Annals, B.L., Add.MSS. 37343, f. 395. In 1648 Holles described Reynolds as one 'who went a long time and a great way with us, but is since fallen off and become thoroughly theirs'; *Memoirs*, p. 210.

but their willingness to listen to a whole range of additional allegations and rumours about the conduct of Holles showed their distrust of him and their desire for proof. They examined the information of one member, Godfrey Bosvile, who claimed that some two years earlier Holles had sent a letter to Sir John Monson at Oxford via Monson's sister, Mrs. Cotton, in which he was said to have asked Monson's favour in making his peace with the King, to which Monson had replied that as Holles showed favour to the Royalists in London, so would he find favour at Oxford. After this it was said that Holles had helped Mrs Cotton in having her sequestration taken off. This information had been circulating for some time, for Vane senior, Salway and Gurdon were all said to know of it, but when Sam Browne's committee was directed to examine the charge, it fizzled out: Mrs. Cotton denied everything 'and cleared Holles'.[1] Lord Saye had earlier tried to establish that Savile told him that when a royalist agent, Mullins, passed through London *en route* for France he enquired where Holles lived, and there were meetings at which members of both houses and the Scots commissioners had been present, but on examination Savile denied connecting these meeting with Mullins's visit.[2]

Holles was saved by the Scots. By 'some strange Providence' the Scots Commissioners received intercepted letters which revealed Savile's royalist sympathies.[3] These letters Holles and Whitelocke advised the Scots to place before the Parliament, and in the favourable climate created by the exposure of Savile's royalism the pair were acquitted of all ill intention in their proceedings at Oxford. Holles was cleared of the charge of being an informer only on the vote that his receiving a letter from Savile in invisible ink was no proof of his corresponding with the Royalists.[4]

Holles and his friends had fought hard over Savile's charges. The whole of that party which Whitelocke referred to as 'Essex's party' in the Commons depended upon it. After the votes of acquittal, Holles and Whitelocke were given leave to prosecute Savile, but they wanted

1 Yonge's diary. B.L., Add.MSS. 18780, ff. 79-79v.; Whitacre's diary, B.L., Add.MSS. 31116, f.221-221v. (18 July 1654); Lords, Main Papers, ff. 260-263; D'Ewes's diary, B.L., Harl. MSS. 166, f. 241v.

2 Information of Saye, examination of Savile, Lords, Main Papers, ff. 244, 246.

3 Baillie, *Letters and Journals*, ii. 303; letters printed, pp. 490-2. I have been unable to discover any clue as to the identity of this anonymous friend.

4 *C.J.*, iv. 213-4. The division on 19 July was whether to put the question 'Whether the receiving this note by Mr. Holles in the manner as he did, be a holding intelligence with the enemy': Stapleton & Lewis – 95; Lisle & Prideaux – 55.

to suppress the whole affair, so they did nothing further. Holles obtained six weeks leave to go into the country.[1] Over the next months there was talk of attempts to revive the charges with further evidence. Pierrepont hinted to Whitelocke early in August that some further enquiry might be made, and later in September Holles's brother, the Earl of Clare, told Whitelocke 'as frighting news' that the Earl of Lindsey was coming to town and they should anticipate further trouble. Holles was undismayed at all this: 'let them do their worst' he told Whitelocke 'we will not care a fig for them, they have spit their venom already, and much to the like effect'.[2] There was an attempt to revive the affair in May 1646 when Savile, who had spent most of the intervening months in the Tower, disclosed that it was the Duchess of Buckingham who said that Holles held weekly intelligence with Lord Digby.[3] Fortunately for Holles the House had other matters on its mind on 6 May 1646 — namely the news of the arrival of the King in the camp of the Scottish army — but in 1647 Savile's original information appeared almost word for word in the articles of impeachment against Holles and others.[4]

Holles's account of the affair as an Independent plot to be rid of him is not correct. There was no deliberate plot, for the charges developed fortuitously and on his own admission they were not mere inventions. Obviously the political Independents were prepared to believe the worst of him and to seek to substantiate their views, but the information against him was so serious it could not be ignored.

The general sense of the contemporary verdict is 'not proven' rather 'not guilty'.[5] Savile was pursuing several devious schemes, but some of his information rang true. Someone *was* sending news to Oxford. Whitelocke said he 'supposed and partly knew' that Savile had delivered to Holles a letter from the Duke of Richmond,[6] and we know from Whitelocke that he and Holles had actually discussed the propositions with the King and drafted a reply for him. Strangely enough Savile never mentioned that they spoke with the King: if he had been

1 Whitelocke, *Annals*, BL, Add. 37343, f. 405; *CJ*, iv. 214, 222.

2 Whitelocke, *Annals*, BL, Add. 37344, ff. Iv., 16-16v.

3 *Memorials of the Great Civil War*, i. 24; *CJ*, iv. 530. Katherine Manners, widow of George, first Duke of Buckingham, was the wife of Randall Macdonnell, Earl of Antrim, in 1646; *DNB*.

4 Whitacre's diary, BL, Add. 31116, f. 268v.

5 Yonge's account was that the House voted 'that there is not sufficient proof that Mr. Holles held intelligence at Oxford with the Lord Digby'; diary, BL, Add. 18780, f.80v.

6 Whitelocke, *Annals*, BL, Add. 37343, f. 406.

there as he claimed, how had he not seen the King? But there are many puzzles surrounding the affair to which the evidence provides no clear answers. Locke recounts a garbled tale of Anthony Ashley Cooper, Holles's cousin by marriage, refusing to testify against Holles at the bar of the House of Commons.[1] Cooper had changed sides a year before Holles was at Oxford, but he may have known something about the charge of corresponding with Digby. Cooper's latest biographer suggests that there was a reconciliation between Cooper and Holles somewhere about this time, for Holles surrendered to Cooper the right to hold the manorial court of Damerham, a right previously contested between the two.[2] Howver, there is no mention of Cooper being asked to testify in any of the records, which might substantiate the story.

Undoubtedly Holles and Whitelocke had pressed a party scheme at Oxford, in advising Charles to address their party so that they might bring him to London where his scattered supporters might rally to him.[3] Later in 1647 Holles again tried to impose a settlement by bringing the King to London and using armed force to support his party's scheme. But although in 1644 and 1645 Holles was probably in communication with those Royalists who, as he did, favoured a speedy settlement of peace, it was most unlikely that he sent weekly information to Lord Digby.[4] Holles's support of peace had brought him so close to the Royalists that he seemed disloyal to Parliament: as one of his opponents remarked, his behaviour was so different from the early days of the Parliament 'and leaning to the court upon all occasions' that this made Savile's accusations credible.[5] The affair cast such doubt upon him that the next time Parliament was negotiating with the King they sent commissioners with propositions for his acquiesence, not for discussion, and they did not choose Denzil Holles as one of their messengers.

1 *The Works of John Locke* (10th edn., 10 vols., London, 1801), ix. 270-1.

2 Haley, *Shaftesbury*, pp. 57-8. Cooper was holding the court by 30 March 1646. The holding of a manorial court Holles later referred to as 'a little point of honour' which he was unwilling to give to his own son: *The Lord Holles his Vindication of Himself and of his Son Sir Francis Holles* (London, 1676), p. 16.

3 Savile's examination, Bodl., Nalson xiv, f. 129v.

4 Although Digby was a fellow countryman, Holles had moved his impeachment in December 1641, and Digby was thought to have named the five members. Holles pointed out that he as Digby 'hateth him as much as any man living', it was unlikely he would put his life and honour in Digby's hands; BL, Add. 32093, f. 227.

5 [Fiennes], *Vindiciae Veritatis*, p. 138.

7

HOLLES, PRESBYTERIANS AND SCOTS,
1645 — 1646.

The Scots had no thought but of settling a peace, laying down of arms . . . and all things to revert into their old channel; therefore they were willing to be gone . . . in confidence that after their departure, the Army under Sir Thomas Fairfax should likewise presently be disbanded. . . .[1]

i.

In mid 1645 Parliament's victory over the King's forces at Naseby gave the Houses a firm confidence in their ultimate triumph, but the prospect of a settlement in the near future exacerbated all their problems. That of church settlement loomed largest, because it most immediately affected both the Scots and the King. If Parliament agreed to establish the presbytery as the Scots wished, this would content them and they would return home; if on the other hand, Parliament refused to establish presbyterianism then the Scots would stay in England and might make their own separate overtures to Charles. Parliament's awareness of the Scots as a complicating factor to any settlement of peace embittered relations between the allies, and there was strong and general hostility to the Scots from mid 1645 until they finally marched away home in January 1647. Part of this bitterness was attributable to the feeling that the Scots had done little, at the last, to secure the parliamentary victory and yet they had reaped rewards disproportionate to their efforts because the King's flight to their army in 1646 meant that their voice in the settlement could not be ignored. Besides, Parliament was paying the Scots; they were the 'mere mercenary army' which the New Model claimed it never was, and the English resented the mercenary army's political influence.

Holles and the Scots shared the desire for a settlement with the King which would establish a church with powers of discipline over the ungodly and would deny toleration to the sects. Both the 'political Presbyterians' and the Scots were conservative, and despite underlying differences, they could work together in 1645 and 1646 united by their common fear of the New Model Army and their hatred of the Independents. 'The Presbyterian party here sought as far as modestly

---

1   Holles, *Memoirs*, p. 64.

they could to support the interest of their brethren of Scotland', said Whitelocke,[1] but it was an uphill task, and, as Holles observed, they were 'decried as Scottish, malignant, and prejudiced in all they did or said'.[2]

So long as the Scots remained in England, Holles and his party had little power at Westminster. With the formation of the New Model Army the political Presbyterians lost control of the military forces, but gained little compensatory power in Parliament. Towards the end of 1645 new elections were held to fill the vacancies in the Commons. Holles later described this recruiting as a plot of the violent party who, finding themselves outvoted in the Savile affair, resolved to 'alter the constitution of the House, and give them infallibly a majority of votes'.[3] He claimed that despite the violent party's corrupt electioneering, the new members 'deceived the expectation of these men' by supporting him and his party whom they found to be the truly public spirited.[4] A recent account of the recruiter elections suggests that Holles was probably correct, for although the middle group and the radicals began electioneering first, the moderates later followed suit.[5]

Holles's credit was shaken by the Savile affair, and he was quiet in Parliament for some time after. A further slur came in November 1645 when the House learnt from captured royalist correspondence that early in 1643 the Royalists had thought Holles and Pierrepont were converts to peace.[6] But the Commons still thought well enough of him in December 1645 to include him among those they would ask the King to reward: they decided Holles should be made a viscount.[7] Furthermore, Holles still offered leadership to those who wanted to resist religious disorder and avert a breach with the Scots.

---

1 Whitelock, Annals, BL, Add. 37344, f.53.

2 Holles, *Memoirs*, p. 53.

3 *Ibid.*, p. 41. The issue was raised on 14 Aug. by a petition from Southwark. Despite the objections of Glyn and Maynard and the proposal of a deferment by Holles, the House decided to issue a writ by a narrow majority on 21 Aug.; Yonge's diary, BL, Add. 18780, f.97v. (14 Aug. 1645). *CJ*, iv. 249; Whitacre's diary, BL, Add. 31116, f.227.

4 Holles, *Memoirs*, pp. 43-4.

5 D.E. Underdown, 'Party management in the recruiter elections, 1645-1648', *EHR* 83 (1968), 263-4; see also Underdown, *Pride's Purge*, pp. 68-9.

6 D'Ewes's diary, BL, Harl. 166, f.267. (1 Nov. 1645). The letter was part of the correspondence between Hotham and the Earl of Newcastle.

7 Whitacre's diary, BL, Add. 31116, f.245v.; Yonge's diary, BL, Add. 18780, f.173 (2 Dec. 1645).

ii.

When the Commons began their debates on church government in 1645 it was apparent that they would not follow the advice of the majority in the Assembly of Divines and establish a *jus divinum* presbytery with full powers of discipline. This was an issue on which the Scots and the 'political Presbyterians' were not of one mind, as Holles for one did not support a *jus divinum* presbytery, and was an Erastian. Thus on this issue the Scots turned to the City and the ministers there to support their campaign for a *jus divinum* or 'High Presbytery'.[1]

> In this case [wrote Baillie] our last refuge is to God, and under him to the City. We have gotten it, thanks to God, to this point, that the mayor, aldermen, common council, and most of the considerable men, are grieved for the increase of sects and heresies, and want of government.

The Scots rightly realised how powerful an ally the City could be to them: 'all know the Parliament here cannot subsist without London: so whatsoever they desire in earnest, and constantly, it must be granted'.[2] In addition the Scots hoped that if their military efforts were more successful, Parliament would heed them more.[3]

At the beginning of the debates on church government in July 1645, Holles was enmeshed in the Savile affair and there is no mention of his playing any active part in the religious discussion. After his acquittal he went into the country, leaving others to debate religion. The ministers of London campaigned for greater powers of discipline, chiefly for unlimited power to exclude scandalous persons from the sacrament, despite the Scots' advice that they should set up what Presbytery they could, and worry about the details of jurisdiction later.[4] The ministers petitioned Parliament for additional powers, and persuaded their friends in the City to move the City government to petition likewise.

---

1 John Goodwin used the term 'High Presbytery' to distinguish those Presbyterians who believed the Presbytery was *jus divinum*, and who would brook no dissent from their all embracing authoritarian church; John Goodwin, *Hagiomastix, or the Scourge of the Saints*, [5 Feb. 1647], TT E. 374.1, preface.

2 Baillie, *Letters and Journals*, ii. 336-7 (15 Jan. 1646).

3 This is a continuous refrain of Baillie's. A typical expression of his view is: 'Had it been God's will to have made our army here this last year successful, we should have had few debates for any of our desires'; *ibid.*, 350 (Feb. 1646). See also 318 (14 Oct. 1645), 325, (Nov. 1645), 336-7 [15 Jan. 1646]. John Maitland, Earl of Lauderdale, shared this view, and expressed the hope in October 1644 that the taking of Newcastle would assist church affairs; *Correspondence of Sir Robert Kerr, First Earl of Ancram and his son William, Third Earl of Lothian*, ed. D. Laing (2 vols., Roxborough Club, Edinburgh 1875), i. 176.

4 Baillie, *Letters and Journals*, ii. 307 (n.d. circa Aug. 1645).

The details of their campaign have been fully discussed elsewhere.[1] Nevertheless, it is important for an understanding of Holles to appreciate his attitude to the demands of the religious Presbyterians. Baillie's letters give an account of the campaign for the *jus divinum* presbytery by the Scots, the Assembly of Divines, the City ministers and magistrates. In January 1646 the Commons suggested that courts of lay commissioners should be established in every shire to judge cases not covered by the parliamentary Ordinance, but this was unacceptable to the High Presbyterians.

> The Parliament will have a court of civil commissioners erected in every shire, on pretence to make report to the houses in every new case of scandal, but really to keep down the power of the presbyteries for ever, and hold up the head of Sectaries. It's our present work to get that crushed. . . .[2]

The Commons were unmoved by protests, and in March completed their Ordinance for establishing the Presbyterian church government which included the lay commissioners. On Saturday 7 March 1646 the whole House of Commons, minus the Speaker, paid tribute to the importance of the Ordinance by all together physically carrying it to the House of Lords.[3] There in fulsome terms Denzil Holles introduced this Ordinance, so hateful to the High Presbyterians, as heralding 'the dawning of a glorious day, which our ancestors hoped to have seen, but could not'.[4] A month earlier one of the leading Scottish Presbyterians, Samuel Rutherford, had described the Ordinance in very different words, which Holles ironically had echoed: 'It is not, I fear, so near to the dawning of the day of salvation but the clouds must send down more showers of blood to water the vineyard of the Lord'.[5]

When the City petitioned Parliament against the lay commissioners, the Commons were enraged. On 14 March they debated how they would convey to the Common Council that they had 'broken the privileges of Parliament and to desire them not to present any more petitions of that Nature'.[6] Undaunted, the Assembly of Divines sent a petition claiming that the power to exclude persons from the sacrament belonged

---

1 Shaw, *History of the English Church*, i. 266-98.

2 Baillie, *Letters and Journals*, ii. 336, 337, 344, 348-9.

3 *CJ*, iv. 467; Whitacre's diary, BL, Add. 31116, f.258v.

4 *LJ*, viii. 202.

5 *Letters of Samuel Rutherford*, ed. A.A. Bonar (Edinburgh, 1891), p. 636. (30 Jan. 1646). Rutherford was not popular with the Commons, for Sir John Evelyn had reported on 28 Oct. 1645 that Rutherford had preached at Covent Garden Church - where Holles was a parishioner - that Parliament had nothing to do with church government; Yonge's diary, BL, Add. 18780, f.154.

6 Whitacre's diary, BL, Add. 31116, f.260 (14 Mar. 1646).

to the church by divine right. The House resented this highly: it was 'by some conceived to be a no less breach of the privilege than that which was lately presented from the City'[1]. Holles and Stapleton unsuccessfully argued against declaring the Assembly's petition a breach of privilege.[2] Much to Baillie's disgust the City opposition collapsed.[3]

Holles made no comment on the campaign for the High Presbytery in his *Memoirs,* and the parliamentary diarists are silent about his views in the Commons. There were no divisions when the Commons censured the petitions of the City and the Assembly, although there was a very long debate in which some defended the ministers, arguing that they had the same rights as others to petition.[4] The only clue to Holles's views at this date is that he did invite Samuel Bolton of St. Saviours Southwark to preach at the monthly fast on 25 March when Obadiah Sedgewick cried off, but if Bolton were a *protegé* of Holles's, his fast sermon tells little of Holles's views. Bolton was so upset at the religious controversy he 'purposely waived all unnecessary controversies',[5] and harangued the Commons on the sinfulness of sin. Francis Cheynell, the other minister, rushed in, and roundly told the Commons that 'Jesus Christ hath not entrusted any state to make new institutions, or create new offices in his Church' and advised them to remove 'the much feared Commissioners'.[6] Both ministers were thanked afterwards by Holles and Sir Peter Wentworth, although one suspects Boltons' sermon would have pleased the Commons better.

The proposed courts of lay commissioners delayed the establishment of the Presbytery while the campaign against them continued. Holles tried to defend the ministers and to arrange some compromise. In April the House debated the Assembly's breach of privilege,[7] and on the

1 *Ibid.,* ff.261-261v. (23 Mar. 1646). What annoyed the House, Whitacre said, was that the petitions were presented before the ministers had made any trial of Parliament's system, 'of the convenience or inconvenience of it'.

2 *CJ,* iv. 506: Haselrig and Evelyn - 88; Holles and Stapleton - 76.

3 Baillie, *Letters and Journals,* ii. 364, 366 (23, 24 Apr. 1646).

4 Whitacre's diary, BL, Add. 31116, f.262v.; John Harrington's diary, BL, Add. 10114, f.11 (1 Apr. 1646).

5 Samuel Bolton, *The Sinfulness of Sin. A sermon before the House of Commons, on the monthly fast,* 25 Mar. 1646, TT E.329.10. Epistle dedicatory. Professor Yule has pointed out to me that Bolton was an irenic Presbyterian who genuinely wanted accommodation.

6 Francis Cheynell, *A Plot for the Good of Posterity. A Sermon to the House of Commons,* 25 Mar. 1646, TT E.329.11, Epistle dedicatory.

7 Harrington says that those who viewed the petition as a breach of privilege found it hard to fix upon particulars, since individually each particular was no breach; Harrington's diary, BL, Add. 10114, f.12v.

17th, Holles, Stapleton, Erle and Ashhurst unsuccessfully protested against clauses in the declaration of censure.[1] In their declaration the Commons bluntly stated their Erastian position: they would 'by no means to part with this power out of the hands of the civil magistrate', nor give unlimited power to 'ten thousand judicatories within this kingdom'.[2] The ministers' dissatisfaction continued, but meanwhile the King's flight to the Scots army made it imperative that Parliament should conciliate them and their supporters in the City. On 21 May Holles and Sir William Lewis were the tellers of a majority in favour of reopening the question.[3] Sam Browne suggested as a compromise, the substitution of a standing committee of Parliament for the lay commissioners, to which the Houses agreed.[4] Finally in June the ministers grudgingly obeyed Parliament and set about establishing Presbyteries.[5]

Although Holles was unsympathetic to the claims of the High Presbyterian ministers for unlimited powers of discipline, he did support them in their campaign against religious toleration. In the Commons, toleration was as unappealing as *jus divinum* Presbytery.[6] Presbyterians of all shades were united in their hatred of toleration. 'Take heed of tolerations', warned Thomas Case, 'they are nothing else but a gunpowder treason to blow up religion'.[7] Publications such as Edwards' *Gangraena* were bitter against the sects and aroused controversy.[8] In the Commons in 3 February 1646 Holles and Stapleton were tellers of a majority limiting this ease for tender consciences: there should be ease only in so far as should stand with the peace of the church.[9] The

1 *CJ*, iv. 512.

2 'A Declaration of the Commons of England . . . of their true intentions concerning the . . . Government of the Kingdom; the Government of the Church', *ibid.*, p. 513.

3 *Ibid.*, p. 552: Holles and Lewis - 110; Haselrig and Evelyn - 99 (21 May 1646). Whitacre's diary, BL, Add. 31116, ff.270-270v.

4 *CJ*, iv. 553; *Acts and Ordinances*, i. 852. Parliament's change of policy was excused as necessary because of the wars, which meant that suitable commissioners were 'absent from their habitations, and so cannot do the service therein, which otherwise they might do'.

5 *Certain Considerations and Cautions agreed upon by the Ministers of London . . . 19 June 1646*, TT E. 341.11.

6 Baillie, *Letters and Journals*, ii. 326 (25 Nov. 1645).

7 Thomas Case, *Deliverance-Obstruction: or, The Set-Backs of Reformation*. 25 Mar. 1646, TT E.329.9, p. 36.

8 *Gangraena: or a Catalogue of many of the Errours, Heresies and pernicious Practices of the Sectaries of this time*. By Thomas Edwards, [26 Feb. 1646], TT E. 323.2, p. 109. See entries for 26 Feb. 1646 in *Catalogue of the Pamphlets, Books, Newspapers, and Manuscripts relating to the Civil War, the Commonwealth, and Restoration, collected by George Thomason, 1640-1661*, ed. G.K. Fortescue (2 vols., London, 1908).

9 *CJ*, iv. 428: Holles and Stapleton - 105, Haselrig and Mildmay - 98.

Presbyterian party in the City continued to protest against toleration, and Parliament became increasingly alarmed at the growing rift between them and the City, especially as they were at odds with their Scottish allies.

iii.

In his *Memoirs* Holles alleged that in 1646 the 'violent party' had sought all means possible to quarrel with the Scots and precipitate a breach between the two nations. They gave credit to false information against the Scots, arranged for their papers to remain unanswered, slighted the committee of both kingdoms, opened and deciphered letters of their commissioners, and altered the peace propositions removing the Scots' interest in the English militia. According to Holles, all that prevented a breach with the Scots was the noble behaviour of the latter, who conceded contested issues and agreed to march away. Even then, the 'violent party' tried to delay them by refusing to pay them properly. By the Covenant, the Scots might have insisted that the English Army should disband at the same time as their own, but they left England on the understanding — subsequently betrayed — that the disbanding of the New Model would follow.[1]

But Holles's account of the Scots' departure from England omitted any mention of those of their activities which aroused English suspicion and hostility. The English Parliament received information of the Scots' transactions with the Royalists, such as the letter of Robert Wright which reached the committee of both kingdoms on 24 February 1646 telling of the Scots' negotiations with the Queen via William Murray.[2] Intercepted letters, especially those of Lord Digby taken at Sherborne and read in Parliament in October 1645, made this information credible.[3] What disquieted the English even more was their appreciation of the strength of the Scots' party in the City, the party for the High Presbytery. The ministers of London were discontented with Parliament's settlement of religion and had already shown how they could influence the City government. Parliament's rejection of the

---

1 Holles, *Memoirs*, pp. 44-68. [David Buchanan], *An Explanation of some Truths,* [3 Jan. 1646], TT E. 314. 15, p. 47, also argues that the Independents deliberately tried to quarrel with the Scots.

2 Bodl., Carte 80, ff.354-5, 'paper of the committee of both houses about Wright', 24 Jan. 1646. *HMC Portland MSS.,* i. 335.

3 Gardiner, *Civil War,* iii. 5. The Scots denied these as a scandal. *The Acts of the Parliament of Scotland* (12 vols., Record Commission, 1844 etc.), vi. pt. 1, p. 544.

petitions for the High Presbytery in March had alienated the citizens, which breach was serious,[1] because Parliament faced the possible combination of the King with the Scots, and a hostile City.[2] The Commons were so jumpy that some members — St. John, Saye and others — insisted on examining the Lord Mayor's house at an untimely hour of night, fearing he intended to aid the King.[3] At the end of April 1646 it seemed as if Parliament's fears might be realised, for hard on the heels of the news of the King's escape from Oxford, came information that he 'intended to go to London and keep in secret and show himself as he saw fit season', which was subsequently confirmed by a letter from Fairfax on 4 May.[4] Deeply alarmed, the Commons postponed the muster of the London forces due to take place at Hyde Park lest the King should use the occasion to show himself, and ordered that anyone who concealed him would be guilty of treason.[5] Suspicion of the City's loyalty was so great that Parliament resumed the control of their militia granted to the City in the Uxbridge propositions.[6]

When the Commons learnt that the King had taken refuge with the Scots, their fears were in no way allayed. The Scots commissioners in London protested their amazement, swore they knew nothing of the King's plan beforehand, and were 'like men that dream' on finding him in their army, but their word was soon discredited.[7] Sir Thomas Hamer addressed a letter to the Speaker of the Commons on 7 June 1646 saying he had already told the committee of both kingdoms of the Scots' plans for the King to escape to their Army.[8] Ormonde published a letter, at Charles's direction, in which the King announced a plan for the Scots, Montrose and the English Royalists to join together against the Parliament of England.[9] The capture of the King's chaplain, Michael Hudson, the man who had guided the King on his escape and whom the Scots had allowed to escape from custody, confirmed the Parliamen-

1   *Memorials of the Great Civil War*, ed. Cary, i. 17, 31 (4 & 11 May 1646).

2   According to Edwards, *Gangraena*, p. 183, a 'great Independent' alleged that King, Scots and Common Council 'did drive on one design'.

3   Baillie, *Letters and Journals*, ii. 365, 368 (23 & 24 Apr. 1646).

4   Harrington's diary, BL, Add. 10114, f.14v.; Whitacre's diary, BL, Add. 31116, ff.267-267v. (30 Apr.); *ibid.*, f.268 (4 May).

5   *Ibid., CJ*, iv. 532.

6   *To the honourable the House of Commons . . . The Humble Remonstrance. . . ,* [26 May] 1646, TT E. 338.7, p. 6.

7   *The Letter from the Commissioners of Scotland, 5 May 1646*, [7 May] 1646, TT 669.f.9 (61).

8   Printed in *Memorials of the Great Civil War*, i. 95-8.

9   *The Kings Letter to the Marquesse of Ormond: 13 April . . .*, 8 June 1646, TT E.340.5*.

tarians' suspicions. The Scots swore that the King's letter to Ormonde was a 'damnable untruth',[1] which was all they could do in the circumstances, but understandably their word carried little weight with the English Parliament or press.[2]

English suspicion and distrust of the Scots made it difficult for Holles and the Presbyterians to support their interests in the House of Commons. When the Royalists sent some overtures for peace, Holles and Clotworthy could not muster enough support to ensure that the Scots would be informed of these.[3] Again, Holles, Stapleton and Sir William Waller were unsuccessful in arguing that the Scots should be informed of the preamble and alterations to the peace propositions which were to be sent to the King in the joint names of the English and Scots.[4] In November 1646 Holles and Stapleton failed in an attempt to insist that the Covenant be a test for office holding.[5] Holles clashed with Cromwell over an ordinance the Lords had sent down for the punishment of those who libelled the Scots: 'Cromwell spoke most vehemently, that it was to discourage their friends, and to encourage their enemies: but Holles took him up so sharply, for calling base libellers friends, that he was glad to recant'.[6] However, on some other occasions, supporting the Scots interest was not so desperate as Holles suggested in his *Memoirs,* and he could muster a majority to prevent unnecessary annoyance of the Scots.[7]

1 *The Declaration of the Commissioners of the Kingdom of Scotland Concerning a Paper Intituled The Kings Letter to the Marques of Ormond,* 9 June 1646, TT E. 340.6, p. 3; Baillie, *Letters and Journals,* ii. 374-5 (26 June 1646).

2 For example, *The Interest of England maintained: the Honour of the Parliament Vindicated,* 8 June 1646, TT E. 340.5, pp. 9-14; *An Unhappy Game at Scotch and English, or a full answer from England to the Papers of Scotland,* [30 Nov.] 1646, TT E. 364.3.

3 *CJ,* iv. 524: Haselrig & Evelyn of Wilts. - 59, Holles & Clotworthy - 38 (27 Apr. 1646).

4 *Ibid.,* 593. The division was on putting the question: Holles and Waller - 46; Brereton and R. Goodwin - 54 (30 June 1646).

5 *Ibid.,* 725: Holles and Stapleton - 115; Haselrig and Evelyn - 133. Whitacre says the issue was debated 'from morning to night', BL, Add. 31116, f.290 (18 Nov. 1646).

6 Gilbert Burnet, *The Memoirs of the Lives and Actions of James and William Dukes of Hamilton and Castle-herald,* (2nd. edn., Oxford, 1852), p. 365. Possibly Burnet had this story from Holles himself. His account of the division figures was 102 to 132 (cp. division figures following). Harrington also mentions a clash between Holles and Cromwell; Harrington's diary, BL, Add. 10114, f.17. Harrington said that the sense of the Commons was to pass a general ordinance against libels, not one against libellers of the Scots only, but Holles and Sir Walter Erle carried the House in favour of a second reading of this particular bill; *ibid.; CJ,* iv. 644: Holles and Erle - 130; Haselrig and Evelyn - 102 (14 Aug. 1646).

7 For example, a majority refused to put to the question whether the Scots had

Contrary to the terms of the Covenant, the Scots were allowed no part in the preparation of the peace propositions to be sent to the King. When they objected, M.P.s spoke darkly of the Scots' interference as an attempt to draw the laws of England 'into a conformity with theirs'.[1] A head-on collision was averted only by the Scots agreeing to everything the English Parliament proposed, and the allies jointly sent the terms to the King at Newcastle.[2] These propositions were for the King's consent, not for discussion.[3] Holles was not even one of the delegation. The King's answer, when it arrived, was unsatisfactory, but in the mean time the Houses began to resolve some of their other problems, chief among which was sending the Scots home.

The departure of the Scots was a difficult question for the Parliament of England to negotiate. So long as the Scots remained in arms in England, Parliament was bound to pay them, by the terms of their alliance. If Parliament failed to satisfy the Scots' financial demands, then the danger was that the Scots would take the King back to Scotland with them, and perhaps make a separate agreement with him. The Scots were determined to bargain with the English Parliament so that the New Model Army, the biggest obstacle to the establishment of the presbytery, would be disbanded as well as their own. Baillie explained in August how the Scots hoped to insist upon disbandment of the New Model through their party in the City.[4]

A partial disbanding of the New Model had already been suggested in the Commons. When the House discussed the plight of Ireland on 30 July, there were many arguments in favour of sending some of the New Model there. The debate continued on the following day, but Holles and Stapleton did not have a majority in favour of sending four regiments of foot and two of horse from the New Model to Ireland.[5] The

---

an interest in the peace propositions relating to England; *ibid.*, 545: Haselrig and Evelyn - 89; Holles and Stapleton - 121.

1 Whitacre's diary, BL, Add. 31116, f.264 (7 Apr. 1646).

2 Interestingly enough, in the list of commissioners for keepers of the peace named in the Newcastle propositions, Holles was listed as *Sir* Denzil Holles. Rushworth, *Historical Collections,* vi. 313.

3 At the Scots' suggestion of a treaty on 6 Aug. 1645 the Commons had objected 'for by a treaty we shall not only be delayed but the king will take advantage against us' and again on 9 Dec. 1645 when the House had considered the King's request for a treaty it was 'moved that it was dangerous to entertain a treaty: for at the first treaty the king fell upon us at Brentford, and the lord Richmond and Southampton being another time here about the peace they underhand laboured to make a party in the city'; Yonge's diary, BL, Add. 18780, ff.91, 117v.

4 Baillie, *Letters and Journals,* ii. 391 (18 Aug. 1646).

5 *CJ,* iv. 632. The division was on putting the question: Holles and Stapleton - 90; Haselrig and Evelyn of Wilts. - 91 (31 July, 1646).

arguments against sending the troops were plain enough: 'a general unwillingness appearing in the house that that Army should be diminished till the Scottish Army were gone out of the kingdom'.[1] The parliamentary diarist, Harrington, was even more specific, suspecting 'a plot to weaken our army in England that after we may be forced to any conditions'. John Gurdon who had clashed with Holles during the Savile affair, argued that the dispersal of the New Model was a plot hatched by some who were not in Parliament (by whom he implied the Scots); 'this offended Mr Holles whose eagerness was excepted against'.[2] Even when the Scots' departure was imminent, the Commons voted in October that Fairfax's Army should be maintained for six months further: 'The Scots will not depart except our army stand firm. Terrible clouds hang over us and will fall on us. Preparations in France against us. . . ,' noted Harrington.[3]

Finally, Holles realised that the Presbyterian party had no chance of disbanding the New Model Army until the Scots Army had left.[4] Consequently, he changed his policy and took a hand in persuading the Scots to leave, as can be seen both from his conduct and the retrospective account of Baillie:

> Stapleton and Holles, and some others of the eleven members, had been the main persuaders of us to remove out of England, and leave the King to them, upon assurance, which was most likely, that this was the only means to get that evil army disbanded, the King and peace settled according to our minds.

A royalist source claims that the political Presbyterians had also promised to bring the King to Parliament.[5]

Holles, Stapleton and the political Presbyterians also tried to support the Scots' financial demands. When the Scots put in their account in August, they claimed that over £900,000 was due to them, but soon declared that £400,000 would content them, of which £200,000 was to be paid at their marching away. On 14 August the Commons voted that the Scots should be paid £100,000.[6] Sir John Clotworthy wanted

---

1   Whitacre's diary, BL, Add. 31116, f.279 (30 July 1646).

2   Harrington's diary, BL, Add. 10114, f.16v.

3   *Ibid.,* f.20 (7 Oct. 1646).

4   For a further discussion of this alteration, see Mahony, 'Presbyterian Party' (thesis).

5   Baillie, *Letters and Journals,* iii. 16 (1 Sept. 1647); *Memoirs of Sir John Berkeley . . .* in *Select Tracts relating to the Civil Wars in England,* ed. F. Maseres (2 vols., London, 1815), i. 356.

6   *CJ,* iv. 644.

them to have more but he was opposed by Cromwell.[1] The Scots wasted no time in letting the Commons know that so small a sum was not enough, and that they needed at least double before leaving. Grudgingly the Commons raised the total to £200,000, of which only £100,000 would be paid at their departure.[2] Still the Scots objected, so on 27 August the House decided to offer them an additional £100,000, to be paid at the end of twelve months, bringing the total to £300,000. Holles and Stapleton still could not persuade the House to increase the payment at their departure to £200,000.[3] On 1 September, after further objections from the Scottish commissioners, Holles and Stapleton finally succeeded in persuading the House to reconsider its offer of a total of £300,000 and to add another £100,000.[4] However, the Commons still adhered to their decisions as to the manner and time of payment, and on the following day the Scots said they insisted on having £200,000 at their withdrawing. 'We much resent this', Harrington notes, and the members resolved to address a few nasty questions to the Scots, such as whether they intended to relinquish English garrisons or not, at which 'Mr Holles nettled'.   Harrington spoke to the Earl of Pembroke afterwards on the matter who said 'it was not of the Scots but of some us [Holles and his party?] that drew the Scots to such demands'.[5] 'Here again' Holles wrote later of the negotiations, 'we had a strong debate: for our incendiaries hung by every twig, sticking fast to their principles to dissatisfy the Scots'.[6]

As Baillie had expected, the House of Commons asked the City for the money.   On 5 September the Commons named a committee, headed by Holles, to discuss raising the money with the Common Council 'as soon as may be',[7] and on the 10th Holles reported the Common Council's proposals for raising and securing the loan. Originally, Baillie had hoped that the citizens might use the House's need

1 Harrington's diary, BL, Add. 10114, f.17 (14 Aug. 1646).

2 *CJ*, iv. 650.

3 *Ibid.*, 655: Holles and Stapleton - 101; Haselrig and Evelyn of Wilts. - 108.

4 *Ibid.* 658. One division was on considering the Scots' reply to the offer of £300,000: Haselrig and Evelyn of Wilts. - 106; Holles and Stapleton - 129. The second division was on adding £100,000 to this: Holles and Stapleton - 140; Haselrig and Evelyn of Wilts. - 101.

5 Harrington's diary, BL, Add. 10114, f.18 (2 Sept. 1646).

6 Holles, *Memoirs*, p. 66. G.F.T. Jones, 'The payment of arrears to the army of the covenant', *EHR* 73 (1958), 459-61, argues that the final payment of the Scots was not unreasonable, but D. Stevenson, 'The financing of the cause of the Covenants, 1638-51', *Scottish Historical Review* 51 (1972), 110, argues that while it was less than they had originally hoped to receive, it was more than the minimum they were prepared to accept.

7 *CJ*, iv. 663.

for money to forward the disbanding of the New Model, but this was not to be. Indirectly, the citizens' proposals helped forward the Presbyterian cause, for the security requested was that of the grand excise, and the bishops' lands. It was Baillie's 'dear friend Dr Burgess's singular invention' to secure the loan by offering all former lenders the opportunity of doubling their original investment and obtaining the bishops' lands in return. As Baillie appreciated, this meant both that the money came in easily, and that the bishops' lands were disposed of 'in a way that no skill will get them back again'.[1] Holles and Stapleton opposed adding to this security the sale of delinquents' estates, but lost on a division.[2] Holles's opposition was prompted by a sense of class solidarity, the feeling that no good would come of the ruin of some of the best families in England.[3]

An interesting omission in Holles's account of events in 1646 in his *Memoirs* is any sense of qualification about the political Presbyterians' commitment to the Scots. To read Holles, one would think that he and his party were behind the Scots all the way, but this was not the case, and the occasions on which the political Presbyterians did not force any divisions on the Scots' behalf are interesting. In particular, although Holles's party had supported to their utmost the Scots' demands for payment, there is no sign that they supported the Scots' claim to share in disposing of the King. Holles and Stapleton had a majority in favour of considering the question of the disposal of the King on 18 September, but there was no division on the resolution that this should be as both Houses of Parliament thought fit, and that the discussion should not retard the departure of the Scots army.[4] Bamfield suggests that by this time the moderate Presbyterians were irritated by the Scots ministers, but there may be a simpler reason: national pride was present in the Presbyterian as well as the Independent party.[5]

In the end, the Scots left England because they realised that since the King would not grant their religious demands there was no future in staying. Their departure, as Baillie observed, improved the position of the political Presbyterians in Parliament, removing 'all ground of

---

1 Baillie, *Letters and Journals*, ii. 411 (1 Dec. 1646).

2 *CJ*, iv. 665. The division was on putting the question; Haselrig and Evelyn - 105, Holles and Stapleton - 100.

3 Holles, *Memoirs*, pp. 128-9. The same sentiment had prompted Holles, Stapleton, and their allies, to support moderate treatment of the King's nephews, Rupert and Maurice; *CJ*, iv. 588 (25 June 1646).

4 *CJ*, iv. 672: Holles and Stapleton - 91; Sir W. Armine and Sir W. Masham - 83.

5 *Colonel Joseph Bamfields Apologie* (1685), pp. 18-19.

jealousy of our joining with the King, the greatest prop of the sectaries's power in the House', a view endorsed by Holles himself.[1] In December 1646 a newsletter commented 'The Presbyterian Party take heart apace and now carry all votes. . . .'[2] The moderates, the remnants of the old middle group, supported the policies of the political Presbyterians, once the threat of Scottish domination was removed. The Presbyterian politicians needed help, for in September their most important leader, the Earl of Essex, had died. Essex was 'the head of our party here', Baillie said, keeping together the House of Lords, the City and the shires. Possibly after his death, since no other aristocrat enjoyed the same position, leadership of the Parliamentary part of the Presbyterian alliance fell more to Holles and Stapleton in the Commons. The aristocratic connection remained, but the Earl of Holland, with whom they were associated, lacked Essex's prestige. Holles was a pall bearer at Essex's enormously elaborate funeral, and was bequeathed a silver watch and a black and silver purse containing old coins. [3]

In the City, the Presbyterian party was weakened and disheartened by the Scots' departure, but nevertheless organised petitions for the disbanding of the New Model and the suppression of heresy during December 1646. The political Presbyterians now had a chance of attaching the City party to their own interest, since in their dislike of the New Model and of heresy the two groups had much in common. Furthermore, the Scots' departure weakened the support for the High Presbytery, which made co-operation between Parliamentarians and citizens easier. In the Commons, Holles and Stapleton found general support for a moderate church settlement. When informed by the City in December that the soldiers of Fairfax's army took it upon themselves to preach, and dragged ministers from their pulpits,[4] the House sat until midnight, and voted by 105 to 57 to suppress the exposition of the Scriptures by the unordained.[5]

Many M.P.s had come to believe that a moderate Presbytery, subject

---

1 Baillie, *Letters and Journals*, iii. 2 (26 Jan. 1647), Holles, *Memoirs*, p. 69.

2 Extracts of Letters of Intelligence, Bodl., Clarendon 29, f.161v. (23 Dec/3 Jan. 1646/7).

3 Baillie, *Letters and Journals*, ii. 401 (2 Oct. 1646); *The True Manner and Form of the Proceeding to the Funerall of the Right Honourable Robert Earle of Essex*, 1646, p. 13; BL, Add. 46189, f.150, f.151v. Among the mourners at Essex's funeral was one, Sir Robert Shirley, whom Dr Mahony suggests may have been a kinsman both of Essex and of Holles's wife Jane Shirley.

4 Baillie, *Letters and Journals*, ii. 413 (8 Dec. 1646); *The Humble Petition of the Lord Major, Aldermen, and Commons of the City of London, in Common Councell Assembled*, 19 Dec. 1646, TT E. 366.15.

5 *CJ*, v. 34; Haselrig and Cromwell - 57; Sir W. Erle and Irby - 105. Whitacre's diary, BL, Add. 31116, f.295v.

to Parliament's control, was for the present the best way of organising the church. Ideally, many of the supporters of such a moderate Presbytery may have preferred moderate episcopacy, but this was not a possibility after the entry of the Scots into the war in 1643. The account of Sir Philip Stapleton's religious views — written after his death by one of his friends, perhaps by Holles[1] — comes closest to explaining this position:

> For his religion, he was a true and zealous Protestant, though not any way new-fangled, yet abundantly careful, and curious enough to discover the saving truths in fundamentals of faith and knowledge. . . Nor was he easily engaged into any thing of change, no not into that way he so much suffered for (the Covenant and church government by Presbytery) though afterwards he looked upon it both in divine and prudent considerations, as the way of God suiting most, and best with the union of the nations, and in that the welfare of both, and the next way under God (moderately advanced) to make the three kingdoms happy;[2]

Although the political Presbyterians may have felt hopeful of settling the kingdom, there were ominous signs. They had not the solid support of the religious Presbyterians in the City: the citizens found the 'Parliament Presbyterians (as they call them) to be the most rigid) called Erastians'.[3] The ministers were dissatisfied with Parliament's settlement of the church, and they looked to the City rather than to the members of Parliament as allies.

More seriously, there were large stirrings of discontent in England. The Parliamentarians had called up the nation to support them in 1642, but by 1646 they began to perceive the fearful dimensions of the monster they had conjured forth. Great multitudes flocked to Parliament with petitions, and Whitelocke observed in September 1646 'that some of those gentlemen who formerly most encouraged such resort were now most fearful of them'.[4] Petitions embraced more than grievances of want. For example, there were petitions against tithes during 1646; as one member said, if they countenanced such complaints they next 'might expect a petition that no tenants should pay rents to the landlords'.[5]

1 C.H. Firth, in his article in the *DNB* on Sir Philip Stapleton, says the account was supposed to be by D. Holles.

2 *A Short and True Narrative of the . . . Death of . . . Sir Philip Stapleton,* [28 Sept. 1647], TT E. 409.3, pp. 1-2.

3 *Perfect Occurrences of both Houses,* 28 Aug. 1646, TT E. 513.7 (24 Aug. 1646).

4 Whitelocke, Annals, BL, Add. 37344, f.66; see also f.74v: in December 'some perhaps were a little awed by the multitudes of Citizens attending at the door of the house'.

5 *CJ,* iv. 534; Whitacre's diary, BL, Add. 31116, f.268 (5 May 1646). White-

There were criticisms in the press of the arrogance of the members of Parliament, and their privileges made them unpopular, especially those which protected them from honouring their debts.[1]   On 10 April 1646 Holles drew the Commons' attention to a pamphlet by George Wither, which complained of 'men of *large fortunes,* and *little conscience'* who had so long monopolised places of power and trust, and suggested replacing them with 'men of middling fortunes'.[2] Wither's criticisms were chiefly directed against Sir Richard Onslow, a friend of Holles's, and Holles was one of the tellers of the majority in favour of ordering Wither to pay £500 damages.[3] *The Last Warning* cautioned its readers against men who desired religious dominance simply because they were wealthier and ate better than other men.[4]   While Holles believed that men with estates ought to control the church, others feared and hated the prospect of Presbyterian tyranny, a pope in every parish, ten thousand judicatories through the land. Holles himself was not the man to allay fears of lordly dominance. His sharp temper had flashed out on several occasions during 1646, and his hostility to Cromwell was marked. In addition to the disputes already mentioned, the pair clashed over who should replace the late Earl of Essex as Lord Lieutenant of Yorkshire. The Commons supported Lord Fairfax, the Lords the Earl of Northumberland: 'Lieutenant General Cromwell and Mr Denzil Holles in some heat upon it'.[5] On 30 December 1646 Stephen Marshall, preaching at the monthly fast, warned the Commons against alienating the hearts of the people. His caution against parliamentary arrogance seems almost prophetic:

> Many great politicans go another way to work, they think the affections of the people are not to be valued, they say, *Populus humiliater servit, superbe dominatur,* that the People (like fire and water) are good servants, but evil masters; and therefore the best way is to subdue them and keep them under, but I am assured that you detest these rules . . . you know what it is to command in the hearts of your brethren. . . .[6]

locke, Annals, BL, Add. 37344, f.86.

1   The Commons took up the subject of their privileges in Dec. 1646, but took no action; *CJ,* v. 9; Whitacre's diary, BL, Add. 31116, f.292 (10 Dec. 1646).

2   George Wither, *Justitiarus justificates* . . . [13 Apr. 1646], TT E.506.30, p. 7.

3   Holles's wife, Jane, was Onslow's cousin, and he was godfather to Onslow's son, named Denzil after him; *HMC Buckinghamshire, Lindsey, Onslow etc. MSS.,* p. 459. Whitacre's diary, BL, Add. 31116, f.264. *CJ,* iv. 640. There was a division on whether to put the question for a fine of £500; Cromwell and Haselrig - No - 54; Holles and Stapleton - Yea - 65. (7 Aug. 1646).

4   *The Last Warning to all the Inhabitants of London,* [20 Mar. 1646], TT E. 328.24, p. 5.

5   Harrington's diary, BL, Add. 10114, f.19 (17 Sept. 1646).

6   Stephen Marshall, *The Right Understanding of the Times. A sermon Preached*

It would have been well for Holles if he had heeded Marshall, since he was prone to losing his temper and to despising the lesser orders in society. The way was clearing for him and his party at the end of 1646, but it remained to be seen whether they could conciliate the grievances of their supporters and be flexible enough in their thinking to propound a satisfactory settlement.

to the House of Commons, 30 Dec. 1646, TT E. 369.5, p. 45.

8

'THE REIGN OF HOLLES AND STAPLETON':[1]
THE CRISIS OF 1647

We have laboured to the utmost of our power, to procure a settlement to the Church and State: We have desired a peace and are
proclaimed guilty of war, as members of Parliament, as members of
the Commonwealth, we have laboured with the loss of our blood,
and the loss of our fortunes, for the health and welfare of the
kingdom; and we are condemned for the firelocks of sedition and
destruction.[2]

. . . if things had been carried by the Parliament's party with moderation, things had been in a calmer condition than now.[3]

i.

1647 was the turning point of Holles's political career. In the first part
of that year he led the House of Commons, but after his attempt to
settle the kingdom failed, he was forced to flee to France. He would
never again be so important a politician, though many more years of
political life awaited him.

Reflecting upon the events of 1647 from his exile, Holles saw a
herculean struggle between two parties; his own good-hearted party
who wanted to settle the kingdom, and the violent party, who sought
to change the government of the state and church so that they might
rise to power.[4]   But recent studies have shown that the politics at
Westminster in 1647 were not a simple two party struggle, and that
there was still a fluctuating body of men uncommitted to either of the
two main groups. Underdown rightly describes the Presbyterian party
as a loose coalition of groups, crystallising around the old peace party.[5]
In some ways it still makes sense to refer to the 'Presbyterians' as a
peace party. Alternatively, they may still be referred to by the names

1   John Milton, *Original Letters and Papers of State, Addressed to Oliver Cromwell;
Concerning the Affairs of Great Britain,* ed. John Nickolls (London 1743), p. 4.

2   *A New Remonstrance of the Eleven Impeached Members . . ,* [14 Aug.] 1647,
TT E.402. 3, p. 4.

3   *A True Account and Character of the Times, drawne by a Gentleman . ,* [9 Aug.]
1647, TT E.401.13, p. 7.

4   Holles, *Memoirs, passim.*

5   Underdown, *Pride's Purge,* pp. 69-72, and ch. iv.

of their leaders, as Holles's and Stapleton's party. While some historians accepted Holles's own term, 'the moderates', there are dangers in taking Holles at his own evaluation, for part of the purpose of his skilfully written polemic was to obscure his own 'fiery' conduct in 1647. His attempt to organise a counter-revolution in the City seems no more moderate than the attempt of the 'Independents' to command the Army for their own purposes. The term 'moderate' seems more properly applied to those members who were committed to neither of the main groups.[1] However, the most commonly used contemporary term and one which Holles employed was 'Presbyterians'.[2] It now seems clear that this label, when applied to Holles's party in the Commons, does not necessarily refer to a group of committed religious Presbyterians; for religious issues could still precipitate new groupings in the Commons.

Holles and the Presbyterians gained the support of many uncommitted members of the Commons when the Scots left England. Although they continued to negotiate on the Newcastle propositions with the King, they concentrated their attention on disbanding the Army. As Holles explained in his *Memoirs*, the Army was expensive to maintain, and so long as it was afoot in England, the burden of taxation continued. Since the Irish revolt of 1641 was still unavenged, Parliament would reduce the Army and send some of the disbanded soldiers there.[3] The Presbyterians hoped that the City would approve and lend the money necessary. Underlying these motives their opponents feared there were others. Holles and the Presbyterians, they believed, intended to settle the kingdom in their own way, which might involve either selling-out the parliamentary cause to the King, or the imposition of a thoroughgoing Presbyterian church government, or both. Whatever the settlement, the Presbyterians wanted to dictate it. Their opponents believed that because the Presbyterians knew that the only power able to resist any settlement they might choose to make was the New Model, they aimed to disband most of it, and keep the remaining soldiers under Presbyterian commanders so that a hostile force would be converted into an ally. 'Holles and Stapleton and the rest', it was later alleged, 'had a design to engross the power into their own hands, and to distribute to the people good or evil at their own pleasure'.[4]

1   MacCormack, *Revolutionary Politics*, p. 7 & *passim*, uses the term 'moderate'. Cf. Valerie Pearl, 'The "Royal Independents" in the English civil war', *TRHS* 5th ser. 18 (1968), 71-2; Valerie Pearl, 'London's Counter-Revolution', in G. Aylmer, ed., *The Interregnum: The Quest for Settlement 1646-1660* (London, 1972).
2   Holles, *Memoirs*, pp. 104, 108. Holles also spoke of 'all the Independent Party'; *ibid.*, p. 117.
3   *Ibid.*, pp. 72-3.
4   *Westminster Projects, or the Mysterie of Darby House discovered*, [23 Mar.

ii.

Many moderates sympathised with the Presbyterians' wish to disband the Army. Seeing the burden of taxation, and the impossibility of relieving Ireland while the New Model remained in England, they supported the Presbyterians' efforts. On 18 February 1647 the Commons resolved to disband the New Model, leaving only 5,000 cavalry. Bellièvre, the French representative in London, commented that 'The Independents, who command it, did what they could to prevent it, but in vain; the Presbyterians carried it with a large majority'.[1] In March Holles and Stapleton were tellers for a majority which stipulated that all the remaining officers should conform to the church government established by Parliament.[2] Faced with Presbyterian majorities, the Independents lost heart: Cromwell was reported to be ill in February, 'whereby his party is now the weaker in the House'. By April it was reported that 'Cromwell and other leading men of them flag much' and that Cromwell and the Independent party were 'exceedingly sunk in spirit'. The Independents were probably staying away from the House — Vane junior, Cromwell and the two Pierreponts were said to be absent in April — because they found themselves powerless in the House so long as Holles had the support of the uncommitted.[3]

Holles and the Presbyterians did not want to send the New Model itself to Ireland — which might have been a simpler solution to the Irish problem — because they considered the soldiers in it a dangerous and disruptive force.[4] Since Holles believed the soldiers were 'a let and hinderance to the settling all government both civil and ecclesiastical', they must be disbanded, and only those conformable with the Presbyterians' policies should be retained for Ireland.[5] Furthermore, by 1647

1648], TT E.433.15, p. 1.

1 *CJ*, v. 90; *The Diplomatic Correspondence of Jean de Montereul and the Brothers De Bellièvre French Ambassadors in England and Scotland 1645-48*, ed. J.G. Fotheringham (2 vols., Scottish History Society, Edinburgh, 1898-9), ii. p. 18 (28/18 Feb. 1647).

2 *CJ*, v. 108. The division was on whether the question should be put; Holles and Stapleton - 136; Haselrig and Evelyn of Wilts. - 108.

3 Bodl., Clarendon 29, f.97, f.165v., f.193, f.203 [letters of intelligence], 8/18 Feb., 1/11 Apr., 15/25 Apr., 29 Apr. 1647. Cf. MacCormack, *Revolutionary Politics*, p. 170 who suggests that Cromwell, Vane and St. John had undertaken to cooperate during Holles's campaign to reduce the Army.

4 Arthur Annesley, M.P. and one of the commissioners for disbanding the Army, wished that the entire Army might be sent to Ireland; *HMC Egmont MSS.*, i. pt. 2, p. 404 (14 May 1647).

5 Holles, *Memoirs*, p. 70.

the financial situation was such that Parliament could not afford both to pay all the soldiers' arrears and continue to employ them all in the Irish campaign.[1]

Ireland was for the Parliamentarians a persistent and difficult problem, and the precise nature of the interests of the Presbyterian and Independent parties there awaits further study. Holles's own interest in Ireland is difficult to explain. He had adventured money in 1642 but there is no record of whether he paid. He was a member of the original committee for Ireland appointed by the King in April 1642.[2] Parliament had gradually taken over from the Adventurers who were committed to the conquest of Ireland for their own profit, which caused resentment among the Adventurers and in the City.[3] Holles was a member of the parliamentary committee for Ireland appointed in July 1645, but he did not attend meetings regularly at first. (He was involved in the Savile affair at the time.)[4] The Presbyterians championed Lord Inchiquin in Ireland, because Lord Lisle, the Lord Lieutenant, was thought to be a 'creature of Cromwell's'.[5] In 1647 Parliament proposed to alter the system of command in Ireland by separating military and civil functions. Two lord justices were to be responsible for the civil government, and a new commander-in-chief appointed for the military forces.[6] When Lisle was recalled he proposed Sir Hardress Waller as his deputy, but Inchiquin objected to this 'planting confiding Independents' in power, and he was reluctant to serve Parliament in Waller's company: 'I confess I would not willingly be joined here with any Independent', he wrote to Sir Philip Perceval in

1   J.S. Morrill, 'Mutiny and discontent in English provincial armies 1645-1647', *Past & Present* 56(1972), 49-74; I. Gentles, 'The arrears of pay of the parliamentary army at the end of the first Civil War', *BIHR* 48 (1975), 52-63.

2   J.R. MacCormack, 'The Irish adventurers and the English civil war', *Irish Historical Studies* 10 (1956-7), p. 50. Holles subscribed £1,000. *Calendar of the State Papers relating to Ireland of the reign of Charles I. 1633-1647* (London, 1901), p. 366. The Earl of Ormonde directed his thanks to the House of Commons to Holles in August 1642; Bodl., Tanner 63, ff. 143-143v.

3   K.S. Bottigheimer, 'English money and Irish land: The 'adventurers' in the Cromwellian settlement of Ireland', *Journal of British Studies* 7 (1967), 12-27.

4   Proceedings of the committee appointed by Parliament, 1 July 1645 printed in *Calendar of State Papers Ireland 1633-1647*.

5   Inchiquin was supported by Holles, Stapleton, Davis, Clotworthy, Sir Philip Perceval, and the Earl of Holland; see correspondence between Perceval and Inchiquin in *HMC Egmont MSS*, i. pt. 2, pp. 385-95. Baillie, *Letters and Journals*, iii. 16 (1 Sept. 47).

6   Whitelocke says that Holles and his friends asked him to be one of the lord justices because they wanted him out of the way, but he avoided the service with the help of his new friend Cromwell, and his party; Whitelocke, 'Diary', Lord Bute's MSS., 1 & 25 April 1647.

April 1647. Inchiquin warned Holles, Stapleton and the Presbyterian party that Lisle was attempting to establish his own faction in command in Ireland.[1] Parliament proposed Skippon as the new commander-in-chief, with Massey as his second in command, but only Skippon was acceptable to the soldiers of the New Model, for Massey was thought to be a Presbyterian by religion, and of loose morals.[2]

In March 1647 the Committee for Irish affairs sent a deputation to the Army to engage the soldiers for Irish service. The Officers raised certain difficulties, the chief of which related to assurances for their pay in Ireland, and satisfaction of their arrears and indemnity for their service in England. These material grievances were taken up by the soldiers in a petition to Fairfax which the Commons, after lengthy debate, ordered Fairfax to suppress.[3] However, on 29 March Colonel Edward Harley informed the House that his lieutenant colonel had read the petition before his regiment and obtained 1,100 signatures on the threat of cashiering all who refused. Perhaps the writer's conclusion goaded the Parliamentarians into action; 'I confess I do much doubt [i.e. fear] the event, except the Parliament take some high resolutions'. After a long day's debate on the soldiers' actions many Independents left the House under the impression that nothing would be done until the following day, but the members accepted a harsh declaration which threatened to brand the soldiers 'enemies of the state'. Holles must bear a large share of responsibility for this provocative measure. Ludlow says that Holles seized the opportunity of a thin house and 'drew up a resolution upon his knee'. Holles later admitted his authorship, but argued that he had acted only in response to a general request.[4] This Declaration, published on 30 March, announced the Lords' and Commons' 'high dislike' of the Army's petition, and their intention to prosecute any soldiers who persisted in disobedience as enemies to the state, and disturbers of the public peace.[5] This threat enraged the soldiers, who claimed that they were simply preparing a petition for

1 *A Particular Charge or Impeachment in the Name of his Excellency Sir Thomas Fairfax . . .* , [9 July] 1647, TT E.397.17, p. 20. *HMC Egmont MSS* i, pt. 2, pp. 385, 394-5.

2 In April Skippon and Cromwell were mentioned as the nominees of one party, Waller and Massey as those of the other; *ibid.*, p. 384. Holles's support of Massey showed his disregard of the complaints of the western counties in 1646 about the outrages committed by Massey's soldiers.

3 Gardiner, *Civil War*, iii, 223-4; 225-6; *CJ*, v, 127; Whitacre's diary, BL, Add. 31116, f.306.

4 Bodl., Tanner 58, f. 16, copy of the letter to Col. Harley, 27 Mar. 1647; *Memoirs of Edmund Ludlow*, ed. C.H. Firth (2 vols., Oxford, 1894), i. 149-50, *A Full Vindication and Answer of the XI. Accused Members*, pp. 14-15.

5 *A Declaration of the Lords and Commons*, 30 March 1647, TT 669.f.9 (84).

submission to their general, and that Parliament had censured them 'upon misinformation'.[1] Parliament's votes against the soldiers seemed so severe some pamphleteers soon argued that they were part of a deliberate plot to provoke the Army to mutiny so as to make it odious to the people.[2]

Parliament's anger did not stop at the *Declaration* for five officers connected with the petition were summoned to the bar.[3] The following day Holles quarrelled with Ireton on the subject of the Army petition, and only the intervention of the House prevented the two men from fighting a duel.[4] Another version of the incident is more colourful. Ireton came into the field without a sword, 'pretending it stood not with his conscience to fight, which confirms the general opinion that all the Independents are deadly cowards'. The clash was subsequently embroidered by Clarendon to make a good story: Holles, Clarendon says, persuaded Ireton to leave the House, and told him

> that he should presently go over the water and fight with him.
> Ireton told him his conscience would not suffer him to fight a duel:
> upon which Holles, in choler, pulled him by the nose, telling him,
> if his conscience would keep him from giving men satisfaction, it
> should keep him from provoking them.[5]

Holles's fiery temper makes the story credible.

The Commons' injunction to Holles and Ireton to proceed no further with their dispute did not end the conflict over the Army petition. Holles believed the soldiers had acted disobediently, and some of their officers dishonestly. He was unsympathetic to the soldiers' material grievances — pay, indemnity, and security from being sent abroad — and considered that the soldiers of the New Model were being treated as fairly as those of Massey's brigade who had been disbanded the previous October. Holles decried the soldiers' contention that they were no 'mere mercenary army', on the not unreasonable grounds that their

1 *For our faithfull and ever honoured commanders (A Manifesto of Loyalty Presented to Sir Thomas Fairfax, Major General Skippon and Lieut.-General Cromwell on Behalf of Eight Regiments of Horse),* [6 May 1647], TT 669. f. 11 (9).

2 *Letters from Saffron-Walden . . . ,* [9 Apr.] 1647, TT E.383.24, pp. 9-10

3 *CJ,* v. 132; *A Perfect Diurnall of some Passages in Parliament,* 29 Mar.-5 Apr. 1647, TT E.515.6, pp. 1541-2.

4 Bodl., Clarendon 29, f.165v., [letter of intelligence], 1/11 Apr. 1647; *CJ,* v. 133. Duelling was a 'scandalous sin' for which a man was barred from the sacrament; 'An Ordinance together with Rules and Directions concerning Suspension from the Sacrament of the Lords Supper in cases of Ignorance and Scandall', [20 Oct. 1645], *Acts and Ordinances,* ed. Firth & Rait, i. 791.

5 Bodl., Clarendon 29, f.193, [extract of letters of intelligence], 15/25 Apr. 1647; Clarendon, *History* (Bk. X, 104), Macray, iv. 238.

concern over their pay showed them to be mercenaries, but he ignored the fact that many soldiers had voluntarily enlisted in a cause he himself had publicised.[1] Holles launched into 'high expressions' upon the *Apology* for the Army in April, but he was not alone in his rage at the soldiers. To Stapleton it seemed a fight to the finish with the soldiers: 'we must sink them . . . or they sink us'. Strode said the soldiers should go to Ireland or be hanged.[2] Locke tells a story, which he had from Holles's cousin by marriage, Anthony Ashley Cooper, of Holles 'in a great heat against Cromwell', determined to attack him.[3] The effect of all this hostility was to weld the soldiers and officers into a suspicious, angry force.

Meanwhile, Parliament proceeded with plans to disband the Army. On 2 April the Commons appointed a committee to borrow £200,000 from the City to pay off the soldiers. The Common Council considered the question of security, and advised that the best means of raising the money for a loan was 'to secure the lenders a like sum as was lately done unto those who advanced the £200,000 for our bretheren of Scotland'. On 20 April Holles reported the City's suggestion that their security should be the bishops' lands, the excise, and the fines and compositions of royalist delinquents not yet received at Goldsmiths' Hall.[4] Although the Lords were prepared to agree to the security requested, the Commons were not, and so there was an impasse. Nevertheless, Bellièvre reported, whatever the City might appear to object, it had let the Presbyterian politicians know indirectly that 'it would not see them at a loss'.[5] Although the Lords finally agreed with the Commons, in the formal negotiations which continued the City insisted that the loan could not be advanced without the security of the delinquents' fines not yet received, so finally the Commons decided to offer half the future composition fines. When the Common Council met on 8 May,

1 Holles, *Memoirs*, pp. 77-8, 81, 111-2.

2 Amon Wilbee, *Plain Truth, without Feare or Flattery*, [2 July] 1647, TT E.516.7, p. 16; *The Clarke Papers*, ed. C.H. Firth (4 vols., Camden Society, 1891-1901), i. 15; *HMC Portland MSS.*, i. 447-8; information of the words of William Strode.

3 Locke, *Works*, ix. 279; W.D. Christie, *A Life of Anthony Ashley Cooper, first Earl of Shaftesbury 1621-1683* (2 vols., London, 1871), i. 79. links the incident with 30 April, but according to his diary, Cooper did not arrive in London until 5 May 1647; *ibid.*, p. xliii.

4 Journal of the Common Council, City of London, Guildhall Record Office, 40, f. 214; *CJ*, v. 146-8.

5 *Ibid.*, 148, 159; *LJ*, ix. 150 (10 for; 6 against). The Commons objected that the fines at Goldsmiths' Hall were their only means of raising money 'if there should be any extraordinary occasion'; Montereul, *Correspondence*, ii. 129 (3 May 1647).

Holles and others informed them of Parliament's votes. Holles was finally able to report to the Commons that, after 'long debate and serious consideration', the City agreed to lend the money on condition it be used only for the disbanding of the Army and the service of Ireland.[1]

The loan of £200,000 was thus negotiated by a compromise both on the part of the Common Council, who moderated their demands for security, and the Commons, who gave the citizens half what they asked for. The Presbyterians have been blamed for niggardliness in dealing with the Army, but their chief difficulty was to persuade a majority in the Commons to approve the conditions requested by the City. After all their trouble, they obtained £200,000 but the soldiers' arrears amounted to nearly £3 million.[2]

In these negotiations, the Presbyterians tried to manipulate the citizens' hostility to the New Model. At the beginning of May the Earl of Pembroke told the citizens 'that did they know so much as he, coming from the fountain's head of the Army, they would not scruple the lending of the £200,000 to be rid of the Army'.[3] In fact, in their negotiations with the City, the Presbyterians were pursuing another, secret, plan for raising an armed force to counter that of the New Model. The financial negotiations with the City proceeded in conjunction with plans for reorganising the City forces, all which was not unobserved by their opponents. Parliament's grant to the City of the right to nominate its own militia committee was publicly described as 'a shoehorn to pull up the £200,000, as though the citizens did not look at the security of their persons, without any regard to that of their disbursements'.[4]

As fears increased, tension mounted. The Presbyterians tried to

1 *LJ*, ix. 165 (1 May 1647); *CJ*, v. 163, 168. Whitacre's diary, BL, Add. 31116, f. 309; Guildhall R.O., Journal of the Common Council, 40, f.216 (3 May 1647); f. 216v.

2 Gentles, 'Arrears of pay', p. 62.

3 *Clarke Papers*, i. 24, 26, anonymous letters of 5 & 6 May 1647.

4 *Acts and Ordinances*, ed. Firth & Rait, i, 928; R.R. Sharp, *London and the Kingdom. A History derived mainly from the archives at Guildhall* (3 vols, London, 1894-5), ii, 241; *A Perfect Diurnall of some passages in Parliament*, 26 April. – 3 May 1647, TT E.515.10, p. 1570: 'after long debate' the Common Council put out from the militia committee Aldermen Penington, Fowkes, Warner, Kendrick, Colonels Wilson, Player, Tichburne and others. Amon Wilbee, *Plain Truth*, p. 10, said that these men were put out because 'they are not absolute for the Faction'. By this means, Wilbee said, 'the Earl of Manchester, M. Holles, Stapleton, Earle senior, and the rest of the traiterous faction . . . do conceive they have well secured themselves from all invasion . . . from any party within the City'; p. 11. *Two Letters, London, May 5. 1647*, TT E.386.2, p. 6.

increase their political strength ready for the coming struggle with the Army by reviving attempts to restore the Earls of Holland, Bedford and Clare to their seats in the House of Lords, but they were unsuccessful. On 25 May the Presbyterians carried a division in the Commons to disband the Army, beginning with Fairfax's regiment. The date fixed was 1 June.[1]

iii.

On 1 June Parliament received a letter from Fairfax announcing the Army's refusal to disband. A long debate resulted, in which Holles claimed that 'vigorous and honourable resolutions' were opposed 'might and main by all the Independent party'. Not until Skippon, the Presbyterian nominee for the Irish command, pleaded moderation did the balance swing against confrontation.[2] The majority agreed, after a debate until 2 a.m. on 3 June, to recall the *Declaration* of 30 March and to pay the soldiers' arrears. Apparently the Independents opposed the Presbyterians' intention to pay all the common soldiers' arrears, 'for it might set division between the officers and soldiers'.[3] While Holles and Baillie both later censured this tame capitulation, it does not seem as if the Presbyterians had the numbers to hold out in the Commons.[4] Holles's surprise at the unexpected nature of Skippon's intervention indicates that there were moderates who could be swayed, and the presence of these uncommitted men helps explain the fluctuations in the Commons' policies. Although the Presbyterians did not dominate the House in June, they had their own plans for resisting the Army, and were engaged in negotiating with the King and enlisting their own forces to resist the New Model.

The next blow to the Presbyterians was the news that Cornet Joyce had taken the King from Parliament's custody at Holmby to the Army at Newmarket.[5] There had been talk of Presbyterian plans to bring the

1   Bodl., Clarendon 29, f. 165 (1 Apr. 1647); *HMC D'Lisle*, vi. 562-5; *CJ*, v. 183: Lewis & Mr Grimston - yea - 136; Sidney & Evelyn of Wilts. - no - 115. Whitacre's diary, BL, Add. 31116, f. 310v., says that Fairfax's regiment was chosen 'to give a good example of obedience to the rest'. A letter of intelligence, *Clarke Papers*, i. 112, stated that the votes on this day were passed 'unanimously (our friends withdrawing)'.

2   Holles, *Memoirs*, pp. 104-5; Whitacre's diary, BL, Add. 31116, f. 120.

3   *CJ*, v. 197. The House divided on putting the question for expunging the Declaration: 96 were for, 79 against; Harrington's diary, BL, Add. 10114, f. 25. The division on considering the common soldiers first was 154 in favour, 123 against.

4   Holles, *Memoirs*, pp. 106-7; Baillie, *Letters and Journals*, iii. 17. (1 Sept. 1647).

5   According to *A True Account and Character of the Times*, p. 5, Joyce had

King to Northampton or Windsor late in May, and the Army feared that with Colonel Graves in command of Charles at Holmby, the Presbyterians might whisk the King to Scotland or to London, as they chose.[1] There were rumours of Presbyterian overtures to the King: the Earl of Dunfermline was the go-between in negotiations between the English Presbyterians, the Scots, and the Queen in France. One account was that the King would be taken to Scotland to head an army which would bring him to London, and that Dunfermline had gone to France to take the Prince to Scotland. Another was that the Prince of Wales should join the forces in Scotland and invade England with the aid of the Presbyterians there. Another rumour was that Dunfermline would bring the Prince to London.[2] The Royalists were suspicious of Presbyterian intentions towards the King. In April 1647 a royalist letter of intelligence reported that once the Army was disbanded, Parliament would send propositions to the King and if he refused them, imprison him in another place. Nicholas afterwards believed that if the Independents had not taken the King from Holmby the Presbyterians would have imprisoned him in Warwick or Pontefract Castle a few days later. The Royalists believed that the Presbyterians intended to impose this settlement on the King as soon as they were powerful enough. Once the Army was down, the King would have to accept the propositions, though they would be a little moderated.[3] How far Holles was embroiled in these plots to join with the Scots and the Royalists it is difficult to say. Not surprisingly, there is no evidence of his involvement, and his later conduct suggests he had reservations about both the Scots and the Royalists. Contemporary references to 'English Presbyterians' negotiating with the Scots and the Royalists may have referred to the Scots' party in the City rather than to Holles and his friends.

What were the intentions of Holles and the Presbyterians towards the King in 1647? In his *Memoirs* Holles wrote as though he and his party had consistently supported Charles against the opposition of the Independents. Certainly there were times after 1642 when he appeared

formerly been 'tailor to Mr. Holles'.

1 Dispatches of the Dutch Ambassador in London, BL, Add. 17677, f. 456, Joachimi to the States General, 7 June [28 May] 1647; *A Letter From the Right Honourable Edward Lord Montague*, 11 June 1647, TT E.400.10, p. 4; Bodl., Clarendon 29, f. 236, [letter of intelligence], 7/17 June 1647; *Memorials of the Great Civil War*, i. 223.

2 *Clarke Papers*, i, xxv, Denton to Verney, 14 June 1647. Bodl., Clarendon 29, f. 240, f. 244 [extracts of letter of intelligence], 10 June, 21 June 1647; Montereul, *Correspondence*, ii. 163, 7/17 June 1647.

3 Bodl., Clarendon 29, f. 203, f. 193, f. 241, [letters of intelligence], 29 Apr., 7/17 June 1647; 14 June 1647; *ibid.*, 30, f.280, [Nicholas] to [Hyde], 3 Feb. [1648].

a crypto-Royalist. But there are two points which should be made here. First, Parliament as a whole was committed to a negotiated settlement with the King. There was a group of Independents who were in favour of offering as moderate terms to the King as Holles and his friends.[1] Secondly, Holles did not favour complete capitulation to the King, as some observers noted. In 1646 Holles and his friends had told the Scots that until the King gave satisfaction over the peace propositions, the Commons 'will never consent that he shall come hither with freedom, nor do they know any one man in either House of another opinion'. They continued, that unless the King consented to the peace propositions, 'they are resolved that during his life the kingdom shall be governed without him'.[2] While this may imply the deposition of Charles — in favour, perhaps, of his son — it may foreshadow a decision such as that made at the beginning of 1648 to ignore Charles, and make no further applications to him. In the context of late 1646, it may also have been an attempt to bully Charles into agreeing to the propositions.

Although in April 1647 there was still talk of Presbyterian intentions to make a council of state and 'new-model' the government if the King refused their terms, Holles was no republican.[3] Evidence from other periods of his life confirms that at no time could he contemplate a constitution without a king. While this may be one of his limitations, his attitude to monarchy is clear, consistent and part of an emotionally held set of beliefs about society. He could no more abandon monarchy than he could abolish all government in the church. Confirmatory evidence of Holles's intentions in 1647 comes from the plans he propounded to the King in 1644 and his ideas in 1648. In 1644 he had begged Charles to throw himself upon London and to worry about the terms later. In 1648 at the treaty of Newport he again begged Charles, on his knees, to consent to the terms so that Parliament might bring him to London. Charles refused on both occasions. The implication is that Holles was asking him to deliver himself into Presbyterian hands, to trust them and all would be well for him. But Charles did not trust them. So in 1647 Holles and the Presbyterians tried to bully Charles into accepting the Newcastle Propositions,[4] for they had not a majority in the House to support the offer of any more moderate

1   Pearl, 'Royal Independents'.
2   *Correspondence of the Scots Commissioners in London, 1644-1646,* ed. H.W. Meikle (Roxburghe Club, London, 1917), pp. 216, 218 (19 Sept., 3 Oct. 1646).
3   Bodl., Clarendon 29, f. 193. [extract of letter of intelligence], 15/25 Apr. 1647.
4   The Newcastle Propositions were sent to Charles for the third time on 21 April 1647; Gardiner, *Civil War,* iii. 243.

terms, and simultaneously tried to secure control over all the armed forces in the three kingdoms so that Charles would have no power — or hope of power — to resist whatever settlement they dictated, and so that they in turn might moderate the peace propositions as they saw fit.

When Charles was transferred from the captivity of the Scots to that of the Parliament of England at the beginning of 1647, he found no very kind treatment. Clarendon says that the Presbyterians treated him 'with the same formality of respect as he had been treated with by the Scots, and with the same strictness'. On 6 February they ordered that the altar plate from the King's Chapel at Whitehall should be melted down — some said for a dinner service for the King's use. They refused to establish a household for him while he continued unco-operative, and in April they ordered a declaration against the superstition of touching for the King's Evil.[1] Although these decisions were designed to demonstrate Parliament's firmness, particularly in religion, they were offensive to the King, and later in the year he found the Army's treatment more lenient and generous. Later historians believed Holles and the Presbyterians were 'willing to make a treaty with the King without adequate security for its performances',[2] but even in 1660, when the tide was running strongly for unconditional restoration, Holles wanted terms similar to the Newcastle Propositions imposed on the King. He had been associated with dangerous schemes — such as bringing the King to London in 1644 — but this does not mean he intended to capitulate in 1647, although he probably would have compromised on some of the issues Charles found distasteful.

Holles in 1647 appears to have believed that the King would have to accept the terms imposed on him. Most of the members of Parliament shared this belief. On such an assumption they had taken up arms in 1642 to fight him into submission. They were reluctant to consider the possibility of Charles refusing. The danger of Holles's schemes in 1647 was that not only Charles but everybody else would have to accept his idea of a settlement, because if his plans had succeeded there would have been no force to resist him. The New Model would be broken, some soldiers dispersed to Ireland. Secure in the City, with the blessing of the Scots, Holles would have been able to dictate to the King.

1 Clarendon, *History* (Bk. X, 69), Macray, iv. 213; *CJ*, v. 66; Whitacre's diary, BL, Add. 31116, f. 301 (9 Feb. 1647); *CJ*, v. 103, 151 (2 Mar. 22 Apr. 1647).
2 Firth, *DNB*, Holles article.

iv.

Presbyterian plans for settlement all depended upon their control in Parliament, the City, and over the armed forces. From the time they had begun to dismantle the New Model in the beginning of 1647, they had proceeded with secret plans for raising a counter force. Professor Pearl has written of their attempts to weld such a force out of three elements: the reformadoes (disbanded officers and soldiers), regiments from the New Model whose commanders they trusted, and the trained bands of the City, suitably reorganised. In April Presbyterian sympathisers had been voted onto the committee controlling the City militia, and other supporters were placed in control of finance committees. The Scots, too, were expected to give some support.[1]

Confronted with the New Model's defiant refusal to disband, the Presbyterians openly prepared for war. Working with the London Militia committee and the committee for Irish Affairs, soldiers were enlisted. Mobs put pressure on Parliament. The reformadoes interrupted Parliament's proceedings on 4 June with demands for pay, and the Presbyterians voted pay and gave soft words.[2] On 7 June Holles, Stapleton, Massey and Colonel Bowyer went to satisfy the importunity of the reformadoes in the Court of Requests, where Holles made 'a short but pithy speech' assuring them of Parliament's good affection, at which 'the soldiery being overjoyed, could no longer forebear but cried out: We will all live and die with the Parliament'. Stapleton spoke after Holles to the same effect.[3] The Presbyterians tried to retain the support of some soldiers of the New Model. When General Points complained on 22 June that his soldiers were likely to decline from their allegiance for want of pay, the Commons immediately voted them £10,000. The Presbyterian politicians were also confident of support from the Navy, for it had never been new modelled as had the Army, and remained a conservative force. There were rumours that the Presbyterian politicians had invited the Scots Army to re-enter England.[4]

---

1 Pearl, 'London's Counter-Revolution', pp. 44-6.

2 *Ibid.*, p. 46.

3 Reformadoes badgered the members on 4, 7 & 14 June; Whitacre's diary, BL, Add. 31116, ff. 312, 313; Harrington's diary, BL, Add. 10114, f. 25: 'we kept prisoners threatened &c.'; *Clarke Papers*, i. 136. *Reasons why the House of Commons ought to suspend the Members charged by the Army*, [1 July] 1647, TT E. 396.1, p. 8, accused the leading Presbyterian members of plotting with the reformadoes, then pacifying them 'by their elegant speeches'. *CJ*, v. 201; *The Kingdomes Weekly Intelligencer*, no. 212, 1-8 June 1647, TT E.391.12, p. 566.

4 *CJ*, v. 219; Whitacre's diary, BL, Add. 31116, f. 314v.; *Clarke Papers*, i, 135; D.E. Kennedy, 'The English naval revolt', *EHR* 77 (1962), 247-56.

But observers recognised that the Presbyterians' chief hope was to persuade the City to resist, by force if necessary. On 6 June Massey went through the streets in his coach 'exhorting the citizens to defend themselves against the mad men in the Army', alleging that the Army would demand the heads of the chief citizens as well as those of the chief Parliamentarians.[1] However, there were intimations that the City's sympathy with the Parliament was not entire. It was reported that at public meetings in early June 'there is a strange and insolent language used against the Parliament; which shows that they have all lost their authority and will soon become very contemptible if they do not speedily prevent it'. The politicians tried to conciliate the citizens by voting on 10 June to remove the protection of parliamentary privilege which prevented M.P.s being sued for debt, in the hope of assuaging one of the City's major grievances.[2]

Finally, on Friday 11 June, the Commons named a committee headed by Holles to join with members of the Lords and the new committee for the London militia to secure the safety of the kingdom. The committee went to the City, where they found the citizens generally disinterested. The Lord Mayor exhorted the citizens to shut their shops and turn out in support of Parliament, but although he persuaded those shops around the Exchange and Cornhill (in the vicinity of the Guildhall) to close, his attempts to involve all the City failed. The trained bands refused to budge and by the afternoon it was business as usual in the City.[3] Holles blamed the Army and its friends for subverting 'the City, and lulling it into a false security, so that they waited to see what this Army would do'. Although there was obviously more to the City's disaffection than the work of a few Army agents, Holles was right about the citizens' attitude in June: they would wait and see what happened.[4]

Their attempt to rouse the City having failed, some time in mid-June the Presbyterian leaders tried to adjourn or dissolve the House, hoping this would interrupt the Army's proceedings. Dyve, who was a royalist prisoner in the Tower with a close ear on events in London

1   Bodl., Clarendon 29, f. 235, [letter of intelligence], 4/14 June 1647; 'The Tower of London letter-Book of Sir Lewis Dyve, 1646-47', ed. H.G. Tibbutt, *The Bedfordshire Historical Record Society* 38 (1958), 60; Bodl., Clarendon 29, f. 236, [letter of intelligence], 7/17 July 1647.

2   *Ibid.* See also Baillie, *Letters and Journals*, iii. 10: 'I know the body of England are overweary long ago of the Parliament' (13 July 1647). *CJ*, v. 205; Whitacre's diary, BL, Add. 31116, f. 312v.

3   *CJ*, v. 207-8; *Clarke Papers*, i. 132-3.

4   Holles, *Memoirs*, p. 110; Pearl, 'London's Counter-Revolution', p. 48.

through his friendship with a fellow prisoner John Lilburne, heard of a motion for adjournment on 17 June which was lost by two voices. Adjournment would have foiled Cromwell's plots since he 'hopes to keep the parliament still on foot to act by colour of their authority, after the Presbyterian party are excluded'. Another source attributes a different motive to the Presbyterians who proposed an adjournment. They intended 'to repair to their counties to raise forces'.[1]

All these rumours of the Presbyterians' activities increased the suspicions of their opponents. The belief that they were attempting to resist by force prompted the Army to demand the removal of the Presbyterian leaders from the House of Commons.

v.

Ever since the *Declaration* of 30 March, the soldiers had been muttering about their enemies in the House of Commons, and on 14 June they named eleven members. These were Denzil Holles, Sir Philip Stapleton, Sir William Lewis, Sir John Clotworthy, Sir William Waller, Sir John Maynard, Major General Massey, John Glyn, Colonel Edward Harley, Anthony Nichols, and Walter Long. The charges were of a general nature: infringing rights, obstructing justice, raising suspicions of the Army, breaking up the Army 'for advancement of their own ends, faction, and design,' and attempting to raise new forces against the Army.[2]

The eleven members continued to sit in Parliament, so on 23 June the Army requested their suspension. The next day Holles made a desperate attempt to defy the Army by moving in the House that the King should come to Whitehall, which was seconded by others, on the proviso that the King should take the Covenant and settle the Presbytery.[3] On 25 June the Army marched from St. Albans to Uxbridge. Realising that to stay in the House would precipitate the occupation of London, Holles requested permission for himself and his fellow impeached members to withdraw. The House, stunned at this

1 *All in an Epistle,* [3 July] 1647, TT E.396.13, p. 3; Dyve, 'Letter-Book', p. 61 (18 June 1647). No reference to adjournment in the Journals of either House; Bodl., Clarendon 29, f. 241, [letter of intelligence], 14 June 1647.

2 *An Unanaimous Answer of the Soldiers to the Commissioners Propositions,* 2 June 1647, MSS., TT E.390.14.; *A Charge delivered in the name of the Army . . . June 14 1647,* 17 June 1647, TT E.393.5.

3 *An Humble Remonstrance from Sir Thomas Fairfax . . . 23 June 1647,* [25 June] 1647, TT E.393.36. Bodl. Clarendon 29, f. 246. [letter of intelligence], 24 June 1647.

unexpected capitulation, did no more than remove hats as the accused members left the Chamber. Satisfied, the Army withdrew to Richmond, and on 27 June in a *Manifesto* approved the members' withdrawal.[1]

The chief reason for the Presbyterians' withdrawal was that their hopes in the City had failed. Right from the start, the sympathy between the members and the City was not entire, as general grievances against the Parliamentarians kept the City cool. The disputes between Parliament and Army were bad for business; by 21 June Papillon, a London apprentice, reported that there was little trade in the City. When the Army moved threateningly towards London on 24 June the Common Council, 'though all Presbyters', collapsed, 'leaving the Faction in the lurch'.[2] The Common Council refused to take Parliament's part against the Army. Holles and his friends should have been warned by the City's refusal to prepare for war on 11 June: the citizens had no intention of fighting against the New Model, especially as it was rumoured that the Army was likely to reach a settlement with the King. Late in June it was believed that the King and the Army were close to a settlement, and the articles of agreement were said to be 'current amongst the best merchants in the City'.[3] But Holles and the impeached members did not give up. Again, as earlier, they pursued two courses of action. One was to press for a vindication of themselves against the Army, the other was to work through the City in the hope of foiling the Army.

The members petitioned for a definite charge to be made. Clearly the Army was not so interested in proceeding against the members as in removing them from the House. Pressed, they agreed to prepare articles, which a group of officers presented to Parliament on 6 July. The articles were not items for an impeachment, but rather a general indictment of the Presbyterian party. Basically, the Army charged the eleven members with having tried to impose their own settlement on the kingdom, and to bring in the King on their terms and to destroy anyone, especially Independents, who opposed them.[4]

The first point was scored against the eleven when the Commons

1 *Ibid.*, f. 249v., [extract of letter of intelligence], 28 June 1647. *A Manifesto from Sir Thomas Fairfax and the Army*, 27 June 1647, TT E.394.15.

2 *Memoirs of Thomas Papillon of London, Merchant 1623-1702*, ed. A.F.W. Papillon (Reading, 1887), p. 16; *All in an Epistle*, pp. 2-3.

3 Bodl., Clarendon 29, f. 244, f. 249, [extracts of letters of intelligence], 21, 28 June 1647; Pearl, 'London's Counter-Revolution', p. 47.

4 *The Petition of the Members of the House of Commons who are accused by the Army, 29 June 1647*, [2 July] 1647, TT E.396.7; Ludlow, *Memoirs*, i. 152; Whitacre's diary, BL, Add. 31116, f. 316 (2 July 1647); *CJ*, v. 236; *A Particular Charge or Impeachment, passim*.

accepted the Army's articles as a charge against the members, and assigned counsel to them. Holles had already begun his legal defence by seeking out Bustrode Whitelocke, who was understandably unwilling to be involved.[1] On 13 July *A Brief Justification* of the eleven members appeared. The blustering tone and vigorous style suggest Holles had a hand in its composition. The author, firmly confident that the Lord was on the side of the accused, criticised those members of Parliament who lacked the courage and conscience to oppose the Army.[2] A lengthier and calmer defence which appeared on 15 July contended that all the actions of the eleven had been authorised by Parliament.[3] On 19 July the eleven delivered their answer to the Commons. Holles defended himself against various specific accusations, and concluded in tones of injured innocence:

> I have had a strict scrutiny over my conscience, . . . and cannot find that I have deserved such a return from any who pretend to be friends to the Parliament, and the peace of the church and kingdom.

Instead of waiting for judgement the members applied for and were given six months leave on the following day.[4]

In the public discussion for and against the eleven members, Holles had his supporters and detracters. The former instanced his past faithful services, the unlikeliness of such a one proving false.[5] His more numerous detractors admitted his past services, but wondered at his fall from grace: 'he that was once one of the five, is as a star fallen from heaven, which was no star, but a comet: 'tis a pity good parts should be employed to make slaves of those entrusted them'. Holles's whole career was attacked as a quest for power: 'his ambition is not to be less than a Duke, or a petty King, though not in title yet in power and domination'.[6] If no one had pinned a charge of treason on this 'man ever factious' earlier, they would have plenty of matter for one

---

1 *CJ*, v. 240, 243 (14 July 1647); Whitelocke, Annals, BL, Add. 37344, ff. 97-98v.

2 *A Brief Justification of the XI Accused Members*, [13 July] 1647, TT E.398.3.

3 *A Full Vindication or Answer of the XI. Accused Members*. The incompatibility of the two arguments - that no Parliamentarian should be accountable for his actions, and publishing a reply - apparently escaped the members.

4 *CJ*, v. 250-2; *A Grave and Learned Speech . . . Delivered by Denzil Holles Esq;* [20 July] 1647, TT E.399.14, p. 6.

5 *A Declaration of the Officers and Armies illegal, injurious Proceedings against the XI Impeached Members*, [8 July] 1647, TT E.397.8, p. 4.

6 *Animadversions upon a Declaration of the proceedings against the XI Members impeached by Sir Thomas Fairfax and the Army*, [13 July] 1647, TT E.398.4, pp. 2-3; *Reasons why the House of Commons ought to suspend the Members charged by the Army*, [1 July] 1647, TT E.396.1, p. 7, Lilburne, *Rash Oaths unwarrantable*, p. 19.

now. The Royalists took a malicious delight in the fact that his own friends had brought him to justice, whereas the King in 1642 had failed to do so.[1] The seeming alteration in Holles's position between 1642 and 1647 interested his contemporaries as it has subsequent writers. Having once been in the van of resistance to arbitrary government, Holles was cast aside in 1647 as a Royalist sympathiser interested solely in monopolising arbitrary power for himself and Parliament. A dire fate was predicted for one who changed his form as it suited his convenience:

> The Protean *Holles,* that will never burn
> Must here or at Tyburn take another turn.[2]

Although the first course pursued by Holles and his fellow Presbyterians to secure their own vindication had apparently failed, the Presbyterian leaders were not yet defeated. Their second plan, for an armed uprising, a counter-revolution in the City, was of necessity secret, but from early July there had been rumours of Presbyterian activity. The City was still enlisting men, and the fiercer Common Council men of the militia committee were endeavouring to raise a new war. Sir Francis Pile told the Army on 6 July that 16,000 were enlisted in the City and would be sent to Kent 'where it was thought the Scots do intend to land'. Dyve said that preparations were being made for a new war on 12 July.[3] It was rumoured that the Presbyterians were trying to make a stir in the western counties, and that the Scots would invade.[4] All this so disquieted the Army that they petitioned Parliament to resume control of the City militia, thus removing it from the hands of the committee named on 4 May when the Presbyterians were in control. This Parliament did on 22 July.[5]

On 23 July the citizens, soldiers, apprentices and watermen of London presented *A Solemn Engagement* to Parliament in which they vowed to bring the King to London for a personal treaty. The Commons declared against this, which angered the citizens. On Monday 26

---

1 Wilbee, *Plain Truth,* pp. 6, 13, *A Letter to the Earle of Pembroke Concerning the Times,* [14 Mar. 1648], TT E.522.5, p. 6: Holles was 'scorned by all mankind ... and not daring to peep in any populous town but by owl-light'.

2 *Cromwells Panegyrick,* [22 Sept.] 1647, TT 669. f. 11 (86).

3 Bodl., Clarendon 29, ff. 263-263v., f. 264, [letters of intelligence], 5 July, 8/18 July 1647; *Clarke Papers,* i. 150. 152; Dyve, 'Letter-Book', p. 68.

4 Bodl., Clarendon 29, f. 263v., [letter of intelligence], 5 July 1647; Clarendon 30, f. 7, [letter of intelligence], 19/29 July 1647. Rumours that the Scots were proposing to send an Army into England were reported in *Reasons why the House of Commons ought to Suspend the Members,* p. 9; *A Copy of a Letter From a Principal Person in Paris,* [17 July] 1647, TT E.398.29, p. 6.

5 Petition of 19 July 1647, printed in *LJ,* ix. 341; *CJ,* v. 254.

July the Mayor and aldermen went to Westminster to present a petition for the restoration of the City's control of its own militia, but the crowd which accompanied them imprisoned the members and forced them to agree to the petition.[1] Still dissatisfied, the mob pushed their way into the House of Commons and forced the members to recall their declaration against the *Solemn Engagement,* which Harrington interpreted as a vote for 'the King's present coming to Parliament'. They would not allow the members to leave until nine at night, and they 'said our guts should be about our ears if we did not vote it', recollected the regicide Thomas Scot in later years.[2]

It was widely believed that the eleven members were responsible for the City's attempt to force the Houses to vote for the return of the militia to Presbyterian hands and for the King to come to London.[3] In their memoirs Waller and Holles went to some lengths to rebut this charge of complicity. They admitted that several of them – Stapleton, Long, Nichols, Massey, Clotworthy, Lewis and Holles – did meet together on 26 July, but Holles claimed that this was to settle their common legal expenses before leaving on their travels, and that they were interrupted by the news of the violent proceedings at the House of Commons. Although Holles denied any foreknowledge of the City petition of 26 July, Waller's admissions make this unlikely. Waller had heard of it two or three weeks earlier, was shown a copy by the Lord Mayor when he dined with him on Friday 23 July, and was consulted by two apprentices about its presentation. Again on Monday morning an apprentice told Waller that the sheriffs had gone to Westminster with the petition accompanied 'with great multitudes out of the City' and asked him to be ready either in Cotton Garden or Westminster Hall so that he might be called into the House.[4] Furthermore although Holles depicts the riots as 'a sudden tumultuary thing of young idle people without design', other evidence makes clear that there was organisation behind the petitions. Bellièvre also mentioned a dangerous meeting on 19 July at which it was proposed that the King should be invited to flee the Army and come to London, and although he did not mention the personnel involved, his letter was about the

---

1   *Ibid.,* 255, 256, 259; Holles, *Memoirs,* pp. 144-5.

2   *CJ,* v. 259; Harrington's diary, BL, Add. 10114, f. 25v. *Memorandums of the Conferences,* p. 34, says the apprentices stood at the bar with their hats on. Burton, *Diary,* iii. 108.

3   *A Declaration of His Excellence Sir Thomas Fairfax,* [5 Aug.] 1647, TT E.401. 2; *A Gilded Pill for a new moulded Presbyter; or, wholesome advice for the holy Synod,* [13 Aug.] 1647, TT E.401.38, p. 6; *A True Account and Character of the times,* pp. 5-6; Bamfield, *Apology,* p. 31.

4   Holles, *Memoirs,* pp. 153-4; Waller, *Vindication,* pp. 103-6.

necessity for supporting the Presbyterian leaders. Whitelocke, however, said that the eleven members directed events from 29 July, which by implication exonerated them from complicity in the tumults.[1]

After the tumults and forced votes on 26 July, Parliament adjourned until Friday the 30th. In the meantime, printed bills were set up to call the mob to Westminster again.[2] Fifty-eight of the Commons and eight of the Lords fled from London to the Army. Although this group has been identified as the Independent party,[3] there were among them men previously thought of as political Presbyterians, such as the Earl of Manchester, and religious Presbyterians, such as Francis Rous.[4] Some thought that worldly advantage had prompted their flight, but those who fled probably did so because they disliked the dangerous courses pursued in the City, and believed that the Army was close to agreement with the King.

When the Houses reassembled at Westminster on Friday 30 July they found both their Speakers and many others missing. Consequently they elected new Speakers, and proceeded to business. They recalled the eleven members, and for a few desperate days tried to settle the kingdom. In control again, the 'Presbyterian' leaders tried to impose a settlement. Obviously their actions were tempered by the Army's threatening stance, and by the need for haste. At first the Commons refused to approve the Lords' suggestion that the King should come to London, then on 2 August they agreed.[5] Bellièvre believed that this initial stumbling showed how unwilling the Presbyterians were to offer anything to the King and how little good will they really had towards him. A contemporary rhymester thought the same:

Den. Holles is a gallant man and was for them too crafty,
What he pretended for the King, was for the Members safety.[6]

1 Holles, *Memoirs*, p. 152; *A Petition from the City of London . . .* [24 July] 1647, TT E.399.35, p. 3. The Petition 'is dispersed into several parts of London, and instructed in the hands of Agitators in the several Wards, to get hands to it . . .'. See also information about engagement of the citizens, 21 July 1647, Bodl., Tanner 58, f. 415; Montereul, *Correspondence*, ii. 198-9, Bellièvre to Brienne, 19/29 July 1647; Pearl, 'London's Counter-Revolution', pp. 50-1; Whitelocke, Annals, BL, Add. 37344, f. 101.

2 Montereul, *Correspondence*, ii. 210, Bellièvre to Brienne, 8 Aug/29 July 1647.

3 Yule, *Independents*, p. 69.

4 Holles, *Memoirs*, pp. 209-10; Manchester was said to have cast off 'the visor of a Presbyter', *Mercurius Pragmaticus*, 14-21 Sept. 1647, TT E.407.39, p. 5. Yule, *Independents*, p. 116, describes Rous as a conservative but mystical type of Puritan. While his tracts do show strong mystical feeling, Baillie identified him in 1647 and earlier as a religious Presbyterian; *Letters and Journals*, ii. 237, 259. *A Letter from an Ejected Member*, pp. 11-12.

5 *CJ*, v. 259-62, 264. *LJ*, ix, 362.

6 Montereul, *Correspondence*, ii. 211, Bellièvre to Brienne, 2/12 Aug. 1647;

Parliament also prepared to resist the Army. On the 30 July they voted
that the Army should not advance within thirty miles of London. On
31 July they empowered the London militia committee set up on 4
May to raise horse. The Commons approved the City's choice of
Massey as commander-in-chief of the City forces and declared that
Fairfax's command did not extend to the trained bands or to the
garrisons. The City, already apprehensive of a further war, had voted to
raise £20,000 on 28 July, and on 30 July they authorized borrowing up
to £100,000. The committee at Trinity House was empowered to raise
mariners for the defence of the King's person, the kingdom, Parliament
and the City. By Monday 2 August there was 'great expectation of
new war'.[1]

All depended on the City and its resolution to stand by the
Presbyterian leaders and Parliament. The soldiers among the
Presbyterian politicians were determined to resist and believed that
they had a fighting chance, with the City's backing. Waller was in
command of horse and dragoons 'in the nature of a flying army', and
Colonel General Points thought 'they would have been able to have
defended themselves against the opposition of many Armies'.[2] But
on 2 August a group of ministers from the Assembly asked leave to
mediate between the City and the Army for peace. This was the work
of Stephen Marshall and those whom Baillie described as 'his seventeen
servants of the Synod'. Marshall, according to Holles, was the villain
of the whole piece. It was Marshall who was Skippon's chaplain and
who had persuaded Skippon to use his voice to moderate the Commons'
wrath at the beginning of June; Marshall who persuaded the Lords to
rescind their votes for the King to come to Richmond; and finally,
Marshall and his friends who influenced the Common Council. The
other ministers — 'good well-meaning men' — were misled by him and
were set on by Aldermen Fowke and Gibbs. In petitioning the Common
Council to pursue a moderate course of non-resistance to the Army the
ministers showed a middle group attitude comparable with that of
many members of the Parliament. At the Guildhall the ministers'
petition led to a tumult, and Points and other supporters of the
Presbyterian politicians drew their swords, but the Common Council
sent a peace-making embassy to the Army on 3 August, and on its

---

The City's Loyalty to the King. The Members Justification, 13 Aug. 1647, TT 669.
f. 11 (62).

1 CJ, v. 259, 261-2; Acts and Ordinances, ed. Firth & Rait, i. 994-5. Guildhall
R.O., Journal of the Common Council, 40, f. 243, f. 244; HMC D'Lisle, vi. 569.

2 The Vindication of Colonel General Points, [Oct.] 1648, TT E.469.23, p. 18.
The Poetry of Anna Matilda . . . written by General Sir William Waller (London,
1788), p. 114.

return decided that they would not protect the eleven members.[1] Thus at the crisis the ministers swung the City away from the Presbyterian politicians and averted civil war on London's streets. The Army entered London through Southwark on 6 August and marched unresisted through the City. The eleven members withdrew from the House and fled soon after.

vi.

Why did the Presbyterian leaders fail in 1647? What did they stand for, and what did it appear to the nation that they stood for?

In religion, the political Presbyterians supported a moderate Presbytery, a state-controlled church which allowed no room for dissent. The civil magistrate would assist the clergy in disciplining the ungodly. As a party they were not High Presbyterians — that is, they did not support an autonomous church with power to discipline — and probably to many of them a moderate reformed Anglicanism, of the variety preached by Archbishop Ussher, would have been more congenial than a moderate Presbytery. They said that they had wanted to establish religion 'according to the purity of it in the primitive times'.[2] Ironically, they were forced by the terms of their political alliance with the Scots to press upon an unwilling King the Presbyterian forms of church government. However, if they were as a party lukewarm in their support of the Presbytery, they were definitely opposed to religious toleration. It was feared that the political Presbyterians would use the Presbytery as a means to their power, and would impose the Covenant, known as the 'Scotch hook', on all the Parliamentarians 'that so they may pack to themselves (as cheats do cards) a set of members for their own game'.[3] Their campaign against heresy was alarming, and it seemed there would be no place in England for those who differed from the Presbyterian form of church government. At a fast sermon on 24 February 1647 the preacher Nathaniel Hardy ominously remarked that although the wolves and lambs had been allowed in the ark, now that the waters were subsiding, it was time to 'send out the wolves from the fold'. Later in 1647 it was argued that the Presbyterian form of church government was a matter of relative

1 *CJ*, v. 265; Baillie, *Letters and Journals*, ii. 17 (1 Sept. 1647); Holles, *Memoirs*, pp. 106-7, 123, 160, 162-3; *A Continuation of Certain Special and Remarkable Passages*, 30 July-6 Aug. 1647, TT E.401.8. For accounts of Fowke and Gibbs, see Pearl, *London and the Outbreak of the Puritan Revolution*, pp. 316-21.

2 *A New Remonstrance of the Eleven Impeached Members*, p. 5.

3 *A Warning for all the Counties of England*, [24 Mar. 1647], TT E.381.13, p. 2.

indifference to the politicians who had exploited religious differences for their own political purposes, engaging people on 'religious pretences'. The Independent barrister and pamphleteer John Cook said that religious differences were fomented by the ministers of the Assembly, but that 'the most zealous promoters of the rigid Presbyterian way are politicians . . . that play their game so cunningly that the godly Presbyterians, not discerning their ambitious aim, which is to make themselves grandees in Church and State, join and concur with them'.[1] Contemporaries criticised the politicians for their unscrupulous use of the ministers. For example, it was said that Massey only had to allege to the Common Council that the Commons were 'swayed by a company of Independents' for the Council to

> send for the Presbyterian Priests, bid them cry out, The cause of God, the cause of God, of Christ, of his Church, and the three kingdoms: let them turn up the whites of their eyes, cry and howl so loud till their voices rend and ruin the whole kingdom and City all to pieces.[2]

Stephen Marshall's account of the political Presbyterians — which he delivered to both Houses on 12 August 1647 as part of the thanksgiving for their delivery from Presbyterian tyranny — was of a political party skilfully and unscrupulously playing upon religious differences for their own self-interest:

> These politicians use to take in the differences of religion which are found among God's people, and weave them into their own designs, and pretend to stand for religion, and join with this and that party for religion-sake, and thereby engage the consciences of such as fear God, when in the mean time religion is no part of their case, but [they] only seek to make use of godly men for their own ends and interests. . . .[3]

John Harris, a pamphleteer who analysed the party situation of 1647, described the Presbyterians as disguised Royalists: under the mask of Presbyterians they were 'royal not real ones'.[4]

Socially, the political 'Presbyterian' party was conservative. Holles believed that the Independents allowed power to fall to the 'wrong people', obscure men who had no conception of public service but

---

1 Nathaniel Hardy, *The Arraignment of Licentious Libertie and oppressing Tyrannie* . . . 24 Feb. 1647, TT E.377.25, p. 16. *Good English* . . . [catalogued 2 May, Thomason's date 8 May] 1648, TT E.441.10, p. 14. John Cook, *Redintegratio Amoris* . . . [27 Aug.] 1647, TT E.404.29, p. 65.

2 *A Speedy Hue and Crie* . . . , [10 Aug.] 1647, TT E.401.20, p.2.

3 Stephen Marshall, *A Sermon preached, to the two Houses of Parliament* . . . , 12 Aug. 1647, TT E.401.29, pp. 16-17.

4 See also [John Harris], *The Royall Quarrel*, 9 Feb. [1648], TT E.426.11, p. 5.

rather sought to enrich themselves with offices and rewards, a thing Holles boasted he had refused to do. He portrayed his opponents as men without wealth of their own, who had nothing to lose in the destruction of property by the war, while the 'Presbyterians' were wealthy men who did not wish to see their property, the basis of their power, destroyed, and both pass to other hands. Holles wanted the nation to return to its normal, pre-war state, to an ordered stratified society.[1]

With Holles's limited view of the objectives of the revolution, the majority of the Parliamentarians might well have concurred. But the political Presbyterans were suspected because in practice their rule seemed as bad as that of the King and bishops before them. They were not interested in the general grievances of the nation, but simply in their own power which, like King and bishops, they wanted to support by an army, voting down the New Model 'because, it is the only block, and stumbling-stone, to their design of Presbytery and lordly predominancy'. It was said that they represented the wealthy men and made a party with the lordly rulers of the City.[2] The M.P.s appeared high handed and arrogant, and as 'perpetual Dictators they forget they are chosen from among the people'. No one might complain of their tyranny for 'Whosoever accused any of these domineering men, was in danger to be crushed'.[3] An incident of March 1647 provided useful propaganda: at a committee Holles and Stapleton had threatened to draw their swords against some petitioners, while Sir Walter Erle waved his cane 'in a most threatening manner' and the committee committed the two ring-leaders, Tew and Major Tulidah, to prison.[4]

Various individuals were named as the chief of these 'ambitious, imperious men . . . [who] would fain be taken for Gods, and sons of the most high' including the Earls of Manchester and Stamford, Sir Walter Erle, and 'the proud covetous priests'. But Holles and Stapleton were the two most frequently mentioned:

1 Holles, *Memoirs*, pp. 4, 6, 8, 43-4, 140.

2 John Lilburne, *The Second Part of Englands New-Chaines Discovered*, [24 Mar.] 1649, TT E.548.16, p. 1; *The Poor Wise-mans Admonition unto all the plain people of London*, [10 June] 1647, TT E.392.4; *Englands Troublers Troubled*, [17 Aug.] 1648, TT E.459.11, pp. 2, 6, 9-10; *A Warning for all the Counties of England*, p. 9.

3 William Ashhurst, *The State of the Kingdom represented to the People*, [25 Jan. 1649], TT E.539.14, p. 10; *A Back-blow to Major Huntington . . .* [1 Sept.] 1648, TT E.461.34, pp. 3-4.

4 *CJ*, v. 118; *Gold Tried in the Fire . . .*, [14 June] 1647, TT E.392.19; John Lilburne, *Rash Oaths unwarrantable*, [catalogued 31 May, Thomason's date 25 June] 1647, TT E.393.39, pp. 39-42.

> if my sight fail not, there is one Stapleton (an Hothamite) and one
> Holles (an Edomite) that have a chief hand in this plot. Long have
> they been hammering of it, and now they have found a time and
> opportunity to act it . . .

Lilburne passionately pleaded with Cromwell not to deliver the people
of England into 'the Hamon-like tyrannical clutches of Holles and
Stapleton . . . that hath designed us to utter ruin and destruction'.[1]

In justification of Holles and his party it should be said that they
were scapegoats for the failure of Parliament to satisfy public hopes
and aspirations of a better world, none of which materialised after
victory in 1646. 'In time of their necessity they promised fair', commented one pamphleteer sourly, 'but having obtained their ends as they
vainly imagine the case is altered'. As the committee at Dorchester
reported to their members of Parliament in May 1647, there were
growing disorders in the country and 'the minds of many were never so
exasperated as now against the parliament'.[2] The people's sense of
grievance was sharpened by the politicians' disinterest. The members of
Parliament, sheltered by and preoccupied with their own privileges,
sat in a cosy, club-like but inevitably somewhat isolated world. Many
had their sons in Parliament, and although there were factions in the
House, Clement Walker pointed out that the members had all sat
together for so long that they were quite happy to oblige each other
day and day about.[3] No longer were M.P.s wooing supporters as they
had been in 1640-1642: they had won the war, and the nation could
wait for them to settle the kingdom. Such faults were common to the
whole Parliament, but the Presbyterians bore the brunt of public
resentment.

1 Wilbee, *Plain Truth*, pp. 3-4. *A Warning for all the Counties of England*, p. 7.
(An Edomite was a rival of the Israelites. The reference to Stapleton as an
Hothamite I have been unable to elucidate). John Lilburne, *Jonah's Cry out
of the Whales belly* . . . , [26 July] 1647, TT E.400.5, p. 3. Hamon, when he saw
that Mordecai refused to bow to him, ordered all the Jews be destroyed;
Esther 3.

2 *The Antipodes, or Reformation with the heeles upward*, [22 July] 1647,
Oxford, TT E.399.16, p. 7; Bodl., Tanner 53, f. 45, 'Letter from the Committee
at Dorchester concerning Assemblies at football', 31 May 1647.

3 [Clement Walker], *The Compleat History of Independency upon the Parliament begun 1640* (London, 1661), p. 16. This part was first published on 24 June
1647. Much public resentment focused on the votes of compensation the Commons
made for their own members on 18 January 1647; *CJ*, v. 55-6. £50,000 at one
breakfast, Lilburne indignantly noted; *Rash Oaths*, p. 14. Bodl., Clarendon 29,
f. 72 v., [extracts of letters of intelligence], 18/28 Jan. 1647: 'the liberal gifts of
Parliament to their own Members are much spoken of among the people, who say
that surely the Parliament is dying, in that they distribute their leagacies so fast'.
Holles's share was £5,000, but he says he refused the money so long as the debts
of the kingdom remained unpaid; Holles, *Memoirs*, p. 140. Holles's statement is

Although the political Presbyterians did not always control Parliament in 1647, they also bore the blame for the failure of Parliament's policy of settling the kingdom by negotiation with the King. Charles was determined never to betray his church, his crown or his friends, so that unless Parliament capitulated to him on these issues, negotiation was hopeless. Ultimately Parliament's failure to recognise this led to the Army's intervention. Nevertheless, the leaders of the political Presbyterians can rightly be criticised for their handling of the Army. All their suspicions of the religious ideas of the soldiers, their fears of egalitarian attitudes, even their personal dislike of the Army leaders and the Army's friends, combined together so that they overreacted to the soldiers' attempts to guard their own interests in March 1647, and their conduct over the next two months gave the soldiers no reason to trust them. Holles played a major part in the measures which discontented the Army.

In 1647, when Holles and the political Presbyterians had support in Parliament for a programme of settlement, they failed to offer satisfactory leadership, and to resolve successfully the new problems created by the war. Basically they were conservative, and if not quite so conservative as they liked to imagine — they did, after all, want to deprive the King of much of his sovereign power — they were nevertheless out-distanced by the more radical groups. Their old ideas had nothing to offer in the way of settling the impasse in 1647, and their contempt for those who had served them deprived them of any general following and sympathy in the nation at large.

borne out by a publication of 1660; *The Mysterie of the Good Old Cause Briefly Unfolded,* July 1660, TT E.1923.2, p. 14.

9

EXILE, REFLECTION AND RETURN

> . . . his *Memoirs* appear to some to have more of the nature of a philippic, and declamation, full of resentments against some persons and things, than of an historical relation of matters, yet they are the more to be valued, in regard they give great light into many considerable actions;[1]

i

Holles's career as one of the leaders of the House of Commons ended immediately when the Army entered London in August 1647. The eleven members absented themselves from Parliament.[2] Glyn and Maynard remained in England, but Massey fled to Holland in the company of his fellow soldier Points. Another group prepared to leave England. On 12 August seven of them - Waller, Stapleton, Nichols, Lewis, Clotworthy, Holles and Long - wrote to Harley saying they had obtained the Speaker's pass for themselves and for him too, and announced their own plans: 'We intend to go away speedily, and the most of us into the Low Countries, from whence we shall (God willing) give you notice in what place we shall stay'.[3] On 13 August the committee for the admiralty informed Vice-Admiral Batten that the members could pass overseas.[4] The members' parting shot was published on 14 August, and bears the marks of Holles's hand. They protested confidence in their innocence and their trust in the Almighty. They compared themselves to the just men of old, such as Aristides, Pericles and Scipio who performed remarkable services for their country and 'willingly afterwards abandoned it, [being] content to adventure and lose their own safety to please the unruly people, made to enjoy only but the shadow and the empty title of liberty'.[5]

Five of the eleven left England for France on 16 August.[6] Holles left England separately a few days later. The committee for the

---

1   Rushworth, *Historical Collections*, vi, Preface p. i.

2   Harrington's diary, BL, Add. 10114, f. 25v. (4 Aug. 1647).

3   *The Letters of Lady Brilliana Harley*, ed. T.T. Lewis (Camden Society 58, 1854), p. 231. Waller, *Vindication*, pp. 200-1, says that the members 'stayed divers days' after the Army's entry before obtaining their passes from the Speaker.

4   'Calendar for the book of entries', 8 Oct. 1646-29 Feb. 1648, PRO, Admiralty 7/673, p. 362.

5   *A New Remonstrance of the Eleven Impeached Members*, p. 5.

6   *A Short and True Narrative of Sir Philip Stapleton*, pp. 5-9.

Admiralty gave him leave to transport himself, his attendants, three saddle horses and household stuff, and directed Batten to convey him to one of the nearest ports of France or Holland 'without prejudice to the service of the state'.[1] 'As for Mr Holles', reported Batten,

> he came not to me till the twenty one, and brought the Speaker's pass of the eleventh: and an order of the committee of the admiralty of the thirteenth, for a ship to transport him, who went out of the Downs the two and twentieth in the morning, upon the Leopard: who was bound toward St. Malo, on another design.[2]

It was not surprising that Holles sought refuge in France, since at some point prior to his exile 'in the time of the troubles' he had sent £2,000 there, his son Francis had a pass to go there in August 1645, and his mother was there in 1646.[3] Moreover his familiarity with French was such that he had been accustomed to act as interpreter for the Commons.[4] He seems to have settled in Normandy.

The flight of the eleven drew to the attention of the Independents the unreliability, from their point of view, of the Navy. On 17 September Batten appeared before a differently tempered admiralty committee - Mildmay, Evelyn, Vane, Rainsborough, Marten - and they accepted his surrender of his commission.[5] 'Nothing was objected, but my suffering some of the 11 members to go beyond the seas, when all of them had the speakers pass', Batten declared. He claimed that at the instigation of the City his opponents were prepared to restore him, but he had had enough: Rainsborough replaced him as Vice Admiral.[6]

Meanwhile at Westminster the Independents and Army supporters had suffered unexpected reversals, and not until Cromwell mustered a few horse in Hyde Park on 20 August did the House conform to the Army's bidding.[7] In September the Commons began to investigate the July tumults and, suspecting that the Presbyterian leaders had been implicated, ordered that seven of the eleven members should appear

1 'Calendar for the book of entries', PRO, Admiralty 7/673, p. 362.

2 *The true Relation of Capt. Will. Batten, Admiral of the fleet,* 26 Aug. 1647, TT E.404.38, pp. 7-8.

3 PRO, SP 78/121, f. 10, Holles to Arlington, 22/12 July 1665. Hyde commented in Oct. 1647 that he had heard of Holles being at Cherbourg, but not of his great wealth; Bodl., Clarendon 30, f. 149, [Hyde to Edgeman], 21 Oct. 1647; *CSP Ven,* xxvii. 245.

4 Whitelocke, Annals, BL, Add. 37343, f. 347v. Whitelocke interpreted for the House once when Holles was absent.

5 'Calendar for the book of entries', PRO, Admiralty 7/673, f. 381.

6 *A Declaration of Sir William Batten Concerning his Departure from London to the Prince of Wales,* [21 Aug.] 1648, TTE.460.13, pp. 2-3; *CJ,* v. 318 (27 Sept. 1647).

7 Gardiner, *Civil War,* iii. 351-2.

on or before 16 October to answer the charges against them.[1] Holles says that this order was simply left at their lodgings, which was inadequate notification because he, for one, had only an old porter and a maid or two there at the time.[2] The Commons proceeded against those of the impeached members who were in their custody, and on 7 September they expelled Glyn and Maynard from the House and sent them to the Tower.[3] Needless to say, none of the other members presented themselves on 16 October. Holles was in Cherbourg at the time. In November he was involved in a brawl with some seamen who called him 'traitor to his face, whereupon he and 7 seamen were at cudgels, and some dry blows passed on each others' shoulders'.[4] In December the Presbyterian party in the City tried to obtain the release of their own citizens, who had been imprisoned for the July disturbances. The City petition for this found such support in the Commons 'as Young Vane openly threatened the bringing up again [of] the Army'. Had the Presbyterian party in the House found support for the citizens, they would have proceeded to recall the ten surviving Presbyterian leaders and to free the seven Lords who were under impeachment.[5] The Royalists abroad noted that Holles, Lewis and Clotworthy met together in December and from London royalist newsletters spoke of a plot by the Presbyterian politicians to meet together 'and by strength of vote to dissolve the Parliament but it went no further'. There were rumours that the Presbyterian party, though weak in Parliament, was acting in collusion with the Scots.[6] But by January 1648 the English Presbyterian plots had collapsed, and it was reported that 'the Presbyterian party are retired to their several Counties in discontent'.[7] On 4 January the Commons passed their momentous votes to make no further addresses to the King, which Holles described in his *Memoirs* as 'the catastrophe of this tragedy'.[8] In the same month Holles sent his son from Cherbourg into England, and Francis took his seat in the House of Commons on

1 *CJ*, v. 291-2.

2 Holles, *Memoirs*, p. 176.

3 *CJ*, v. 295. The House divided on Glyn's case, which was discussed first. 58 were in favour of his expulsion, only 52 against.

4 Bodl., Clarendon 30, f. 149, [Hyde to Edgeman], 21 Oct. 1647; *ibid*., f. 178, [Nicholas] to Edgeman, 11 Nov. 1647.

5 *Ibid*., f. 211, [extract of letter of intelligence], 2/12 Dec. 1647.

6 *Ibid*., f. 218, Wilcocks [i.e. Nicholas] to [Edgeman], 16/26 Dec. 1647. Nicholas had better hopes of Lewis than of Clotworthy; *ibid*., f. 210, [extracts of letters of intelligence], 13 Dec, 1647; *ibid*., f. 233, [letter of intelligence], 30 Aug. 1647.

7 *Ibid*., f. 256v. [letter of intelligence], 6 Jan. [1648].

8 Holles, *Memoirs*, p. 200.

14 January, under age, as a member for Lostwithiel, Cornwall.[1] At the end of January 1648, when the Commons had a little more leisure, Haselrig revived the question of impeached members whose leave had expired. Although the proceedings expelling the Presbyterian leaders were expunged at the Restoration, Boys' diary shows that the House divided on the question of expelling Holles; 65 were in favour of his expulsion, 54 against. The House also expelled Lewis, Waller, Clotworthy, Massey, Long and Nichols, and sent articles of impeachment against Maynard to the Lords.[2]

ii

Various pamphlets appeared in January 1648 justifying the accused members of Parliament,[3] and it is in the context of this discussion that Holles wrote his *Memoirs* in France. He did not publish the work during his lifetime; it appeared in 1699 when John Toland prepared an edition which he dedicated to the Duke of Newcastle. Dr. Blair Worden, in studying various civil war memoirs edited by Toland, found that in the case of Edmund Ludlow, Toland had distorted the original manuscript most markedly.[4] However, his recent discovery that a manuscript of Holles's *Memoirs* among the Wentworth Woodhouse Muniments is in Holles's own hand establishes the authenticity of the printed version. But for minor variations in spelling, punctuation, capitalisation and paragraph structure, the manuscript and printed versions are identical.[5]

The title of the work, which was not Holles's own, is misleading, for Holles was not writing his memoirs or a history, but a political pamphlet

1   Bodl., Clarendon 30, f. 258, Wilcocks [i.e. Nicholas] to Edgeman, 6/16 Jan. 1648; *Perfect Occurrences of every dayes Journall*, no. 55, 7-21 Jan. 164[8], TT E.520.27, p. 401.

2   *CJ*, v. 445 'The parliamentary diary of John Boys, 1647-8', ed. D. Underdown, *BIHR* 39 (1966), 158-9 (27 Jan. 1648).

3   *The Lords and Commons first Love to, Zeale for, and earnest Vindication of their injuriously accused Members and violated Privileges*, [8 Jan.] 1648, TT E.422.10 (attributed by D.G. Wing, *Short-title Catalogue . . . 1641-1700* (3 vols., New York, 1945-51), to William Prynne). *The Case of the Impeached Lords, Commons, and Citizens, truely Stated*, [22 Jan.] 1648, TT E.423.16 (also attributed by Wing to Prynne).

4   Blair Worden, 'Edmund Ludlow: the puritan and the whig', *Times Literary Supplement*, 7 Jan. 1977, pp. 15-16.

5   Sheff. C.L., W.W.M., MS. vol. 12. I am grateful to Professor Charles Hoover for drawing my attention to this manuscript, and to Dr Worden for informing me of Dr D.M. Barratt's identification of the manuscript as Holles's holography. The manuscript confirms one small but important detail: the date of composition was printed incorrectly. Holles dated his preface 'this 14 of February 1647 stilo veteri', which was printed as 'this 14th of February 1648. S.V.' This subsequently misled Maseres whose reprint dated the work to 1649.

justifying himself and his party! At the time of its publication in 1699, it was the acrimony of his attack upon Cromwell and St. John which provoked comment. Subsequently, the merit of the work has been variously judged. Collins, by some stretch of imagination, thought the *Memoirs* showed Holles 'great disinterestedness', while the author of the *Biographia Britannica* entry thought that 'his indignation was indeed that of a patriot, indisputably just and noble'.[2] Most modern historians would consider the *Memoirs* so biased as to be unreliable, but they reveal much about Holles and his views of society, politics and religion. While his ideas are not set out as a formal *credo,* they can be deduced from his general comments and even his use of language.

Holles believes in an ordered society. His prose expresses vividly his outrage at the violation of order, and he reiterates that all he and his friends want is to return to the known laws, 'to the ancient and ordinary course'.[3] The natural and proper order is that king, nobility and gentry should rule; lesser .persons should obey. The *Memoirs* open with epigrammatic forcefulness: 'The wisest of men saw it to be a great evil, that servants should ride on horses, and princes walk as servants on the earth: an evil now both seen and felt in our unhappy kingdom'.[4] Part of his outrage at the Army's intervention in politics springs from scorn for social inferiors, 'a notable dunghill, if one would rake into it, to find out their several pedigrees'.[5] He resents the opportunities for social change offered by the war. While he and his kind have too great a stake in the kingdom to want to continue the war to confusion, his political

1 Holles himself refers to his work as 'this Discourse' and elsewhere as a 'Memorial'; *Memoirs,* p. xiii, p. 3. John, 2nd Earl of Clare, recorded among his books at Haughton in 1654 'Manuscript of Mr. Holles Observations' which could refer to this work; Nott. U.L., PW V 4, f. 195.

2 Harley papers, BL, Loan 29/183, f. 84, [Robert Harley] to [Sir Edward Harley], 9 Apr. 1699; Collins, *Historical Collections,* p. 158; *Biographia Britannica,* iii. 2047.

3 Holles, *Memoirs,* p. 131; See also p. 211: 'to return into the way whence we were put out, of a free quiet parliamentary proceedings', and p. 26, 'all things must have returned into their proper channel'.

4 *Ibid.,* p. 1. Holles was not alone in holding this view, and even his political opponents, such as Nathaniel Fiennes, shared his hatred of the confusion of the many-headed multitude; *Vindiciae Veritatis,* p. 6. John Cook, another political Independent, believed that 'the God of order hath appointed several degrees of men, and set them in their several stations';. John Cook, *Unum Necessarium; or the Poore Man's Case . . .,* [1 Feb. 1648], TT E.425. 1, p. 36. The metaphor of master riding and servant walking was a common one. For example, *The Vindication of Points,* p. 16, bemoans the state of the kingdom 'when the master must laquey it, by his footman, whiles he rides in the saddle'. There is also a verse of poetry on the subject among the Nicholas Papers, in BL, Egerton 2541, no. 24.

5 Holles, *Memoirs,* p. 149.

opponents introduced into committees men of no social standing, men known 'only by their faces', who, lacking estates and private concerns, are able to monopolise power, ruining in the process some of 'the best families of England'.[1]

To express the relationship between king, parliament and kingdom, Holles uses the metaphor of the human body with its connotations of mutual dependence and inviolable unity. For parliament to cut itself off from the king, as it does by the votes of no further addresses, was as if a limb were to detach itself from the body, and be deprived of life and nourishment. To prevent the king and parliament from settling terms of peace 'is casting the kingdom into a mortal disease, putting it past cure, past hope'.[2] As for the head of the body politic, Holles's view differs from that of Elizabeth I, who saw herself as the head, Parliament as the toe, for King and Parliament together are the head and the Army the toe. For that Army to usurp the place of the head is to invert the whole body, to make it a monster.[3] On another occasion, Holles uses the image of the kingdom as a diseased body to introduce ideas of sacrifice and healing: if God, the surgeon, had determined that some blood should be drawn for the kingdom's better health, then the true patriots offer their own.[4]

For the King, Holles displays constitutional respect and a degree of reverence, but he shows neither affection nor any personal feeling for Charles Stuart. Charles is the prince 'whom nature, duty, the command of God, and the laws of men, oblige them to reverence, and to love as the head and father of the people', but Holles shares the parliamentary view of how the king is best served: each individual should support the public cause, even in opposition to the king himself, and should prefer to risk his displeasure 'by promoting the public cause, than (as they thought) his ruin by deserting it'.[5] Interestingly enough, Holles betrays a confusion in his thinking about the king, for although recognising that Charles was the prince he is obliged to love and honour, he realises that there were aspects of Charles's character which merited neither. His only response to this difficulty is to ignore its existence, and he castigates those who attack Charles and his family because this inhibits settlement of the kingdom. Reviling and reproaching the King, impeaching the Queen 'make the distance wide, the wound

1 *Ibid.,* pp. 8, 41-2, 129, 149.
2 *Ibid.,* pp. 200, 201.
3 *Ibid.,* p. 207.
4 *Ibid.,* pp. 4, 6.
5 *Ibid.,* pp. 4-5.

deep, that there might be no closing, no binding up'.[1] Yet when Holles comes to clear Charles of the allegations made against him in the Declaration justifying the votes of no further addresses, his defence is a qualified one. As a rational man, he cannot believe that Charles destroyed the Protestants of France, fomented the rebellion in Ireland, or poisoned his father King James: charity obliges us to think better of any man, especially of a king 'whom Solomon tells us we are not to curse, no, not in thought, much less, which Job blames, tell him, and tell the world he is wicked and ungodly, least of all when there is not a clear and undeniable proof'.[2] Having proposed this tenuous defence for Charles, that Parliament should not broadcast his offences, least of all without proof, Holles hurries on to the point about which he is far more confident: that the crimes of the King pale into insignificance beside the offences of Parliament 'whose little finger has been heavier than the loins of monarchy'. Under the King 'we were chastised with whips, but now with scorpions'.[3] Thus although Holles sets out to justify Charles, he is carried away by the momentum of his argument and exposes his true view of the King's rule, that it is metaphorically a chastisement with whips. But while nothing in the *Memoirs* shows any love or trust of the King, Holles never faces up to the implication of his mistrust. Since a king is necessary for the orderly settlement of the kingdom, and no alternative candidate for this role was legally possible, Holles is reluctantly prepared to accept Charles. This explains how he would be able to welcome back Charles II in 1660: it was not Charles II he longed for so much as he longed for a king.

Holles has an idealised view of parliament. According to its 'fundamental constitution' there should be no acknowledgement of internal divisions, for the minority is comprehended in the majority, and both are 'one entire agent' in all they do.[4] Parliament is destroyed by any outside body which limits its freedom and independence. Without its proper Speaker, and under Army control, 'a wounded body that lies in a trance without sense or motion', it ceases to be a parliament.[5] The Army, the perpetrator of this attack, is depicted metaphorically as 'the spleen in the body by the concourse of all ill humours', a malignant growth drawing all nourishment from the frame it starved.[6]

1 *Ibid.,* p. 7.
2 *Ibid.,* p. 206.
3 *Ibid.,* p. 207.
4 *Ibid.,* pp. 120-1.
5 *Ibid.,* p. 167. The metaphor is a well known one, and appears, for example, in Donne's poem, *The Extasie.*
6 *Ibid.,* pp. 69-70.

Holles presents the Civil Wars and their sequel as a tragedy, and his description of the successive acts gives the reader a dramatic sense of events hurrying towards an inevitable disaster. His political opponents are naturally cast as the villians, whose dark purposes were to do all the mischief they could by undermining the basic structure of society. Even though he admits he cannot accuse them of plotting the whole tragedy, as not even the Devil himself could have done that,[1] Holles believes they intended to cause all the confusion they could so that they might pursue their own self-seeking ends of power and financial rewards.[2] His account of their political tactics is one of villainous rogues setting upon honest, good hearted men: a naive version of the conspiracy theory generally accepted by the Royalists.

Holles discredits his political opponents with sarcasm, ridicule, irony, and invective. He portrays them in animal images - frozen serpents, wolves, whelps, and blood suckers - while he refers to his own party through the image of 'the Lamb', with its overtones of innocence and sacrifice. His opponents are 'these visible saints', 'the crew', 'that faction', 'those firebrands', 'that gang', 'sharp and implacable spirits', 'children of darkness' and 'hocus-pocuses'. Chief among those he names are Haselrig and Fairfax, but the two he singles out for most virulent abuse, Oliver Cromwell and Oliver St. John, are 'the two grand designers of the ruin of the three kingdoms'. They are a pair of witches, cozening the world and plotting destruction.[3] He seeks to undermine Cromwell's military reputation, in order to demonstrate that Cromwell is 'far from the man he is taken for', 'as errant a coward, as he is notoriously perfidious, ambitious and hypocritical', illustrating his view with anecdotes of Cromwell in a pitiful state at Marston Moor with a little burn in his neck, 'out of gun shot behind a hedge' at the siege of Basing House, and incapable of even finding the battlefield at Edgehill.[4] Yet of the two men, St. John is the more dangerous, for he is both a man of law, respected for his keen mind and intelligence, and a subtle and successful politician. In an emergency St. John discards legality, as is illustrated by his argument in Strafford's case, 'that some persons were not to have law given them, but to be knocked on the head'. Such behaviour enrages Holles, who sees in it an attempt by St. John to place himself above both king and parliament, 'to frame, new

1   *Ibid.*, pp. 3-5.
2   *Ibid.*, p. 201.
3   R.T. Davis, *Four Centuries of Witch Belief* (London, 1947), p. 139 treats this passage in Holles's epistle dedicatory as evidence that Holles believed in witches. Holles's style is highly metaphoric, and should not be viewed literally.
4   Holles, *Memoirs*, pp. 16-17.

mould, alter and destroy as he thinks good'.[1] Although Holles has a number of political charges to make against St. John, such as his devious schemes for new elections and his attempt to ruin Holles himself in the Savile affair,[2] he hates him and Cromwell chiefly because they betray what he considers to be 'the cause' which they had started out together to defend.

Of the other men Holles attacks, Haselrig was a regular political opponent,[3] whose career in some ways matches Holles's: he too was singled out by the King as one of the five members, engaged in military service and then politics. Holles mocks Haselrig as 'one of their invincible champions' for the way he came to the Commons after the loss of Donnington Castle in 1644, 'all in beaten buff, cross girt with sword and pistols as if he had been killing his thousands, when 'tis more probably if there was any danger, that he had been crying under a hedge'.[4] Holles depicts Fairfax as a willing dupe who did nothing to prevent the disorders in his Army, of which he apparently disapproved.[5]

Religion is part of the ordered framework of society. Holles makes no positive statement about the kind of church he wants, but this can be deduced from his attacks on the Independents and their allies, whom he detests equally. The Independents, he said, want no power exercised to preserve religion and society.

> They would have bishops so they may be just ciphers, and all acts to be repealed which hinder men from being aetheists or Independents; for nobody must be enjoined to come to the church, and there may be meetings to practise anything of superstition and folly.[6]

This of course took away all church discipline, all power to enforce godliness. Those 'visible saints', with their new light and tender consciences, who pulled ministers from their pulpits, removed them from their livings for small faults, and petitioned against tithes, all attack the social order and property rights.[7]

Although Holles begins with the confident assertion that the causes

1 *Ibid.*, p. 33.

2 *Ibid.*, p. 40.

3 For example, in 1646 Holles was a teller 62 times, and on 42 of these occasions Haselrig was one of the tellers on the opposite side.

4 Holles, *Memoirs,* pp. 11, 27.

5 *Ibid.*, p. 34. In 1699 it was remarked that Holles had not known Fairfax very well; Harley MSS., BL loan 29/74, [Anne Clinton] to Sir Edward Harley, 8 April 1699.

6 *Ibid.*, pp. 177-8.

7 *Ibid.*, pp. 103, 71, 129, 179-80.

of the wars and the kingdom's misery would be 'no difficult thing to discover, and make so plain, that he who runs may read', in his conclusion he confesses that the reasons for the miseries of the kingdom seem beyond the wit of man to fathom. He himself sees no ultimate sense or purpose in the events he depicts, but as a Christian submits to the will of God.[1] The major part of his explanation of events is in terms of the malice of wicked men, and this mode of thinking affects his ideas about how a settlement might be achieved. Although he writes constantly of returning to the known ways, the established course, he shows no real understanding of how this might have been achieved. Only the obduracy of evil men prevented the settlement of peace with the King. Thus the *Memoirs* state even more clearly what his actions during 1647 had suggested: that he was a conservative politician who, despite his personal feelings about the King, believed that only by agreement between Charles and Parliament might the kingdom be settled and social order restored.

The *Memoirs* are Holles's best work, and display his literary talents, with prose which is both rhetorical and homely. His use of metaphor is vivid and colourful, and while his allusions bear testimony to his learning, religious and classical, he could also cite common fables or a tale from Chaucer. The work's chief value lies in its revelation of Holles: his passionate conservatism, his limited vision, and his skill with words. His vituperativeness towards his opponents displays his limitation as a politician, for while all that his opponents do is scorned and mocked, there is on his side only self-righteousness.

iii

During 1648, while Holles was in exile, the Scots invaded England in pursuance of their Engagement made with the King at the end of 1647. Many Scots did not consider this Engagement bound Charles closely enough to the Presbyterian form of church government, and their army set forth denounced by the Kirk. Success depended on the extent to which the English Presbyterians would support the Scots, which placed the English Presbyterians, laymen and ministers, in an awkward dilemma, since they wanted neither the Scots nor the New Model to impose a settlement. Some notable individuals, such as Lord Willoughby of Parham, Massey and Batten, and many lesser figures supported the Scots Royalist alliance. The Royalists were not unhopeful of Holles's support. In February 1648 Nicholas enquired if Holles were in correspondence with the Queen's party at St. Germains, while in March it was rumoured

1 *Ibid.*, pp. 2-3, 213.

that Massey, Waller, Holles and Long had thrown in their lot with the Engagers and were lurking 'privately in Scotland'[1] Actually Holles remained in France until Parliament altered its policy towards the King.

Although neither the City nor the Parliament supported the Scots invasion, the Lords were unwilling to declare the Scots enemies and all who supported Prince Charles traitors.[2] Reopening negotiations with the King appeared desirable. Recent research has revised interpretations of politics in 1648; whereas Gardiner attributed every proposal for agreement with the King to a Presbyterian majority, the work of Pearl, Underdown and Worden has revealed the general support for the monarchy among the 'royal Independents' and the middle group.[3] During the second Civil War, both Houses reconsidered their policy to the King, and although the Lords were more eager for a treaty with him than the Commons, the Commons finally agreed to negotiate without preliminaries when the Lords agreed the King should not come to London, but remain in the Isle of Wight for the negotiations. The Lords, *Mercurius Melancholicus* commented, hastened on the treaty, but the Commons 'come on like slow paced dromedaries'[4] However, the Houses finally agreed to repeal the vote of no further addresses and to negotiate with the King on the propositions submitted to him at Hampton Court. On 5 August the Commons passed an ordinance to establish the Presbyterian church government so that they might confront the King with a *fait accompli.* [5]

In conjunction with an alteration of policy towards the King, the Houses revised their attitude to the excluded Presbyterian leaders. On 3 June 1648 the Commons discharged the votes impeaching the eleven members, and revoked the orders which disabled them from sitting on the 8th. Some of the members resumed their seats, but not until 14 August did Rushworth note that 'Col. Denzil Holles came this day to the House and sat'.[6] He had been waiting cautiously in Dorset since early August,[7] for what motives are not clear. Possibly he wished to

1   Bodl., Clarendon 30, ff. 248, 280, Wilcocks to Edgeman, 3/13 Jan. and 3 Feb 164[8] ; f. 310, [letter of intelligence], 6 Mar. 1648.

2   *CJ*, v. 639-43 (18, 21, 22 July 1648).

3   Pearl, 'Royal Independents'; Underdown, *Pride's Purge;* B. Worden, *The Rump Parliament 1648-1653* (Cambridge, 1974).

4   *Mercurius Melancholicus,* no. 52, 14-21 Aug. 1648, TT E.460.14, p. [154].

5   *CJ*, v. 617, 622.

6   *Ibid.,* 584, 589; Rushworth, *Historical Collections,* vii. 1226. I have found no mention of Holles's presence in the *Commons' Journal* until 16 Aug. 1648; *CJ*, v. 673.

7   BL, microfilm, Northumberland 548, f. 20, letter of John Fitzjames, 5 Aug. 1648: 'Mr Holles is come over and lives privately at his country house here at

see how the war would go and whether there would be any further overtures to the King. He took his seat at Westminster on the eve of Cromwell's great victory over the Scots at Preston, which victory probably hastened the treaty with the King. The Houses named Holles as one of a delegation of five Lords and ten Commoners to negotiate with Charles in the Isle of Wight and allowed forty days for the treaty.[1] The parliamentary commissioners lost no time in pressing the King to consent to the propositions. Holles and Grimston told Burnet later that they had both begged the King on their knees to make speedy concessions: if he would 'send them back next day with the concessions that were absolutely necessary, they did not doubt but he should in a very few days be brought up with honour, freedom, and safety to the Parliament'.[2] Thomas Coke, a Royalist, later gave further details of the Presbyterians' pleas. Coke claimed they wanted to convey the King to London before the Army marched southwards, where the City would raise an army under the command of Major General Browne, and other parts of the kingdom would rise to their assistance. Holles was intimate with the Earl of Lindsey at the negotiations, 'and by him conveyed all his opinions and projects to the King', as he had done at Oxford in 1644. Charles proposed various offices for Parliament's commissioners, including that of Secretary of State for Holles.[3] At the Newport treaty the King offered more substantial concessions than ever before, but Parliament nevertheless voted them inadequate during October and November. Although many historians believe that there was still a real possibility of agreement between King and Parliament, it seems more likely that the threatening stance of the Army rendered the M.P.s desperate.[4] The members were only too well aware of the Army as another party whose assent was crucial to any agreement with the King. As Vane pointed out, any agreement, without Army approval, 'would prove but a feather in their caps'.[5] Furthermore,

Cerne'. I am indebted to Mr. J. Ferris for this reference.

1   *CJ*, v. 697.

2   Burnet, *Own Time*, i. 74.

3   *HMC Portland MSS.*, i. 592-3, papers of Thomas Coke, April 1651. While the Newport negotiations were in progress, the Dorchester corporation ordered the minister, William Benn, to ride to the Isle of Wight at this time to confer with the ministers Marshall, Caryl, Vynes and Seaman, about the abilities of Stanley Gower to succeed John White; *Municipal Records of Dorchester*, p. 604. It is tempting to think that they may have been invited to comment upon the religious debates.

4   I have argued this at greater length in my M.A. thesis, 'A Study of the Attitudes of the Parliamentary Opposition to the Crown, 1642-1649', (Western Australia, 1964).

5   Ludlow, *Memoirs*, i. 208.

Charles had conceded his personal powers, but not the prerogatives of the Crown, which did not satisfy Parliament.[1] During October and November the commissioners at Newport begged their friends in the Commons to persuade the House to accept the King's concessions, but the Commons were unreceptive.[2] While the 'Presbyterian' demands were one of the chief stumbling blocks, it was not Holles and his friends who created this problem, but a combination of 'rigid Presbyterians' and radicals who wanted the wreck the treaty. As Sir Dudley North explained, although he thought that the commissioners 'and something else' had done wonders in bringing the treaty so near to success, if the King did not yield all there was no hope of acceptance in Parliament, let alone outside.[3] Probably the majority hoped that Charles might be bullied or persuaded to yield. Underdown has shown how the middle group, working with the Presbyterians and crypto-Royalists, did all in their power to bring about agreement, but although the time for negotiations was extended, the Army fulminated against the treachery of Parliament for dealing with 'the man of blood'. On 20 November the Army demanded exemplary punishment on the 'capital author' of all the kingdom's miseries - to wit, the King - and although the Commons decided not to consider this *Remonstrance,* the Army was not so easily set aside.[4] In fact, Parliament could not ignore the *Remonstrance,* and the knowledge of the Army's desperate intentions coloured all views of the King's concessions.

The Commons thanked their commissioners on their return on 1 December, but they delayed consideration of the treaty papers presented by Holles until the following day. On Monday 4 December, when there were nearly three hundred members present ('a great house in those days'), the King's answers were debated through the night until eight o'clock next morning, when a majority of 129 to 83 accepted the King's answer as a satisfactory basis for a settlement.[5] But the

1 Besides, Charles said he made concessions only in order that he might escape; C.W. Firebrace, *Honest Harry: Being the Biography of Sir Henry Firebrace* (London, 1932), pp. 344 ff. For the negotiations, see Sir Edward Walker, *Historical Discoursed upon Several Occasions . . .,* ed. H. Clopton (London, 1705).

2 Underdown, *Pride's Purge,* pp. 110, 113-4. *HMC Portland MSS.,* iii. 165 (21 Oct. 1648); *CSPD, 1648-9,* p. 319.

3 *Memorials of the Great Civil War,* ii. 35, 38.

4 Underdown, *Pride's Purge,* ch. 5, esp. pp. 112-5; *A Remonstrance of Lord Fairfax and the Generall Councell of Officers,* 20 Nov. 1648, TT E.473.11, p. 64; *CJ,* vi. 81, 90. See my article, 'Charles Stuart, That Man of Blood', *Journal of British Studies* 16 (1977).

5 Speech of Bulkeley, 7 Feb. 1659, in Burton, *Diary,* iii. 106; [Walker], *History of Independency,* pt. ii. 29; *CJ,* vi. 93: Lisle and Stephens - 83; Cranborne and Ashton - 129; *Mercurius Pragmaticus,* no. 36-7, 5-12 Dec. 1648, TT E.476.2.

following day Colonel Pride purged the House, and all the treaty proceedings were cancelled on 13 December. Holles's description of the situation in the previous year when the Parliament took pains 'like children, to build castles of cards' seems appropriate: 'a puff from their faithful army blows it all down'.[1] There is no clear evidence of Holles's whereabouts when Pride stood at the door of the Commons with a list of members in his hand, turning away those the Army objected to. Some sources suggest Holles was imprisoned, but the silence of others suggest that he had already absented himself.[2] By the end of the week the soldiers were encamped on his doorstep in Covent Garden, 'and the pavement under the Piazzo they make their stable, and tie their horses to the doors of noblemen's, knight's and gentlemen's houses'.[3] Probably Holles had fled. There was no question of his taking his seat in the Rump, for although the Army leaders encouraged the return of those members who had absented themselves after Pride's Purge, their welcome did not extend to certain leading Presbyterians, among whom was Holles.[4] There was not much sympathy for the excluded members. Royalists were quick to point out that the Presbyterians had fallen into their own pit; having taught the people to despise the King, they were themselves despised and cast aside. This fate was richly deserved, argued Milton, since they had fallen away from their first principles.[5]

Although the Isle of Wight negotiations and Holles's part therein may have been a fiasco in 1648, these negotiations later assumed an important place in the thinking of many Parliamentarians, because of the concessions the King finally made. The terms have been described as Presbyterian, but apart from the demand that the King agree to establish the Presbytery, and enjoin everyone to take the Covenant, they rather reflect the position of the Parliament as a whole. However,

1 *CJ*, vi. 96. Holles, *Memoirs*, p. 104.

2 Holles was included in *A List of the Imprisoned and Secluded Members*, [26 Dec.] 1648, TT 669.f.13 (64), and his name appeared to *A Vindication of the Imprisoned and Secluded Members . . .*, [23 Jan.] 1649, TT E.539.5. Rushworth, *Historical Collections*, vii. 1355, did not include him among the imprisoned members.

3 Bodl., Clarendon 34, f. 7v., John Lawrans to [Nicholas], 4 Dec. 1648.

4 *A Declaration of the Commons in Parliament . . .*, 15 Jan. [1649], TT E.538.23, p. 3.

5 *The Recoyle of ill-cast and ill charged Ordinances*, [13 Dec.] 1648, TT E.476.12, pp. 9-10, displays 'the wonderful judgement of God in returning the mischiefs of this present rebellion, upon the authors and contrivers thereof'; *The Works of John Milton*, (18 vols., New York, 1931-8), v. 'The Tenure of Kings and Magistrates', pp. 1-3.

on the eve of the Restoration, when there was an attempt to revive the terms, all who supported them were indiscriminately termed 'Presbyterians'.

10

THE COMMONWEALTH AND THE RESTORATION

The desire for the king is universal, some upon rigorous conditions,
some on moderate ones and some freely, without any arrangement,
referring everything to the clemency of his Majesty.[1]

i

Holles's activities during the Commonwealth and Protectorate illuminate
the general questions of how the Presbyterian party faced the Interregnum
and their part in the Restoration. Here, as earlier, questions of defini-
tion arise: who were the Presbyterians, between 1649 and 1660?
Pride's Purge once seemed to offer historians a splendid opportunity
to separate the sheep from the goats, and Holles's political Presbyterian
party was equated with those secluded. But not all those who served in
the Rump can be counted as Independents (for many attended only
because they thought it better than to desert Parliament altogether)
and not all those secluded were political Presbyterians.[2] Pride's Purge
did shatter the corporate existence of the political Presbyterian party
and thereafter the name 'Presbyterian' was often applied in a general
sense to conservatives who favoured a restoration on terms.[3]

The political Presbyterians of 1648 responded as individuals rather
than a party to the death of the King and establishment of the
republic, as can be seen by the reactions to the Commonwealth of
the surviving eleven members, which ranged from acquiescence to
active royalism. Nichols sat in the first Protectorate Parliament and
Glyn accepted the post of Chief Justice of the Court of Common
Pleas. Clotworthy, Harley and Waller suffered imprisonment for three
years, and were viewed as suspect under the Commonwealth. Harley
said he devoted his estates and abilities to the King's restoration.[4] Long

---

1 *CSP Ven. 1659-1661,* pp. 136-7 (16 Apr. 1660.)

2 Worden, *Rump Parliament.* Underdown argues that after 1648 the term
'Independent' has no meaning when applied to the political group at Westminster;
'Independents reconsidered', pp. 68-76. Among those secluded was Sir John
Evelyn of Wiltshire, but he was not a political ally of Holles's in 1648.

3 G. Abernathy, *The English Presbyterians and the Stuart Restoration,
1648-1663* (American Philosophical Society, n.s. 55, 1965). Introduction, pp. 5-6,
defines the Presbyterian party in religious as well as political terms, but later
seems to adopt a purely political usage.

4 BL, Portland loan, 29/47, copy of a letter Sir Edward Harley to Clarendon,
12 Dec. 1665.

joined the royalist exiles. Massey was an active Royalist, escaping from prison in January 1649, and taking service under the King. He tried to persuade the Lancashire Presbyterians to join the invading Scots.

The Presbyterian party outside Parliament was generally divided too. One group of Presbyterians - laymen, ministers and exiles - plotted for the restoration of the monarchy.[1] Briefly, the plan developed between 1649 and 1651 was that the English Presbyterians should rise in support of the invading army of the Scots and the Prince. Holles's name is mentioned on the periphery of the plot. In May 1650 the Royalists were interested in his whereabouts, although Nicholas, who had been Secretary of State to Charles I, knew he was not with the active plotters in Holland. However, these activists - Massey, Bunce, Alexander and Wood - proposed Holles as one of the 'good counsellors' who should be placed about the King. In May 1650 Nicholas told Hyde that Holles did, through 'his cousin Colonel Gervase Holles, make a kind of offer of his service to the King at Jersey, which was not so accepted as perhaps he expected'.[2] But although some Royalists hoped for Holles's support, he did little for their cause. He offered wagers that the King would shortly be restored, but when his brother-in-law Colonel Fitzwilliam was asked by Lord Jermyn to ascertain the attitude of the English Presbyterians to the King's planned invasion from Scotland, Holles offered only 'a confidence (but no assurance)' that the Presbyterians would fight for Charles. In March 1651 Charles offered a secretaryship of state to Holles, but Nicholas believed Holles would not accept the office 'until he shall see the King more likely and nearer the recovery of his just rights'. Although Holles was at Caen with the royalist agent Silas Titus in April, and was said to be meeting with Jermyn near Rouen, he refused the proffered secretaryship.[3]

Meanwhile, to further the Presbyterian uprising and to assist the Royalists in England, Charles sent Holles some blank commissions, which he filled in with the names of English Presbyterians, but dispatched them into England so carelessly, 'the parties are discovered'.[4]

---

1 L.L. Carlson, 'A history of the presbyterian party from Pride's Purge to the dissolution of the Long Parliament', *Church History* 11 (1942), 108-22.

2 *The Nicholas Papers*, ed. Sir G.F. Warner (4 vols., Camden Society, 1879-1892), i. 171 (4 May 1650); *Calendar of the Clarendon State Papers preserved in the Bodleian Library* (5 vols., Oxford 1869-1970), ii. ed. W.D. Macray, p. 59; *CSPD 1650*, p. 25.

3 *Nicholas Papers*, i. 186 (17/27 June [1650]); 227 (11/21 Mar. [1651]); 237 (14/24 Apr. [1651]); 261 (9/19 June 1651).

4 *CSPD 1651*, p. 127, [Lord Hatton] to [Nicholas] (2/12 Apr. 1651).

How far Holles's carelessness contributed to the discovery of the proposed uprising under the Earl of Derby in the north of England, as a Royalist suggested, is hard to determine.[1] On his capture, the royalist agent Thomas Coke betrayed all he knew of royalist plans, including those of a group of Presbyterian ministers in London for an uprising.[2] The Council of State ordered the sequestration of Holles's estate on 17 April 1651, on the grounds that they had information of his designs against the government, but when subsequently no specific accusations were presented, the county committee discharged the sequestration.[3] On 2 May 1651 the Council ordered the arrest of three ministers and five laymen. Among the laymen was 'Holles his man', one John Gibbons. The Presbyterian minister Love was tried, and sentenced to death on 5 July and Gibbons, who had attended various meetings at Love's house, was also condemned.[4] Love and Gibbons were executed on 22 August and were the sole victims. In his scaffold speech Gibbons vindicated the Presbyterian party and their actions, and affirmed his faith in a Presbyterian church government: 'Ever since I had my knowledge, I have looked upon the Presbyterian government as the only most excellent government . . . that shall bind the Devil a thousand years'.[5] Gibbons was said to have been Holles's secretary; Holles had taken him to the treaty of Uxbridge,[6] and his connection with Gibbons in 1651 appears from a letter Holles wrote to his wife in October 1651 from France. Discussing one of his servant's failure to write, he observed that it was no crime for a servant to write

1   S.R. Gardiner, *History of the Commonwealth and Protectorate 1649-1656* (4 vols., London, 1903), ii. 11-12, argues that when an officer seized a group of Royalists at Greenock in the second week of March 1651, this shows Cromwell had prior knowledge of the plots.

2   For the best discussion of Love's plot, see Worden, *Rump Parliament*, pp. 243-8. See also D. Underdown, *Royalist Conspiracy in England, 1649-1660* (New Haven, 1960), p. 46; *Nicholas Papers*, i. 237 (18/28 Apr. 1651). Abernathy, *English Presbyterians*, p. 18, does not attach much importance to Presbyterian involvement in the London plot, but his account is inaccurate. For example, he dates Coke's arrest to 1650, not 1651. Cp. I.D., *The History of His Sacred Majesty Charles II*, [14 June] 1660, TT E.1935.2, pp. 93-4, who attacks the Presbyterian ministers for their involvement in the plot, and also Carlson, 'History of the presbyterian party', pp. 108-22.

3   *Calendar of the Proceedings of the Committee for Compounding, etc. 1643-1660*, ed. M.A.E. Green (5 vols., London, 1889), p. 2772; *CSPD, 1651*, p. 149.

4   Milton, *State Papers*, (3 May 1651); *Mr. Love's Case*, 22 Aug. 1651, TT E.790.1, pp. 8, 9, 10.

5   Gibbons planned an unsuccessful escape; *CSPD 1651*, p. 441; *A True and Exact Copie of Mr. Gibbons' Speech . . .*, 22 Aug. 1651, TT E.796.24, pp. 1-2.

6   Milton, *State Papers*, (3 May 1651); *The True and Perfect Speech of Mr. Christopher Love . . .*, 22 Aug. 1651, TT E.790.3, p. 7: 'Mr Gibbons (formerly Secretary to Col. Holles)'; *A Collection of the State Papers of John Thurloe, Esq.*, ed. T. Birch, (7 vols., London, 1742), i. 59.

to his master, 'and if John Gibbons had meddled with nothing else but what I gave him order for, it had been no crime in him neither, nor had he ever had blame for it': tantalisingly Holles does not indicate what he had ordered Gibbons to do in 1651; this letter was mainly concerned with domestic matters, including his mother's declining health.[1] (She died later in the year.)[2]

Holles remained in France. Early in March 1654 Hyde heard that Cromwell, seeking to reconcile all factions to his regime, had sent a pass to Denzil Holles, 'the chief pillar of the Presbytery, and who hath since the suppression of that party lived privately in base Normandy' so that he might return to England. Denzil availed himself of the opportunity, and returned early in May 1654. After spending a month or so in London, he retired to his estates in Dorset.[3] Little is heard of him in the following years prior to the Restoration. He participated neither in the affairs of Commonwealth nor the Royalist conspiracies. He was convinced that Cromwell and his Council opened his letters, and in 1656 Hyde observed that Cromwell had vowed revenge against Holles, believing him to be the author of a critical pamphlet which he himself had written.[4] Holles was not implicated in Penruddock's rising in the west in 1655, although his wife Jane was stepmother to Penruddock's wife.[5] He was in contact with the royalist agent Silas Titus in 1657, and he, his arms, horses and other goods, were seized after Booth's uprising, but the Council of State ordered the release of his person and goods on 2 September 1659.[6] Apart from these few events, he was isolated from national politics. His personal affairs, however, kept him occupied.

When he returned to England in 1654 Holles found his estates in some disorder. Three years earlier his wife complained of their estate manager, Ezekias Lambe, and the account of Holles's difficulties with

1 BL, Add. 32679, ff. 7-7v., Holles to Jane, 6/16 Oct. 1651.

2 Her will was proved on 26 Nov. 1651. Her lands she bequeathed to her son John, for life. To Denzil she bequeathed £300, to his wife £100. In a codicil she cancelled a bequest to Eleanor of £500 and furniture and linen and transferred these to Denzil's son, Francis; PCC 207 Grey (1651).

3 *Clarendon State Papers*, iii. 224; *Calendar of the Clarendon State Papers*, ii. 323 (14 Mar. 1654); Copy of joint answers of the honourable Denzil Holles Esq. and Dame Jane Covert his wife, defendants to the bill of complaint of Ezekias Lamb Gent., in Chancery, Nott. U.L., Ne L.506, pp. 5-7, 10 Feb. [1660].

4 PRO, SP 78/118, f. 266, Holles to Bennet, 25/15 June 1664; *Calendar of the Clarendon State Papers*, iii. 171 (11 Sept. 1656).

5 Arundel Penruddock was the daughter of John Freke. Jane actually referred to Arundel in her will as 'daughter'; PCC, Jane, Lady Holles, 1667, 55.

6 *Clarendon State Papers*, iii. 331; *CSPD, 1659-60*, p. 165.

Lambe reveals the tensions in the master-servant relationship intensified by the war. Lambe had been in Holles's service for many years. He had paid off Holles's regiment out of Holles's estates in 1642, and had removed his goods to the Isle of Wight in 1643. But by 1651 Lambe grew 'every day more than other weary of a servile life, as he calls it', and threatened to leave Holles for more profitable service in the Commonwealth. When Holles asked for his estate accounts, Lambe delayed, and before the appointed day when William Constantine, Holles's old legal adviser and a former fellow Dorset M.P.[1], was to audit the accounts , all Lambe's papers were burnt. Much later Holles and his wife complained to Chancery of Lambe's mismanagement.[2] Holles was also litigating in Chancery with Arthur Shirley from 1656-1659 over Shirley's receipts of rents from lands since Michelmas 1647. Certainly around August 1654 Holles's estates were in a bad way. His wife was forced to sell some property, Lambe having sold some of Holles's lands earlier (and subsequently refused to give account).[3] However, by 1655 Holles was consolidating his estates again, and buying land.[4] He also engaged in several pieces of litigation over his property.[5]

In July 1654 Denzil's son Francis Holles was one of the ten members elected to the first Protectorate Parliament for Wiltshire. It was alleged that the 'Scotified' clergy had canvassed a list of ten names and secured their return.[6] The ministers admitted to canvassing, but denied that they were wedded to the Scots interest. The clergy who took a leading part in the campaign were Adoniram Byfield, (formerly the scribe of the Westminster Assembly of Divines, 'a busy clergyman', minister of

1 William Constantine, elected for Poole to the Long Parliament, was disabled from sitting in December 1645 because he had advised Poole to surrender to the King. He and another, Nicholas Lechmere, were bound for Francis Holles when he was admitted to the Middle Temple on 9 February 1648; *Middle Temple Records*, ed. C.T. Martin (3 vols., London, 1904-1905), ii. 960.

2 Joint answers of Holles and his wife, Nott. U.L., Ne. L. 506, pp. 1, 4. Holles complained that all the estate papers were in chaos, 'thrown together in sacks and tubs in a very disorderly manner', p. 34.

3 PRO, C 22/258, 19 [Holles v. Shirley, 1659] ; PRO, C 5. 26/88 Testimony of Constantine. The purchaser said he had paid the money to Francis Holles; *ibid*. PCC Will of Jane, Lady Holles.

4 *Victoria County History*, Surrey, iii. 51.

5 Cases listed by F.J. Pope, Notes on depositions in Law Suits taken in or near the county of Dorset; manuscript in Dorset Natural History and Archaeological Society Museum, i. 185, 262; ii, 299; iv, 221; viii, 260.

6 Ludlow, *Memoirs*, i. 388-9. Ludlow blamed a combination of 'the Cavaliers and the imposing clergy, the lawyers and court interest'. *The Copy of a Letter sent out of Wiltshire to a Gentleman in London*, [5 Sept.] 1654 printed in *ibid*., app. v, p. 545. The pamphlet was possibly the work of the unsuccessful candidate Ludlow himself.

Collingbourn Ducis, Wiltshire), Humphrey Chambers, John Strickland and Peter Ince.[1]

After his return to England, Holles exercised ecclesiastical patronage, which gives some insight into his own religious views. On 23 June 1654 he, his wife Jane and her son John Freke presented Edward Deare to Ibberton, but as he died shortly after no conclusion can be drawn about how conformable a minister he was.[2] On 16 October 1654 he and his wife presented Samuel Watson to Cerne Abbas. Watson was B.A. from Caius College, Cambridge, had been lecturer in Wiltshire, and had certificates of worthiness from Peter Ince, Nathaniel Webb and others. He was 'faithful pastor' of the church for eighteen years until September 1672, and was thus conformable to the religious settlement after the Restoration.[3] In November 1657 Thomas Freke, Holles and his wife presented Henry Glover to Iwerne Courtney, where he was inducted on 30 August 1660. Glover was from Corpus Christi College, Oxford, and had certificates of his worthiness from Stanley Gower, White's successor in Dorchester who had a background of service to Archbishop Ussher and Sir Robert Harley, William Benn, rector of All Hallows Dorchester from 1629 but one who was ejected at the Restoration, and Robert Cheeke. Glover conformed to the Restoration settlement and remained in the living until his death in 1668.[4] Thus both the ministers patronised by Holles who were alive in 1660, Watson and Glover, accepted the established church and avoided eviction.

1 Humphrey Chambers, John Strickland, Adoniram Byfield, Peter Ince, *An Apology for the ministers in Wilts . . .,* [12 Aug.] 1654, TT E.808.9. Chambers, Strickland and Ince were all deprived of their livings at the Restoration in 1662; A.G. Matthews, *Calamy Revised* (Oxford, 1934), pp. 107-8, 288-9, 467-8.

2 Deare had received a B.A. from Exeter College Oxford, and had certificates from nine people; E.A. Fry, 'The augmentation books (1650-1660) in Lambeth Palace Library', *Proceedings of the Dorset Natural History and Antiquarian Field Club* 36 (1915), 54. The Commissioners investigating the value of livings in Dorset in 1650 reported that Ibberton had an incumbent at that date and was worth £60 p.a.; Returns of the Commissioners appointed to enquire into the value of livings in Dorset, 1650, Do.R.O., ff. 133-133v.

3 The Commissioners reported that the parsonage of Cerne Abbas had been vacant for seven years, and was worth £47 p.a.; *ibid.,* f. 107; D.G. Squibb, 'Dorset incumbents, 1542-1731', *Proceedings of the Dorset Natural History and Archaeological Society* 70-72 (1949-51), 24; Fry 'Augmentation books', p. 60. Ince had been one who campaigned for Francis Holles earlier in the year; Hutchins, *Dorset,* iv. 30.

4 Squibb, 'Dorset incumbents', p. 54. In 1650 the commissioners had found an able minister at Iwerne Courtney, and the living was worth £130 *p.a.*; Do.R.O., Returns of the Commissioners, f. 131. Fry, 'Augmentation books', p. 75; Preface by Stanley Gower to *Eighteen Sermons preached in Oxford in 1640 . . . By James Usher,* 1660; Stanley Gower, *Things Now-a-doing,* 31 July 1644, TT E.3.25. See also *Municipal Records of Dorchester,* pp. 605-7; Matthews, *Calamy*

Cromwell's death in September 1658 and the increasing conflict between the Council of State and the Army which followed persuaded many former Presbyterian politicians to support the civil power. But there is no sign that Holles participated in these struggles. In the game of in-and-out between the Army and the remnants of the Rump, many sought a more permanent settlement. Holles was in a good position to mediate because he had held aloof both from the English government after 1648 and from the Royalists. Uncompromised, he occupied the same political position he had held in 1648: restoration of monarchy upon terms which guaranteed some independence to Parliament. His situation was in many ways similar to that in 1640 when, after opposition and isolation from government, he reappeared upon the public stage. But in 1660 he was sixty-one years of age.

ii

On 21 February 1660 Colonel Monk restored the secluded members to the Commons on the understanding that they would provide for the Army and dissolve themselves after arranging for new elections. There is no sign that Holles participated in the discussions leading up to the restoration of the secluded members.[1]   Holles probably took his seat again on 21 February, for the Commons included him in the new Council of State on 23 February. The 1648 votes against him were discharged on 2 March.[2]   The Commons dissolution was announced for 16 March and new elections for 25 April. In this fluid situation there were many plans and schemes. Some members opposed the dissolution, and there was talk of the recall of the 1648 House of Lords so that both Houses might treat with Charles upon the Newport terms, but Monk

Revised p. 47. In September 1660 Benn was reported to scorn the Church of England; presentment at Dorset Assizes, Bodl., Clarendon 73, ff. 218-9, and he was later ejected; *Municipal Records of Dorsetshire*, p. 615. In 1617 Sir Francis Ashley had granted tithes of Puddle\Walterston to All Hallows, Dorchester, *ibid.*, p. 620.

1   *Clarke Papers*, iv. 264; Ludlow, *Memoirs*, ii. 228; *Mercurius Politicus*, 16-23 Feb. 1660, TT E.775.7, p. 1117; *The Speech and Declaration of Generall Monck . . .*, 21 Feb. [1660], TT E.1016.2.

2   *CJ*, vii. 849, 859. Abernathy, *English Presbyterians*, p. 36, reads William Prynne's tract, *Seven Additional Queries in behalf of the Secluded Members*, [4 Jan. 1660], TT E.765.1, p. 3, to mean that Holles had actually taken his seat before 4 January 1660. However, Prynne was discussing whether Parliament had cause to adjourn, as it had in January 1642, and 'whether Haselrig . . . can in justice . . . oppose them and Denzil Holles (another of the impeached and secluded Members) therein now'. 'Therein now' I take to refer to Haselrig's right to oppose Holles in this matter of an adjournment, and not to mean that Holles was sitting in Parliament, as Haselrig was. On 16 March 1660 Slingsby mentioned to Hyde that 'Mr Holles sits in the House', which implies he had not sat earlier; *Calendar of the Clarendon State Papers*, iv. 602.

would not permit this! Unbeknown to the M.P.s, he had already begun his negotiations with Charles[2] In the end Charles was restored unconditionally. The Presbyterian leaders have been blamed for the unconditional nature of the restoration, especially for selling out on the religious issue. Professor Abernathy depicts Holles as one of the lost leaders who had long since made his peace with Hyde[3] While Holles may not have supported the interest of the Presbyterian ministers, he was one of the group of Parliamentarians who tried to ensure the restoration upon conditions which would secure the issues they had fought for in the 1640s. The term 'Presbyterian' was used indiscriminately for those who supported the Presbyterian ministers and those who wanted a conditional restoration[4] However, there is another term contemporaries used, although less frequently; 'old Parliament men', which seems more appropriate[5] for 'Presbyterian', a religious term, does not contrast sufficiently with the term 'Royalist'.[6]

Although Royalist agents were in touch with Holles early in March 1660 and reports of him seemed promising, Holles was a member of the Council of State which began to discuss the terms for the restoration of the King as soon as Parliament dissolved. There were divisions in the Council, the French ambassador Bordeaux reported, but the principal members wanted to settle the manner and place of a treaty 'so that the matter may be thoroughly digested' before the Convention should meet.[7] Holles was associated with an unofficial cabal discussing

1   Ludlow, *Memoirs,* ii. 247; R. Wodrow, *The History of The Sufferings of the Church of Scotland, from the Restoration to the Revolution* (2 vols., Edinburgh, 1721), i, p. xi, Sharp to Douglas, 10 Mar. [1660].

2   F.P.G. Guizot, *Monk: or the Fall of the Republic and the Restoration of the Monarchy in England, in 1660,* trans. A.R. Scoble (London, 1851), p. 91.

3   Abernathy, *English Presbyterians,* p. 34; see also p. 41.

4   For example, 'The Presbyterians were the people that restored the King to his throne . . . It's most certain they are of a republican spirit'; Mons. Sorbière, *A Voyage to England* (London, 1709), pp. 23-4; M.P. Schoenfeld, *The Restored House of Lords* (Hague, 1967), p. 76, Roberts, *Growth of Responsible Government,* p. 142, and Abernathy, *English Presbyterians,* p. 19 describe Lord Saye as a 'Presbyterian', because he wanted a restoration on the Isle of Wight terms.

5   Bramston, *Autobiography,* p. 116. In 1666 Milward referred to 'Serjeant Maynard and all the old Parliamentary gang'; quoted in H.N. Mukerjee, 'Elections for the convention and cavalier parliaments', *Notes and Queries* 166 (1934), 417.

6   J.R. Jones, 'Political groups and tactics in the Convention of 1660', *Historical Journal* 6 (1963), p. 159; see also G.F.T. Jones, 'The composition and leadership of the Presbyterian party in the Convention', *EHR* 79 (1964), 320. Haley, *Shaftesbury,* p. 134, writes of 'former Parliamentarians and so-called Presbyterians'.

7   *Calendar of the Clarendon State Papers,* iv. 59 (9 Mar. 1660); *Ormonde Papers,* ii. 317-8 (23 Mar. 1660); F.P.G. Guizot, *History of Richard Cromwell and the Restoration of Charles II,* trans. A.R. Scoble (2 vols., London, 1856), ii. 409 (26 Apr. 1660).

terms, in which the former parliamentary Lords were prominent, although the House of Lords was not yet sitting. Meetings were held at the Earl of Northumberland's house, and those attending included the Earls of Bedford and Manchester, Lords Wharton and Fairfax, and Pierrepont, Popham, Waller, St. John, Holles, Lewis, Sir Gilbert Gerard, and Anthony Ashley Cooper.[1] Holles was associated with Lady Carlisle and a pro-French interest. He wanted the King to be in France during the negotiations - a move against Hyde's influence - but the rest of the Council did not support this.[2] The Royalists were alarmed at the Council of State's discussions. By mid March they feared that the majority supported the Isle of Wight articles, or even terms 'more insolent than ever they had demanded of the late King'. There were suggestions that the Council should treat with the King before the Convention met, but as Monk opposed this, the Council contented itself with drawing up articles to be offered to the Convention.[3]

A letter from Holles to his wife from early April 1660 has survived, but unfortunately contains little information about his own plans and hopes. He seemed weary of Westminster, wishing he could meet her at Cerne: 'I wish with all my heart, I could slip my neck out of the collar here, for in good truth I am not ambitious of this employment, and will get out of it as soon as I can'. He reports how her cousin, Sir Richard Onslow, had lost the county seat for Surrey because he wanted the second seat for his son, but says little of general affairs in London: 'Here is no news at all, things go on quietly, and no changes at all'.[4]

By mid April the Royalists had persuaded Annesley to spy out the secrets of the cabal who sought a conditional restoration. The news was disquieting, for they agreed that only the old Lords who had sat in 1648 should sit in the restored House of Lords. Their second meeting, Mordaunt sarcastically noted to Hyde,

> produced those moderate conclusions; first, that all should be nulled since the carrying away the Great Seal to Oxford; next,

1   *Clarendon state Papers*, iii. 705, 729-31 (23 Mar. & 19 Apr. 1660); Clarendon, *History* (Bk. XVI, 160), Macray, vi. 191. There is no sign of his brother in this cabal, although Clare had been associated with an offer of restoration on the Isle of Wight terms late in 1659; *The Letter-Book of John Viscount Mordaunt 1658-1660*, ed. Mary Coate (Camden Society, 3rd ser. 69, 1945), p. 95.

2   Bodl., Clarendon 71, f. 339v., [Coventry] to [Hyde], 20 Apr. 1660; French transcripts, PRO, 31/3, f. 14v., Bordeaux to Mazarin, 6 May 1660. The Queen and her party were thought to support the Presbyterians; Baillie, *Letters and Journals*, iii. 444 (31 Jan. 1661).

3   *Clarendon State Papers*, iii. 703, 705, 726 (23 Mar. & 11 Apr. 1660); Wodrow, *History of the Sufferings*, i. p. xix (Apr. 1660).

4   BL, Add. 32,679, f. 9v., Holles to Jane, 5 Apr. 1660.

that the Articles of the Isle of Wight should be sent to the King,
the preface excepted, and his Majesty to sign them before he was
to treat further in person.

The old demand that officers should be appointed with Parliament's
approval was revived. These were harsh terms, and among those
'debauched' by them, were Fairfax, Holles, Lewis, Pierrepont, Gerard
and Cooper.[1] Apart from imposing terms on the King, it was believed
that these 'old Parliament men' wanted to monopolise offices for
themselves. Bordeaux said that the principal posts were designed for
'the party leaders'. Holles was proposed as Secretary of State. 'They
have already shared the bear's skin (according to the proverb) amongst
them' wrote Nicholas.[2] Lambert's escape from the Tower on 11 April
and his attempt to raise the army for the Commonwealth seemed to
offer the Parliamentarians an even stronger bargaining position. The
cabal 'promised to themselves the advantage of fishing in troubled
waters', but after Lambert's defeat and capture, Holles and Sir William
Lewis were thought more moderate, although Evelyn and Pierrepont
'stick at the mark' and Holles's cousin Cooper was shifting again.[3]

Meanwhile the elections for the Convention were keenly contested
and there was a high poll in many places. The Venetian Ambassador
thought that many of 'the chief men of the counties' were rejected lest
they should support a conditional restoration.[4] Dorchester again
returned Holles. Gervase Holles commented from Holland that Holles
and his brother 'labour very much [for] the best . . . And I hope my
cousin Holles will make good what he said to me the last time I saw
him, that at the last he should prove himself an honest man'.[5] But
cousin Denzil's conduct was still not in accord with Royalist hopes.

When the Convention met on 25 April the Royalists believed they
outnumbered those 'Presbyterians' who wanted to impose terms on the
King by four or five to one, but the skilful political tactics of the latter
gave them some nasty moments.[6] The first points the 'Presbyterians'

1 *Clarendon State Papers*, iii. 729-30 (19 Apr. 1660).

2 Guizot, *Richard Cromwell*, ii, 384, Bordeaux to Mazarin, 29/19 Mar. 1660.
Clarendon State Papers, iii. 705, 730 (23 Mar., 19 Apr. 1660).

3 Bodl., Clarendon 72, f. 19, Mordaunt to the King, 24 Apr. 1660.

4 Mukerjee, 'Elections', pp. 401-2; *CSP Ven. 1659-1661*, p. 137.

5 *Municipal Records of Dorchester*, p. 436 (9 Apr. 1660); Bodl., Clarendon
71, f. 324, Gervase Holles to Hyde, Rotterdam, 20/30 Apr. 1660.

6 Bodl., Clarendon 72, f. 180, [Henry Coventry] to Kirton [i.e. Hyde], 4/14
May 1660, says the Royalists were four times more numerous than the 'not well
contented party'. Mordaunt said that the Royalists had five voices to their
opponents' one, *ibid.*, f. 19v. [Mordaunt] to Hyde, 24 Apr. [1660]. G. Davies,
The Restoration of Charles II 1658-1660 (London, 1955), p. 333 points out

gained were control of the Speaker and the clerk. Mordaunt and the Royalists supported the election of Sir Edward Turner as the Speaker but while they were busy at their prayers, 'Mr Holles, Sir William Lewis and the General had lugged the Speaker to his chair'. Sir Harbottle Grimston made the usual professions of inability, but coupled these with the practical suggestion that 'Mr Jesop might be clerk, without whose assistance he should be at a loss'. The choice of Jesop, wrote Mordaunt 'was likewise slabberd up before the fifth part of the members could get into the House'.[1] Both appointments were 'highly to our prejudice', for both were 'rigid Presbyters'. The next tactic was to examine the returns.

> Mr Holles began with saying there were many faces near to him he knew not, and therefore desired the election might be examined. Yet he came a little off and said he knew not but these gentlemen who were strangers to him might have as much right to sit as he. Upon this near 100 were put out.

Actually, the manoeuvre was not a success, as the committee for privileges to whom the disputes were referred was captured by the Royalists. Abernathy concludes that the persons discharged were Independents, not Royalists.[2]

The Presbyterians wanted only the old parliamentary lords of 1648 to sit in the House of Lords, but the young peers claimed their seats when the Convention assembled, and soon more joined them. Mordaunt says that 'Holles his interest, and party' miscalculated on this issue, expecting Monk to exclude the young peers until the terms of settlement were completed. It was rumoured Monk was displeased at the young Lords' action, but when Holles and Lewis complained he refused to interfere.[3]

Holles still wanted a conditional restoration. On 24 April Mordaunt reported 'Mr Holles is solicitious in sending conditions to *your Majesty* which must prove to *your prejudice* since tis known they will be more

the difficulty of generalising about the relative strengths of the different groups who wanted Charles recalled.

1   Bodl., Clarendon 72, f. 19v, f. 62, Mordaunt to Hyde, 24 & 27 Apr. 1660.

2   *Ibid.*, ff. 19v.-20. Bordeaux said that it was proposed to exclude 100 or 120 members for fear 'they will be too violent for the King' and in case the question of the composition of the upper house should arise; Guizot, *Richard Cromwell*, ii. 412 (3 May/Apr. 23, 1660); Abernathy, *English Presbyterians*, pp. 55-6.

3   Diary of Parliamentary business kept by Sir Edward Dering, M.P. for Kent in the Convention Parliament, 25 Apr. - 15 Aug. 1660, the property of Doreen, Lady Brabourne, on loan to Kent A.O., 27 Apr. 1660; Bodl., Clarendon 72, f. 19v., f. 63, M[ordaunt] to the King & to Hyde, 24 & 27 Apr. 1660; BL, Egerton 2618, f. 70, Strafford to Monk, 26 Apr. 1660: 'we hear your Lordship is much displeased with the young Lords that went into the House'.

rigid than your Majesty will expect'. Again three days later, he reported that the King's friends would find 'high opposition' in the Commons, where they were prejudiced by the exclusion of members 'and likewise the propositions Mr Holles and that cabal are finishing'[1] On the same day (27 April) Coventry wrote that although the recall of the King was no longer doubtful 'there is a party amongst the old secluded members that would have the treaty grounded upon the Isle of Wight propositions, and the old Lords are thought generally of the design'. Hyde found the 'Presbyterians' plans 'contrary to their professions to the King', although they tried to hide their activities by pretending Monk was in control.[2]

Time ran out for those who wanted to negotiate on the Isle of Wight or any other terms. After the King's letters were read to the Commons on 1 May, a committee was directed to prepare some propositions, which reported that before Charles should be received, 'the treaty ought first to be made with the King, and conditions of security' be agreed to.[3] Between 3 and 5 May Monk joined the 'Presbyterians' in supporting propositions along the lines that the present possessors of lands might enjoy these on generous leases, all but five persons should be pardoned, and the army be entrusted to him for life. More serious in relation to the King's power were proposals that he annul all acts under the Great Seal since 22 May 1642 (which would affect the composition of the House of Lords) confirm all the acts and ordinances of the Long Parliament submitted to him, and finally, agree to the settlement of the church by King, an Assembly and Parliament.[4] But before any terms could be agreed upon, the Commons resolved to invite the King to return.

At this critical point the Commons had to choose messengers to the King, and some Royalists saw the advantage of sending away the older parliamentary leaders. Broderick filled out his ballot paper with the names of 'the old ones'. 'I wish that Pierrepont, Holles, Sir Wil: Lewis and Maynard were there', he wrote, since they would not be a trouble at home, and might 'be sweetened by his Majesty's most excellent temper and acquainted with his princely prudence, that would at the same time force both love and reverence from the most inveterate malice . . .'. Henry Coventry also favoured sending Rumpers and the

1   Bodl., Clarendon 72, f. 20, (words *underlined* in cipher), f. 63, Mordaunt to Hyde, 27 Apr. 1660.

2   Bodl., Carte 30, f. 576; Bodl., Clarendon 72, f. 172, draft by Hyde to Sir J. Grenville, 4/14 May [1660].

3   Clarendon, *History* (Bk. XVI, 215), Macray, vi. 217.

4   Abernathy, *English Presbyterians*, pp. 58-9.

most rigid Presbyterians[1]. In these circumstances Holles's name appearing high on the poll was a qualified honour[2]. However, to the nation at large it appeared the height of happiness to be chosen to fetch the King, and this mood appears to have animated Holles who sailed to Holland where he delivered an oration to Charles on behalf of the House of Commons[3]. 'All agreed that never person spoke with more affection nor expressed himself in better terms than Mr Denzil Holles'[4]. The nation longed for him, he told Charles:

> You are the light of their eyes and the breath of their nostrils, their delight and all their hope; to have been so long banished from them into a strange land, it is no wonder that the news of your return should put a new life into them; what then will it be when their eyes shall be blessed with the sight of your royal person?

He gracefully alluded to the interregnum as a period when 'other lords have had dominion over them, have reigned and ruled over their bodies and estates; but their better part, their hearts, and minds, and souls, were free . . . and still continued faithful and loyal to your majesty'. They hoped that under Charles they might 'enjoy again their laws and liberties, and, which is above all, their religion in purity and truth'. Holles was confident they would not be deceived: 'a king of so many vows, and of so many prayers, cannot but crown the desires of his people'[5]. His audience had 'tears of joy in their eyes'[6].

The 'Presbyterians' ' attempts to control the King's restoration had failed, and the King arrived in London on 29 May. Nevertheless, they had put up a good fight, preparing terms to be offered to the King. Although they miscalculated in thinking they would lead the House, when they perceived the royalist strength they mustered all their political skill, to the success of which the royalist writers testified. Initially, the Presbyterians secured a *coup* in gaining control of the Speaker and the clerk and suggesting a review of elections, but their

1 Bodl., Clarendon 72, f. 15v., Broderick to Hyde, 3 May 1660; f. 180, 4/14 May. Annesley opposed sending twelve members, double the number of Lords, simply to carry a letter, but he was overruled; Dering's diary, Kent A.O., 4 May 1660.

2 *CJ*, viii. 15 (7 May 1660).

3 Holles was said to have raced the other commissioners in a pacquet boat; *HMC*, Report V. 184. The Speaker gave Holles the Commons' letter to deliver to Charles; *CJ*, viii. 22-3 (11 May 1660).

4 *The Diary of Samuel Pepys*, ed. H.B. Wheatley (10 vols., London, 1917), i. 159 n.3.

5 Printed in *A Collection of Scarce and Valuable Tracts . . .*, ed. W. Scott (13 vols., London, 1809-1815), iv. 417-9.

6 *The Letters of Elizabeth Queen of Bohemia*, ed. L.M. Baker (London, 1953), p. 308.

failure to prevent the young Lords from taking their seats both weakened their numerical strength in the Lords, and conceded the legality of Charles I's acts under the Great Seal after 1642. After this, they attempted to secure the cause by making the present Parliament legal and fixing its existence for some years.

Thurloe thought attitudes to the restoration fell into three main groups early in April 1660: strict Presbyterians, who wanted to bind the King to the presbytery, to exclude the King's former party, and to confirm all the land sales; 'the peers and others of the more moderate party [who] speak of the Isle of Wight Treaty'; and a third group who wanted to see the King as strong as if his father had been victorious in the war.[1] Holles belonged to the moderate group who supported the Isle of Wight terms, and although some thought the politicians did not really want to impose conditions on the King, but only to increase their own power in bargaining with the Court for offices, Holles's whole political life to this point and after argues in favour of his genuine desire for a limitation of the power of the King.

iii

Initially neither Charles nor Clarendon knew how strong the Presbyterians were, and so chose some of the foremost for the King's service as part of their policy of reconciliation. Charles admitted Holles to the Privy Council on 1 June 1660. Probably he was promoted at Monk's insistence. Monk had embarrassed Charles with a list of seventy names of persons 'who were thought fittest to be made Privy Councillors' and had explained that he knew most of them were no friends, but that 'his service would be more advanced by admitting them, than by leaving them out'.[2] When Holles became a Privy Councillor, the details of the settlement had still to be worked out. It is at this point he appears one of the 'lost leaders', for whereas he had been active from March until May in the schemes to restore the King upon terms, thereafter he was less outspoken. When the crucial details were debated in the Commons, he was already a member of the King's government.

Holles's speeches in the Commons show a conciliatory spirit and a great willingness to trust the King. This can best be illustrated by his contribution to the debate on voting supply before the Act of

1 Thurloe, *State Papers*, vii. 887 (6 Apr. 1660).
2 PRO, PC Register 2/54, f. 27; *The Life of Edward Earl of Clarendon . . . Written by Himself* (2 vols., Oxford, 1857), i. 275-8.

Indemnity had passed the Lords or been accepted by the King. Since money was vital to pay off the Army, the Commons' sole bargaining power lay in delaying supply until the Lords abandoned their desire for further punishment of former Parliamentarians. In the debate,

> Mr Holles next said, If he thought the stopping the bill of indemnity, at present, was meant to injure the subject, he would not open his mouth for the money bill; but, as he was assured the King would do, and had done, all he could to hasten the bill of indemnity, if, after this, it stop only at the House of Lords, the Commons had acquitted themselves.[1]

Holles's trust in the King and his support for the Court are obvious. Nearly twenty years earlier, when the Lords were unco-operative, Holles threatened that the Commons would act without them, but in 1660 he tamely surrendered responsibility, suggesting that the Commons had done their part, and could do no more. In the event the Commons were foolish not to have insisted on their bill. Holles was among those who indirectly advised Ludlow, a regicide, to surrender in June 1660, as the House 'would never be guilty of so unworthy an action' as to proceed against men who surrendered, yet this was precisely what the Lords forced the Commons to do by refusing their bill. (Fortunately for Ludlow, he had not surrendered.)[2]

In divisions on the fates of former Parliamentarians, Holles was moderate. He voted against excepting Lenthall from pardon, and on 4 December in the debate about the attainder of the regicides Holles said 'he had as great an abhorrence of that black crew as any one' but he moved that their creditors, wives and children be considered.[3] However, he was named one of the commissioners to try the regicides. When from the dock Harrison contended that he had acted his part in the King's trial by the authority of Parliament and therefore no inferior court could judge him, Holles launched into a bitter tirade, denying Parliament existed after Pride's purge.

> That House of Commons, which you say gave you authority, you know, what yourself made of it when you pulled out the Speaker, therefore do not make the Parliament to be the author of your black crimes. It was innocent of it. You know yourself what esteem

---

1 *The Parliamentary or Constitutional History of England* [hereafter cited as *Old Parliamentary History*] (24 vols., London, 1751-1762), xxii. 406 (27 July 1660). The House passed the bill for supply.

2 Ludlow, *Memoirs*, ii. 280.

3 *CJ*, viii. 118 (13 Aug. 1660). Holles was more moderate than others about imposing oaths on Papists; *Old Parliamentary History*, xxii. 370-1; xxiii, 37-8. Holles wanted those members who had been active after 1647 to be punished, but some proposed all those who had been active against the King since 1642 should be excepted from pardon; *ibid.*, 43-4.

> you had of it, when you broke, and tore it in sunder, when you
> scattered, and made them hide themselves, to preserve them from
> your fury, and violence. Do not make the Parliament to be the
> author of your crimes.

Holles was obviously angry that Harrison should make the same plea he
had made in 1629, that members of Parliament were answerable only to
Parliament, hence the vehemence of his denial that Parliament in 1649
was not free. However, there is another point. Holles assumed that a
member was directly responsible to his constituents: 'Did you', he
taunted Harrison, 'go home to advise with your country, that you
represented?'[1] The accountability of members of Parliament to their
constituents was not normally part of Holles's political creed, but in
his anxiety to dissociate himself and his party of the 1640s from the
regicide and the Commonwealth he failed to perceive the inconsistency
of his own position.[2] Others felt the inconsistency, and a certain
indelicacy in Holles's actions. Manchester and Holles, two of the
members who had contributed their utmost to engage men to the
cause, Ludlow says, 'were not contented to abandon them in this
charge, but assisted in condemning them to die for their fidelity to the
cause, which themselves had betrayed'.[3] Although Ludlow and Holles
had never really espoused the same cause, the spectacle of Holles in
judgment on his former associates is not attractive.

Holles has been blamed for not supporting the Presbyterian ministers
during the negotiations for the settlement of the chuch, but those who
have censured him have expected that a 'Presbyterian' politician was
Presbyterian in religion. His contemporaries did not make the same
mistake. As Baxter explained, 'he that was for episcopacy and the
liturgy was called a Presbyterian if he endeavoured to procure any
abatement of their impositions, for the reconciling of the parties, or the
ease of the ministers, and people that disliked them'. Baxter explicitly
states that although the Earls of Manchester and Anglesey and Holles
were called Presbyterians, 'I have heard them plead for moderate
episcopacy and liturgy myself, and they would have drawn us [the
ministers] to yield further than we did'.[4] Holles wanted to compromise.

---

1 *An Exact and most Impartial Accompt of the Indictment, Arraignment,
Trial and Judgment . . . of Nine and Twenty Regicides,* 31 Oct. 1660, TT
E.1047.3, 52.

2 All 'the old parliament men' were enraged with Lenthall on 12 May 1660
when he argued 'that he that first drew his sword upon the King committed as
great offence as he that cut off his head'; Dering's diary, Kent A.O.

3 Ludlow, *Memoirs,* ii. 302.

4 Baxter, *Reliquiae Baxterianae,* pt. II, p. 278; see also p. 373: Baxter says that
he and his friends were called Presbyterians after 1662 'though we never put up
one petition for Presbytery, but pleaded for primitive Episcopacy'.

He said in the House of Commons that he was never averse to the Book of Common Prayer, and although this may have been an exaggeration, he was never committed to *jus divinum* Presbyterianism.[1]

Baillie found the re-establishment of the Anglican Church quite incredible: 'the overturning of all the reformation of England, without a contrary petition, to me was strange, and very grievous, and I suspect we know not yet the bottom of that mystery'.[2] It was indeed a strange and unexpected event, and the history of the re-establishment of the Anglican Church and the creation of non-conformity outside the church is extremely complex.[3] The problem here is Holles's role. Did he support the Presbyterian ministers in the debates in the Convention and in Parliament, or in the discussions between the clergy, the bishops and the King?

It was of great importance to the Puritans that religion should be settled by the Convention. Even before the King returned, there was an attempt to confirm the ministers in their positions and livings, which alarmed the Royalists.[4] An act of Parliament was necessary because the King's policy of reconciliation was being undermined all over England as returning Anglican patrons ejected Puritan clergy from their livings, with the support of the justices of the peace.[5] Time was on the Anglicans' side, perceiving which they filibustered to delay the religious settlement.[6] Holles gave little backing to the Presbyterian cause. Cooper moved for a three month adjournment on the question of religion on 9 July, a move which conceded the issue to the Royalists, and which Holles supported. On 21 July Bowman reported he was 'for the petition' to prevent further legal proceedings being taken against ministers in sequestered livings, a stop-gap measure, prior to establishing the ministers' rights. On Friday 27 July when a bill to this effect was read for the first time Holles followed Sir Heneage Finch in recommending it be read again on Monday, to which the House agreed. The reason for deferment was that the bills for money needed to be

---

1   D.R. Lacey, *Dissent and Parliamentary Politics in England, 1661-1689* (New Jersey, 1969), p. 370, suggests that initially some, such as Lords Delamer, Holles and Anglesey, gravitated towards the Anglican church in 1660, and later swung back to a position best described as Presbyterian.

2   Baillie, *Letters and Journals,* iii. 444 (31 Jan. 1661).

3   See R.S. Bosher, *The Making of the Restoration Settlement* (London, 1951; revised 1957); Abernathy, *English Presbyterians,* and A. Whiteman, 'The restoration of the Church of England', in G.F. Nuttal and O. Chadwick, eds., *From Uniformity to Unity 1662-1962* (London, 1962).

4   *Clarendon State Papers,* iii. 747 (Broderick to Hyde, 10 May 1660).

5   Bosher, *Restoration Settlement,* pp. 161, 164-5.

6   For example, *HMC,* Report V. 204a. (4 Aug. 1660).

passed. Holles also urged the House to defer reading the ministers' petition until Monday.[1] Nevertheless, by August 1660 the Presbyterians appeared strong enough to carry the bill to confirm the ministers in their livings.[2] On 13 August Townshend confided a rather unlikely story to his diary:

> It is said Mr Denzil Holles at Council Table made a speech for the settling presbytery and abolishing episcopacy, the King present, when he expressed himself with some disgust to the Speaker therein.[3]

Presbyterian strength so alarmed the King and Lord Chancellor Clarendon that they adjourned the Parliament on 13 September, and attempted to settle the contentious issue of religion outside Parliament through discussions with the ministers. On 4 September Clarendon offered the ministers various concessions which they, led by Baxter, declared unsatisfactory. Baxter's plain speaking was objected to by some, and the better to effect a compromise they called in 'the Earl of Manchester (with whom as our sure friend we still consulted . . . .): And he called the Earl of Anglesey and the Lord Holles to the consultation as our friends'. Clarendon assembled the parties for a discussion of the altered Declaration at Worcester House and Holles was again among those present. After this, the King ordered that two from the Episcopal party and two of the Presbyterian ministers should revise the Declaration, with Holles and Annesley deciding any differences.[4] The outcome was the King's Declaration of November 1660 offering concessions to dissentients. A group in Parliament attempted to legalise this Declaration by having Parliament declare it law, but when this failed[5] it undermined the King's power, leaving the Declaration in an equivocal position. The Convention dissolved with the religious issue still unsettled. The ministers had no security for their livings, and all depended on the next Parliament summoned for 8 May 1661.

1 The diary of Seymour Bowman, Bodl., Salway Deposit 9, ff. 83-84v.; ff. 90v-91; f. 96v. There is no evidence of his speaking when the bill was brought in on Monday 30 July.

2 'Manifest it is, that the Presbyterian party is at present at a great height in the Commons House'; Collection of letters to Dr. William Sancroft, BL, Harl. 3784, f. 2, H. Thorndike to William Sancroft, 17/27 Aug. 1660.

3 *Diary of Henry Townshend of Elmley Lovett 1640-1663*, ed. J.W. Willis Bund (Worcestershire Historical Society, 2 vols., London, 1920), i. 58.

4 Baxter, *Reliquiae Baxterianae*, pt. II, pp. 265, 277-8.

5 The reason for the King's opposition to the attempt to enact the Declaration into law is debatable. Bosher, *Restoration Settlement*, pp. 194-9, argues that the Government had no real intention of compromising with the Presbyterians, but Whiteman, 'Restoration of the Church of England', pp. 71-2, suggests that opposition may have been as much dictated by dislike of Parliament's interference with the prerogative.

Charles still pursued a compromise in religion, calling a conference at the Savoy to revise the Prayer Book in April 1661, but the bishops refused to compromise. The Presbyterian ministers had already revealed that they would not accept toleration if this included toleration for Independents, sectaries and Catholics, thereby antagonising potential allies. When the Cavalier Parliament debated the religious settlement, they made confirmation of the ministers in their livings dependent upon their submission to episcopal ordination.[1] Many ministers found they could not conform, and left their posts.[2] Meanwhile, there were other Acts which enjoined all members of Parliament to accept the Anglican sacrament, or face exclusion. At the end of 1662 Charles attempted to grant indulgence, but the Episcopal leaders resisted him.[3] Thereafter the Presbyterian ministers were dependent on the help of individuals who might keep them in their livings or appoint them to posts at their disposal.

Before the completion of the religious settlement, Holles ceased to be a member of the House of Commons. On 21 April 1661 Charles created him Baron Holles of Ifield - for his service to the Restoration, the patent declared. On 11 May 1661 he took his seat on the barons' bench in the House of Lords, introduced by Lords Robartes and Lexington.[4] Was it a reward for services rendered or the fulfillment of a promise? In 1660 Charles's supporters had advised him to be chary of granting honours and preferments, 'The hope being of infinite more use as affairs stand'. Holles may have earned his peerage by not obstructing the settlement once the King was in England, and some historians find his acceptance of a reward repulsive.[5] On the other hand, it may be that in conferring honours Charles was fulfilling prior

---

1   Baxter, *Reliquiae Baxterianae*, pt. II, pp. 303-72, 277; Bosher, *Restoration Settlement*, pp. 226-30, 239-41.

2   Some ministers, such as Zachary Crofton, found themselves able to conform to the church as laymen after resigning from the ministry; Whiteman, 'The Restoration of the Church of England', p. 82.

3   Bosher, *Restoration Settlement*, pp. 259-64.

4   Holles's creation, Bodl., Ashmolean 838, f. 63; *LJ*, xi. 250. John Lord Robartes supported Parliament in the Civil Wars, although in 1641 he had refused the Protestation. He was proposed as general of the west instead of Holles at the end of 1642. He was said to be a religious Presbyterian, but he refused to take the Covenant until May 1645; Pearl, 'Oliver St. John', p. 511 n.7. Robartes disavowed Presbyterian views in- 1660, but was thought sympathetic to the Presbyterian cause; article by C.H. Firth, *DNB*. See also Lacey (*Dissent and Parliamentary Politics*, pp. 470-2) who considers him a possible Presbyterian. Robert Sutton, Lord Lexington, was a former Royalist, but he came from Nottinghamshire and this may explain his connection with Holles; *DNB*.

5   Bodl., Clarendon 72, f. 157v., Broderick to [Hyde], 3 May 1660; D.H. Pennington, review in *History* 52 (1967), 334.

promises, for although there is no evidence of any promise to Holles before the Restoration, his relations with the Royalists at that point are obscure.[1] Possibly Charles rewarded him for a combination of reasons, among which may have been the need to reconcile the former parliamentary party, and a desire to neutralize an experienced Parliamentarian by elevating him to the safer and more conservative House of Lords. Furthermore, Charles had to consider, in conferring peerages, men who might be able to support their new dignity with suitable wealth, and although Holles's estates had been in some disorder during the Commonwealth, he was still a wealthy man.[2]

The following year, in 1662, Charles chose Holles for the most important of the foreign embassies, that of France. Offices and a peerage had come his way at last. Was this at the expense of his principles? Edward Harley, one of his fellow eleven members, was so fearful of seeming self-interested that he refused any honours, although he accepted the post of governor of Dunkirk.[3] Holles had done what he could to insist upon terms, but since he had wanted the restoration of the King to Parliament since 1642, it was no *volte face* to welcome Charles II. Once the King was restored unconditionally, he accepted office. Probably he hoped it would be a means of influencing the monarch by providing him with good counsel. He showed later that office was not the be-all and end-all of his existence, and was in opposition again by the end of the reign.

---

1 Unfortunately a letter from Hyde at Breda to Holles 1660 calendared in the *HMC*, Report IV, 238, No. 18, is no longer among the Bath MSS. It might have provided a clue on the subject of Holles's relationships with the Royalists.

2 For comments on Holles's wealth, see Appendix 2.

3 *DNB*.

II

LORD HOLLES: AMBASSADOR AND OPPOSITION PEER

Lord Holles acted zealously for the Restoration, and, while the dawn of the King's reign was unclouded, accepted employments and embassies from the crown, consistent with his honour and duty to his country. As soon as the Catholic rudder was uncovered, he again reverted to patriot opposition.[1]

i

In May 1662 Charles II appointed Holles his ambassador to France. D'Estrades, the French ambassador in London, who had been disturbed to hear that the anti-Clarendon faction had tried to gain the post for Henry Bennet, explained that Holles was of Clarendon's faction, and not at all attached to the interests of Spain. Although Charles said he would dispatch Holles within a month, not until May 1663 did he take up his appointment.[2]

Contemporary literary accounts described the ideal ambassador as a man of universal parts, a paragon of virtue. English diplomats at this period generally fell somewhat short of such perfection. For many men a diplomatic post was a stepping stone to political office at home, rather than the climax of a professional career.[3] But Charles probably appointed Holles as a stop-gap, until the lines of his foreign policy should have clarified. English policy was being pursued against the background of the growing power of France, which Holles attributed to the weakness of Louis XIV's neighbours, and his own 'vast treasure and an absolute power'.[4] Louis was defining diplomatic procedures at his Court to recognise French supremacy while Colbert pursued an aggresive commercial policy which threatened English trade.

1 Horatio Walpole, *Royal and Noble Authors*, p. 393.

2 *Lettres, mémoires, et négociations de M.le Comte d'Estrades. By Godfroy, Comte d'Estrades* (9 vols., London, 1743), i. 232-3, 236-7, 263; C.H. Firth and S.C. Lomas (eds.), *Notes on the Diplomatic Relations of England and France 1603-1688* (Oxford, 1906).

3 Francis Thynn, *The Application of Certain Histories Concerning Ambassadours And their Functions* (composed 1579; London, [29 Aug.] 1651); [J. Howel], *A Discourse Concerning Precedency of Kings . . .* (London, 1664), section iv; K. Feiling, *British Foreign Policy 1660-1672* (London, 1930), pp. 19-22; Phyllis Lachs, *The Diplomatic Corps under Charles II and James II* (New Brunswick, 1965), pp. 63-5.

4 PRO, 30/24 Bundle 4, no. 127, ff. 59v.-60.

Holles occupied his diplomatic post at a difficult stage in Anglo-French relations. In addition to procedural and commercial conflicts, Anglo-French relations were complicated by England's relations with Holland. Charles assumed that in any conflict with Holland, France would assist him, but Louis made a treaty with the Dutch in April 1662, and although Charles professed his desire to be bound in a close alliance with Louis, negotiations did not prosper. To add to the difficulties of Anglo-French relations, Charles's Council was divided: Bennet was basically pro-Spanish and clashed with Clarendon who, in addition to being pro-French, was a stumbling block in the way of Bennet's further political advancement.[1]

Paris was the most lucrative of the diplomatic posts, and in June 1662 Holles's salary was fixed at £400 per month and £3,000 for equipage, but lack of public money prevented his departure. He received his credentials and his instructions in June 1663, and arrived in Dieppe on 21/11 July 1663. Charles sought a commercial treaty, prior to the establishment of closer union between the two Kings, and Clarendon wanted the negotiations transferred to France to by-pass Secretary Bennet's increasing influence. Holles was to insist on all previous commercial concessions England had enjoyed. In private instructions he was ordered to keep an eye on Orange interests in Holland, those of the Palatinate, and to assess French designs on Germany.[2]

From the time of his landing in France, Holles showed determination to uphold his own and his master's honour which was entirely in accord with contemporary notions of diplomatic behaviour. He quarrelled over the right of the French customs officers to search his baggage, disputed precedence at his formal entry, quarrelled with the French nobility because they failed to honour his notions of his own importance, and took various slights as insults.[3] The most widely commented on dispute concerned procedence at his formal entry before his first formal audience with Louis. As one measure designed to increase the

1 Feiling, *British Foreign Policy*, Ch. 2.

2 Bodl., Clarendon 104, f. 77; PRO, SP 78/117, f. 105, f. 270; Instructions *ibid.*, f. 278, f. 280. Another copy of his instructions, BL, Stow 191, f. 3, is endorsed 'Penned by the Earl of Clarendon', 16 June 1663; PRO, SP 78/116, ff. 7-8; Feiling, *British Foreign Policy*, p. 65; Lachs, *Diplomatic Corps*, p. 82; Violet Barbour, *Henry Bennet, Earl of Arlington. Secretary of State of Charles II* (Washington, 1914), pp. 70-1.

3 T. Fuller, *Of the Ambassador*, p. 303; PRO, SP 78/117, f. 105, f. 111, f. 128, f. 138. These disputes have been discussed briefly by Feiling, *British Foreign Policy*, pp. 64-5, and at length by W.L. Grant, *A Puritan at the Court of Louis XIV*, Bulletin of the Departments of History and Politics, Queen's University (Ontario, 1913).

prestige of the royal family, Louis had recently insisted that the coaches of the Princes of the blood should precede those of foreign ambassadors. As Holles refused to concede precedence he was unable to begin his duties until Louis gave him his first audience at St. Germains without any formal procession.[1] The reason the dispute lasted so long was not Holles's fault: neither Charles nor Louis would give way. As Holles recognised, 'ceremony is substance, and who carries it in that will carry it in the essentials'.[2] At a formal entry to London in 1661, the French ambassador had contested his right to precede the Spanish ambassador to the loss of five lives and thirty-three injured, as a result of which the French ambassadors gained the right to precede the Spanish on all occasions. Louis did not wish to omit Holles's formal entry since this might deprive him of the advantage he had so recently gained in all other courts.[3] Charles was no more inclined to give way than Louis. Although Bennet took little notice of Holles's difficulties initially, when Sir George Downing wrote in indignation from Holland, he mentioned the matter to the King and the Duke. Thereafter Holles was simply a pawn, for after a frantic search for precedents, Charles directed that he was determined 'that we would not depart with a right'.[4] Holles's own attitude to the dispute was not entirely humourless: 'sometimes I am very angry, sometimes I laugh at myself to be served so' he wryly observed. His opposite number in Spain commiserated with him: 'I agree with your Excellency, that the ceremonious part is the most troublesome in our employments'.[5]

After the matter of the entry was settled — and the next English ambassador, Ralph Montagu, was allowed precedence without any dispute in 1669 — Charles insisted that Holles should not give way to the princes, but should wait for them to visit him. However, after further difficulties, Charles weakened.[6] He began to think that his

1 PRO, SP 78/118, ff. 110-110v. Pepys thought Holles's audience was 'in the most dishonourable way that could be'; Pepys, *Diary*, iv. 52.

2 PRO, SP 78/119, f. 33v.

3 J.J. Jusserand, *A French Ambassador at the Court of Charles the Second Le Comte de Cominges* (London, 1892), pp. 26-8; Letters to Sir George Downing, BL, Add. 22920, f. 19. In 1664 the English ambassador in Holland disputed his rights of precedence with the Duke of Holstein; Edward Browne, *Journal of A Visit to Paris in the Year 1664*, ed. G. Keynes (London, 1923), p. 21.

4 PRO, SP 78/117, f. 161, f. 193, f. 228v., f. 261; *ibid.*, 118, f. 25, f. 30; Bodl., Clarendon 106, f. 224.

5 PRO, SP 78/117, f. 214; *Original Letters and Negotiations of his Excellency Sir Richard Fanshaw, the Earl of Sandwich, the Earl of Sunderland, and Sir William Godolphin* (2 vols., London, 1724), i. 211 (18 Aug. N.S. 1664).

6 Lachs, *Diplomatic Corps*, pp. 110-1; Julia Cartwright, *Madame: A Life of Henrietta, Daughter of Charles I and Duchess of Orleans* (London, 1900),

ambassador was causing unnecessary trouble, and when Holles showed willingness to dispute forms of address with the French ministers, Charles recalled him to the task of the treaty.[1] When Holles demanded satisfaction for the insulting words some Dutchmen had uttered about Charles and the Duke of York on French soil, Charles vented his exasperation to his sister, Henrietta:

> I am sorry that my Lord Holles had asked for justice upon a point of honour that I should never have thought of. You know the old saying in England, the more a t.— is stirred the more it stinks, and I do not care a t.— for anything a Dutch man says of me.[2]

Increasingly Charles pursued his diplomacy through his sister, who in addition had to smooth over difficulties between Holles and the French Court.[3]

Charles sought a commercial treaty, but negotiations were complicated by disputes over customs duties and the rights of merchants. England demanded that her merchants be given equal privileges with other foreigners, which involved the remission of shipping dues. The Dutch were already exempt from these dues, as part of a reciprocal treaty, and the French refused to remit the English dues unless their merchants received similar concessions in England. As Henrietta explained, if Charles would treat Louis's subjects in England 'as the English, he consents that the English in France should be treated as French', — apart from the customs dues'.[4] But the underlying difficulty of Colbert's aggressive commercial policy could not be resolved. Holles appreciated Colbert's power and doubted his friendship to England. Conflicts between England and France in the New World, Canada and the West Indies and East India trade all obstructed the commercial treaty.[5] Furthermore, while England was skirmishing with the Dutch in 1664, English privateers seized French merchants' goods carried in Dutch ships, which was bitterly resented: 'I tell them I am sure justice

pp. 151-2 (Charles to Henrietta, 28 Dec. 1663, 18 Jan. 1664); PRO, SP 78/118, f. 25, f. 115.

1 *Ibid.,* 119, f. 81.

2 Cartwright, *Madame,* pp. 208-9, Charles to Henrietta, 27 Feb. 1665. An eighteenth-century writer considered these words 'could hardly have been expected from a royal hand'; J. Dalrymple, *Memoirs of Great Britain and Ireland,* (2 vols., London and Edinburgh, 1771-3), ii. 4. Holles was annoyed that the matter was not pursued further; PRO, SP 78/120, f. 71v.

3 *Ibid.* 118, f. 261; Carwright, *Madame,* p. 160. In 1664, at the height of Holles's dispute with the French ministers over the style of address they should employ towards him, he found there was a play at Court in which a bear 'is very forward and unruly, till he be stroked with the name of Altress [Highness]'; PRO, SP 78/118, f. 244v.

4 *Ibid.,* 119, f. 192, ff. 154-154v.; f. 218.

5 *Ibid.,* 118, f. 155v., f. 228v., f. 272.

will be done to them', wrote Holles, 'which is all I can say'. He thought the English privateers damaged Anglo-French relations, and retarded the remedy of English grievances. From February 1665 onwards the commercial treaty negotiations lagged and finally halted. Clarendon believed that Holles had done all he could, but the French did not really want the treaty.[1]

Assisting the English merchants trading in France was one of Holles's duties, but even to sustain their customary rights was difficult. There were attempts to organize the English merchants into companies, and although Holles said he was 'no great friend to companies', he thought a regulated trade would assist them.[2] He supported the Bordeaux merchants who opposed the establishment of a consulate, but was overruled by the home government who found consuls useful as purveyors of information.[3] Holles also assisted individual merchants as best he could.[4]

As the alliance with France was no nearer after Holles had been in France for over a year, Charles sent a personal friend, Charles Berkeley, Viscount Fitzharding to promote the alliance. Charles assured Holles that although he was under 'some small prejudices', he was graciously pleased to attribute these to 'serving me well and maintaining the dignity of our character'. While the deterioration in Anglo-French relations was hardly due to Holles's ineptitude, his isolation from the French Court limited his utility.[5] He could not penetrate the secrets of Louis's policies, but although he may have underestimated French strength, his dispatches show that he was sure the French Court was pro-Dutch, and intended 'to fall foul of us'.[6] Finally, when French attempts to mediate in the Anglo-Dutch war failed, both Kings recalled their ambassadors. Holles had his audience of *congé* on 26 December 1665, refused a parting gift from Louis, and was said to have 'taken his leave in very big words'.[7] But misfortunes dogged his plans for

1 *Ibid.,* 120, f. 230; *ibid.,* 121, f. 72; Clarendon, *Life,* i. 461.

2 PRO, SP 78/119, f. 174; *ibid.,* 117, f. 112.

3 *Ibid.,* 118, f. 282v.; P. Fraser, *The Intelligence of the Secretaries of State and their Monopoly of Licensed News 1660-1688* (Cambridge, 1956), p. 5.

4 PRO, SP 78/118, f. 219; *ibid.,* 120, ff. 64-64v.; *ibid.,* 118, f. 48; BL, Stow 199, f. 1.

5 PRO, SP 78/119, f. 248, Copy, Charles II to Holles, n.d.; *ibid.,* 118, f. 201; *ibid.,* 119, f. 172; see also, Longleat, Coventry Papers 33, f. 6.

6 T.H. Lister, *Life and Administration of Edward, first Earl of Clarendon, with original correspondence* (3 vols., London, 1837-8), iii. 393, 412, 413.

7 Jusserand, *French Ambassador,* ch. ix; PRO, SP 78/121, ff. 204-7, Relation of audience of congé; *ibid.,* f. 190, f. 222, ff. 224-224v; *ibid.,* 122, f. 20; *The Rawdon Papers* (London, 1819), p. 216.

departure. All the English in the town, anticipating war, wanted to accompany him, he was delayed for want of money and a ship, and he fell ill with gout.[1] He heard from England that his brother had died, and his wife in France was ill. France's declaration of war on 6 January 1666 added to his difficulties. At the end of January his wife died, and since she wished to be buried at Shroton, beside her son of a former marriage, he had the problem of conveying her body to England. Personal difficulties confronted him, and he was most annoyed to learn that her son Thomas Freke had taken immediate possession of his deceased wife's estate 'fearing it would run away', and was rifling through his papers: 'done like a Dorsetshire country gentleman' he growled. To top his distress the French doubted the authenticity of his sufferings from the gout — they think it is more policy than sickness' — and it was so construed in England.[2]

However, Holles's continuing presence in France was of some value. He obtained from Louis a statement granting such Englishmen as were in France three months' grace to remove themselves and their goods, and presented a memorial to Louis on 20 January on Charles's reasons for refusing the peace terms Louis's ambassadors had proposed.[3] In March Henrietta advised him to 'be lame still a little longer', as some peace overtures were under consideration. Although Holles considered he had no power to treat, he reported the terms offered, which were so unsatisfactory Charles ordered his immediate return. Poor Holles was again too ill to obey immediately, suffering this time from an overflow of bile 'caused as they say by occasion of much chagrin of which I have had store'. Finally he set off, accompanied by the comte de Gramont, a French nobleman of distinguished family, finding at his departure 'great civilities everywhere'.[4]

Shortly after his return to England, Holles married for the third time. De Gramont had noticed that during his last days in France 'une Mme de Cambremont, de Basse-Normandie, a presque toujours été avec lui', and this was the woman he later married. By September 1666

1   PRO, SP 78/121, f. 199, f. 217; *ibid.,* 122, ff. 4-5; Holles's father had also suffered from gout; Nott. U.L., Ne C 15 405, p. 201, Clare to Bourchier, 18 July 1636.

2   PRO, SP 78/122, f. 19, f. 67v., f. 116, f. 105; *Miscellanea Aulica;* ed. T. Brown (London, 1702), p. 388; *The Right Honourable the Earl of Arlington's Letters: to Sir W. Temple . . .,* ed. T. Bebington (2 vols., London, 1701), i. 66. Subsequently Holles's stepson Thomas Freke was a prominent Dorset Whig.

3   PRO, SP 78/122, f. 36, f. 39; Bodl., Clarendon 83, ff. 263-267v.; D'Estrades, *Lettres et Négotiations,* iv. 47-50.

4   PRO, SP 78/122, f. 109, ff. 137-157v., ff. 161, 170, f. 184; Arlington, *Letters,* i. 75.

there was talk in England of Holles's new wife, 'some say married in France, and others say not married but come to be married'. Holles married Esther le Lou, daughter of Gideon le Lou, widow of Jacques Richer, 'seigneur de Cambrernon, en Normandie' on 16 September, and she was naturalised by a private act of Parliament which received the King's assent on 8 February 1667. She outlived Holles, dying in 1683 and was buried beside him. Esther, according to her own testimony, was born of parents who instructed her 'that the reformed religion is the true one', and in her will she testified she found Denzil an excellent husband.[1]

Public affairs drifted from bad to worse after Holles's return from France. The disaster of the plague in 1665 had demoralised the nation, and the great fire of September 1666 seemed another adverse judgment from heaven. Holles, as a member of the Privy Council, took part in trying to quiet the disturbances, and with his cousin Anthony Ashley Cooper, now Lord Ashley, saved a servant of the Portuguese ambassador from lynching by a hostile mob.[2] The war with Franch was going badly for England, and by November 1666 Holles wept to his friend Carteret 'to think in what a condition we are fallen'.[3] The Government was divided in policy towards peace, but the problem was difficult because it involved determining England's future foreign policy. However, by 1667 the cry for peace was so great that, after disputes about the location of the treaty, Charles dispatched Holles and Henry Coventry as plenipotentiaries to Breda to negotiate a treaty, while preparing limited strategy for the summer war. Although Charles initially instructed Holles and Coventry to negotiate a peace upon reasonable terms, English policy continued inconsistent because of the two factions within the Council.[4] The English government, believing that Louis's conquests in Flanders would drive the Dutch to a speedy peace, tried to by-pass the peace negotiations and treat with the Dutch and the French separately. It was vaguely assumed that the negotiations could be accepted as a cessation of hostilities, although no such cessation was in fact made. While Holles's and Coventry's negotiations at Breda proceeded slowly, the Dutch prepared their summer fleet. The English had no

1   Guizot, *Portraits Politiques*, p.40; *HMC*, Report VII.485b; *Marriage, Baptismal, and Burial Registers of St. Peter, Westminster*, p. 4; *LJ*, xii. 11-5, 82, 110; Will of Esther Le Lou, 24 Aug. 1683, translated from French, Somerset House, P.C.C., 1684/162.

2   Clarendon, *Life*, ii. 283-4.

3   Sir George Carteret, Treasurer of the Navy; Pepys, *Diary*, vi. 63.

4   Feiling, *British Foreign Policy*, p. 219, says that the choice of plenipotentiaries reflects conflicting policies. Lachs, *Diplomatic Corps*, p. 61, says that Arlington had wanted to go himself with Clifford.

fleet ready, and when the Dutch sailed up the Thames, and destroyed English ships in the Medway, English humiliation was complete.

After an initial impulse to recall their plenipotentiaries, the home government instructed them on 21 June to conclude a peace as soon as possible: 'if you get a speedy peace, you will be very welcome home' wrote Clarendon. Fortunately the Dutch were anxious for peace also, so reasonable terms were negotiated. Coventry, who seems to have taken the leading part in the negotiations, returned to England for Charles's approval, and the Treaty was signed on 21 July, ratified and proclaimed on 14 August 1667. On 23 August Charles recalled his plenipotentiaries who arrived back at Whitehall on 13 September.[1] England had gained better terms than her strength might have warranted, but contemporary comments were hostile, betraying wounded pride. 'The Dutch have the best of us, and do end the war with victory on their side' was Pepys's conclusion, which was hardly surprising since Pepys had thought the decision to negotiate was a national disgrace. Holles felt that they had done the best they could in the circumstances.[2]

Despite the inglorious background to this treaty, it was a more successful venture for Holles personally than his residence in France. His salary was appointed at £200 per week. The formal entry of the two Englishmen into Breda was a splendidly triumphant affair — trumpets, horsemen, footmen in livery alongside, rich coaches, escorts, lined streets. 'Nothing of this nature', observed the author of the *Narrative* of the embassy, 'hath ever been performed with more advantage to the honour of the English nation' which was in marked contrast to the shabby affair of Holles's reception in France. The *Narrative* makes no mention of the humiliating circumstances in which Holles and Coventry found themselves when the Dutch achieved so signal a triumph in the Medway, and merely remarks that 'every thing [was] carried on with mutual civilities and kindness'.[3]

The embassy to Breda marks the end of Holles's diplomatic career. It has been suggested that Holles owed part of his wealth to his enjoyment of office, particularly to this post in France,[4] but this seems

1   Arlington, *Letters,* i. 171-2. BL, Add. 32094, f. 186; Longleat, Coventry Papers 44, f. 181, Morrice to Holles and Coventry, 23 Aug. 1667; *A Narrative or Journal of the Proceedings of their excellencies . . . Lord Holles and the Lord Coventry,* (London, 1667), pp. 19, 31.

2   Pepys, *Diary,* vii. 43-4, vi. 177; Lister, *Life and Administration of Clarendon,* iii. 466 (16 July 1667).

3   *CSPD 1667,* p. 65; *Narrative,* pp. 9-12, p. 16. The author may have been Holles himself.

4   O.R.F. Davies, 'The wealth and influence of John Holles, Duke of Newcastle 1694-1711', *Renaissance and Modern Studies* 9 (1965), 27 and n. 2.

unlikely. Although his salary was £400 per month, like most other diplomats, he had trouble obtaining his money.[1] The perquisites of the office were few, and Holles refused the gift of the King of France. Possibly he, like many other ambassadors, failed to return the plate, with which he had been supplied, to the Jewel House. He obtained a lease of the Prince's Woods in Dorset at the time of setting out, and may have looked for further leases as a reward.[2]

Verdicts on his ability as a diplomat have been unfavourable. The French were critical of him after he refused to give way to the Princes of blood, while at Breda D'Estrades thought that the English ambassadors had made unnecessary points of honour, and were inexperienced.[3] Later judgements have been equally uncomplimentary: Holles is described by Cartwright as 'too punctilious and too irascible' and by Feiling as basically old fashioned and insular.[4] Holles professed to care nothing for his own status — 'of my self and concerning my self I am the most indifferent man in the world' — and everything for his master's honour, but the post of ambassador puffed up that sense of self-importance he always possessed.[5] Frequently his complaints were petty, and if the home government overruled or criticised him, he wrote lengthy self-justifications. He corrected Sir George Downing's French, and wrote tediously on numerous occasions of his patent method of sealing letters so they could not be opened undetected because he did not care for the use of ciphers which the home government advised. However, although Charles recognised that in personal matters Holles 'may possibly be formal and punctilious enough', he thought him well affected to the proposed alliance between England and France. Coventry told Holles that the King was entirely satisfied 'both with your address and resolution in retrieving and maintaining his just pretensions', and that Charles appreciated, 'how hard the game you had to play would be, and . . . applauded himself that he had set so good a gamester to play it'.[6] The

1 PRO, SP 78/117, f. 270; ibid., 118, f. 143; BL, Add. 32679, f. 11, f. 12, f. 13. Lachs, Diplomatic Corps, pp. 91-5. Holles received a warrant for his extraordinary expenses in April 1668; Calendar of Treasury Books, 1667-1668, ed. W.A. Shaw, p. 543.

2 Lachs, Diplomatic Corps, pp. 87-8, 94. Prince's Woods had previously been leased to the Frekes. The lease to Denzil was 10 July 1663; Nott. R.O., Portland deposit, DD 4 P 75/13.

3 Guizot, Monk's Contemporaries, p. 18; D'Estrades, Lettres et Négotiations, v. 357.

4 Cartwright, Madame, pp. 154-5; Feiling, British Foreign Policy, pp. 64-5. See also Jusserand, French Ambassador, p. 80; C.H. Hartmann, Charles II and Madame (London, 1934), p. 169.

5 PRO, SP 78/121, f.1.

6 Hartmann, Charles II and Madame, p. 117 (17 Oct. 1664); Longleat, Coventry

diplomatic situation in France was difficult, but Holles was not well suited to his role either by temperament or previous experience. As Burnet said

> He stood too much upon the points of an ambassador, and considered more what an ambassador ought to be than what this age can bear or that court did like; so he was looked on there as a sort of stubborn hero, but as a very ill courtier.[1]

Querulous, self-opinionated, and perhaps somewhat out of his depth, Holles seems to have made few friends and exercised little influence at Versailles. Nevertheless he did succeed in maintaining some of the rights which Kings of England had previously enjoyed in the face of the growing power of the French King.

ii

Contemporary and later accounts have presented Holles as a complaisant courtier of 1660 who was transformed into a Whig patriot by the time of his death in 1680. Another aspect of his Restoration career stressed by Professor Lacey is his leadership of a Whig group concerned with protecting Protestant dissent which led to his being 'counted for many years the head of the Presbyterian party', who numbered according to Lacey about forty in the Commons and half a dozen in the Lords.[2]

Was Holles genuinely interested in religious reform and Protestant unity in the years between 1660 and 1680? His own religious position merits careful consideration, for the evidence is not easy to interpret. As a member of Parliament and a Privy Councillor, Holles conformed to the Anglican Church. However, there were various ways in which he could manifest sympathy for Dissent – by attendance at Nonconformist meetings, employment of Dissenters as chaplains, protection of Dissenters, personal contact with ministers, and his own religious practices, as well as by his conduct in Parliament.

There is no evidence that Holles attended any religious conventicles,

---

Papers, 80, f. 37v.

1 *A Supplement to Burnet's History of My Own Time . . .*, ed. H.C. Foxcroft (Oxford, 1902), p. 95.

2 Burnet, *Own Time,* i. 174-5; J.R. Jones, *The First Whigs. The Politics of the Exclusion Crisis 1678-1683* (London, 1961), pp. 9-10. Jones distinguished the Presbyterian section of this party by its 'genuine and positive zeal for religious reform and Protestant unity'. Lacey, *Dissent and Parliamentary Politics,* Appendix II.

although his third wife may have done so.[1]   He appointed as chaplains both respectable Anglicans and men with Puritan sympathies.   His first chaplain, Richard Russell, had been an assistant to Stanley Gower in Dorchester.[2]   One, Henry Compton, was later Bishop of London,[3] and another, Roger Morrice, was a Presbyterian and also a chaplain to Sir John Maynard.[4]   He dismissed one chaplain, Richard Pettys, while he was in France, allegedly because of Pettys's scandalous life, although Pettys claimed it was 'because he [Pettys] was so exact a conformist to the discipline of the Church of England'.[5]   Holles's personal relationship with ministers show the same two faces of Anglicanism and Dissent. His physician, Nicholas Cary, was an ejected minister,[6] but he helped Gilbert Burnet, later Bishop of Salisbury, to the Chaplaincy of the Master of the Rolls.[7]   As already mentioned, the two ministers he patronised in the 1650s who were still alive at the Restoration both accepted the Anglican church.[8]   There is no clear evidence that in the

---

1' In 1674 several members of the Holles family subscribed to a new chapel for Richard Baxter, including a Lady Eleanor Holles. Since Eleanor, Countess of Tyrconnel, was separately listed, this presumably refers to Holles's third wife, Esther; Baxter's *Reliquiae Baxterianae*, pt. III. 172. A Lady Holles was mentioned among Baxter's congregation in Great Russell St. in 1676, but this may have referred to Sir Francis Holles's wife, Anne. Holles helped to settle a dispute in the French Church in Threadneedle St. in 1675 when Herault was dismissed. I am grateful to Dr R. Gwynn for this information.

2 *Municipal Records of Dorchester*, pp. 608, 618. In 1658 the corporation had directed Gower, Benn, and Russell to take every opportunity 'to the stirring our cold hearts'. In 1663 Russell as permitted to hold the livings of both Brixton and Frome Billet although the two were more than thirty miles apart; *CSPD 1663-1664*, p. 67. Lacey, *Dissent and Parliamentary Politics*, p. 467, considered Russell an Anglican, but his connections with Dorchester, and with Stanley Gower suggest he was a Presbyterian able to conform.

3 *DNB*.

4 Mathews, *Calamy Revised*, p. 355. Morrice was ejected from a Derbyshire living in 1662. He witnessed Holles's will on 26 July 1670; Somerset House, PCC, Will, Holles, f. 6.

5 PRO, SP 78/120, ff. 136-136v. Pettys also said Holles objected to his reading the Apocrypha. According to Protestant divines the Hebrew Bible was the source of the authentic text and the Apocrypha was therefore uncanonical. Baxter, for example, *Reliquiae Baxterianae*, pt. II, p. 318, thought it 'of dubious and uncertain credit'.

6 Lacey, *Dissent and Parliamentary Politics*, p. 467. Lacey says Holles supported another ejected minister, John Hodges, by allowing him to live with him for a time. Baxter says Hodges was 'a grave, ancient, godly moderate divine'; Baxter, *Reliquiae Baxterianae*, pt. III, p. 96.

7 Burnet, *Supplement*, p. 484.

8 The case of a third minister Edward Damner is less clear cut. Matthews, *Calamy Revised*, p. 156 says that an Independent minister of this name was ejected in November 1660 and 'Some time after his ejectment, he was steward to Denzil Lord Holles, and preached occasionally'. Knowing Holles's dislike of Independency this seems strange. There was one John Damner in Holles's service in the 1660s; BL, Add. 32679, f. 12v., Holles to his son Francis 8 Apr./

1660s he objected to legislation aimed against the Presbyterians, such as the burning of the Solemn League and Covenant and the Corporation Bill.[1]

Little is known of his private religious practices and beliefs. In the preamble to his will, he professed his sole trust and confidence for salvation 'in the merits and mediation of the Lord Christ my God and my Redeemer'. He exulted at the prospect of change from an earthly condition full of sin and misery

> to the palace of heaven, the heavenly Jerusalem, a City not made with hands, but whose builder and maker is God, and the building is as the builder, infinitely glorious, the gates pearls, the foundation of the walls precious stones, the streets of pure gold, and the light above sun and moon, God himself is her light, this so represented in the vision to set forth the incomparable glory of it.

Burnet said 'he had a true sense of religion, and was a man of an unblameable course of life'.[2] Samuel Reyner, preaching Holles's funeral sermon, said he

> stuck close to the reformed religion, understood its principles, well and thoroughly . . . He thought it not beneath him . . . upon his bended knees daily to worship that God that made him . . . Prayers and tears, and supplications, these he thought the most proper way of addressing himself by, to the eternal God.[3]

His body was returned to his own parish church for burial, a tradition which has been described as moderate Presbyterian but may have more to do with his wish to be buried beside his first wife.[4] In his will Holles ordered that there should be no 'solemn funeral . . . but a decent burial as befits a sober Christian, without any thing of pomp and charge,

29 Mar. [16]64. In the 1690s, after Holles's death, there was both a John and an Edward Damner who were agents for the estates; Nott. R.O.; DD P 54/126, Abstract of accounts [1697]; DD 4 P.54/84, list of agents, by Anthony Guidott, 1694. Calamy, who compiled his account at the end of the seventeenth century, may have confused the two men.

1 Holles was already a member of the House of Lords when these measures passed the Commons in 1661. In 1670 he protested when the Lords agreed to a clause in the Conventicle Act permitting J.Ps. to search the houses of peers; *LJ*, xii. 340.

2 Somerset House, PCC., Will, Holles, f. 4; Burnet, *Own Time*, i. 175. Burnet wrote elsewhere that Holles 'was a very sincere and devout Christian, allowing somewhat for pride and passion'; *Supplement*, p. 63.

3 Reyner, *Funeral Sermon*, p. 24. Samuel Reyner had been ejected for nonconformity after the Act of Uniformity; Matthews, *Calamy Revised*, p. 408. He was rector of Holy Trinity Dorchester in 1670;*Municipal Records of Dorchester*. He claimed he had not known Holles well, nor had he been briefed for his sermon by any who did.

4 Lacey, *Dissent and Parliamentary Politics*, p. 468, n. 15; Somerset House, PCC, Will, Holles, f. 5.

which I ever disliked' and he absolutely forbade any feastings, since funerals required 'sad and retired thoughts'.[1] Thus although he conformed to the Anglican church, he maintained Presbyterian sympathies.

Holles's attitude to religious toleration underwent a real change. In 1660-1661 he supported the policy of reconciliation and hoped that the puritan clergy would conform, but the Anglican triumph and the exclusion of moderate Presbyterian ministers altered his attitude. In 1672 the King's Declaration of Indulgence offered the ministers permission to conduct services outside the Anglican Church under licence from the Crown, and although some doubted the King's power to grant indulgence, most of them applied for licences, thereby recognising separation from the Anglican church.[2] Holles applied for fourteen licenses for persons and places on 16 May 1672, and the seven ministers were all Presbyterians,[3] indicating that he accepted separation as an alternative to comprehension.

Throughout his life, Holles showed great concern for issues of honour and justice, but in his later years many of the issues he contested seemed of less public concern. Matters which touched his honour and his privilege as a peer he brought to the attention of the House of Lords, and whereas in earlier years his privileges as an M.P. were bound up with issues of freedom of Parliament, after the Restoration these related to his personal affairs.[4] His honour was as sensitive as ever. He published a lengthy vindication of himself and his son in 1676 against the aspersions of his son's wife's family.[5] In 1671 his defence of two young Frenchmen who were wrongfully imprisoned earnt him the censure of the Chief Justice of King's Bench. Unintimidated, he secured the release of the two unfortunates, appealed to the Lords for his own vindication, and received a public apology from the Chief Justice.[6] A typical dispute was that of 1678, when one of Holles's neighbours, forbidden to take any more hares, indicated he valued Holles 'no more than I do Thomas Booby', claimed that he was a gentleman before Holles was a lord, and made further disparaging remarks about Holles's

---

1 *Ibid.*, f. 5.

2 R. Thomas, 'Comprehension and indulgence', in Nuttal and Chadwick *From Uniformity to Unity*, pp. 206-10. Presbyterian ministers, who were doubtful about the King's power to grant indulgence, delayed applying for licences. Baxter did not apply until October.

3 *Original Records of Early Nonconformity under Persecution and Indulgence*, ed. G. Lyon Turner (3 vols., London 1911-1914), i. 349.

4 *LJ*, xii. 140, 312, 365; xiii. 415.

5 *The Lord Holles, his vindication of himself and of his son Sir Francis Holles.*

6 Denzill Holles, *A True Relation of the Unjust Accusation of certain French Gentlemen* (London, 1671); *LJ*, xii. 440, 444, 452.

greed and covetousness: Holles took him to law and was awarded £2,000 damages.[1]

Nevertheless, Holles was still concerned with national as well as personal issues. He protested at the banishment of Clarendon in 1667 against the wishes of the King.[2] There were rumours at the same time that Charles would remove him from the Privy Council,[3] and although Holles remained in the Privy Council, he was associated with the opposition. From 1667 the Lords and Commons were at loggerheads over the case of *Skinner v. the East India Company*. An anonymous work, attributed to Holles, was published before the 1669 session of Parliament which fanned the dispute by claiming that the Lords could act as court of first instance, and championing their right as beneficial to the subject:

> It was well for Skinner, That the Lords took cognizance of his [case] : otherwise this powerful Company had trampled him in the dirt and ruined him . . . And well will it be still be for many a poor man to have such an asylum, such a city of refuge to fly unto, to save himself from the violence and oppression of power and greatness.[4]

The dispute so incensed the Commons that the King was forced to prorogue Parliament until February 1670 when he persuaded both Houses to drop the case and expunge all references to it from their Journals. Charles and his ministers were angry with Holles, believing that he was using Skinner's dispute to force the King to dissolve Parliament and to summon a new.[5]

By 1670 Charles perceived Holles was not so pliable in his service as others. It was no use soliciting him in a private cause before the House of Lords, since he was one of the 'stiff and sullen men'.[6] More significantly, he was part of the developing opposition, motivated partly by dislike of the penalties against Dissenters and partly by fears of absolutism and Catholicism. In 1674 it was said that 'the Cabal is kept at Lord Holles's house , Halifax and Shaftesbury are of it, and Bucking-

---

1   Dr Williams Library, Morrice Entering Book, vol. 1, f. 226.

2   *LJ*, xii. 167-8: BL, Egerton 2539, ff. 139v.-140, 14 Nov. 1667.

3   Pepys, *Diary*, vii. 253 (30 Dec. 1667).

4   [Denzil Holles] , *The Grand Question concerning the Judicature of the House of Peers* . . . (London, 1669), pp. 70-1; See Appendix 1 for Holles's authorship.

5   J.P. Kenyon, *The Stuart Constitution 1603-1688 Documents and Commentary* (Cambridge, 1966), p. 414. The Lords made no further attempts to act as a court of first instance, except in the process of impeachment. French transcripts, PRO 31/3, 123, f. 20, Colbert to de Lionne, 24 Oct. 1669.

6   Burnet, *Own Time*, i. 493.

ham is got in'.[1] This group, 'and all those that were thought the country party', opposed a new Test Act in 1675 which would have required all office holders to swear that any attempts to alter the government of church or state, or any resistance to the King, were unlawful. They believed this was part of a design to erect an arbitrary and absolute government by undermining the independence of Parliament. For seventeen days they contested the issue in the House of Lords, arguing that the proposed test struck 'at the very root of government', and, by imposing an oath which could make a peer incapable of sitting, deprived him of his birthright. To prohibit any alteration in the church, they protested, showed a want of 'Christian compassion to Protestant Dissenters'. Outraged, the majority voted this a reflection upon the honour of the peers, at which the opposition claimed that their right to protest was being threatened. Holles defended the right to enter protests with reasons 'with so great ability, learning and reason' that their opponents abandoned their attempt to prohibit it.[2]

The opposition failed to stop the Test Bill, but before it could become law, a judicial dispute developed between the Lords and Commons over the case *Shirley v. Fagg* which it was thought the opposition deliberately fostered to force the King to prorogue Parliament. The contest, which concerned the Lords' right to act as a court of appeal, survived the prorogation, and a pamphlet attributed to Holles supporting the Lords was attacked in the Commons when Parliament reassembled.[3] Holles's proxy supported an unsuccessful attempt to ask the King directly for a dissolution. The following January 1676 Charles removed Holles and Halifax from his Privy Council, 'and no cause assigned for so doing'.[4]

---

1 *Essex Papers*, vol. i. ed. O. Airy (Camden Society, n.s. 47, 1890), p. 168 (27 Jan. 1674).

2 G.N. Clark, *The Later Stuarts 1660-1714* (Oxford, 1934), pp. 76, 82; *A Letter From a Person of Quality, to His Friend in the Country* (London, 1675, repr. *State Tracts*, 1693), pp. 45-6. Marvell wrote that 'in order to make their Episcopal Cavalier Party, they contrived before hand a politic test to be enacted'; *The Poems and Letters of Andrew Marvell*, ed. H.M. Margoliouth (2 vols., Oxford, 1927), ii. 319, J.T. Thorold Rogers, *A Complete Collection of the Protests of the Lords* (3 vols., Oxford, 1875), i. 43-4, 46.

3 Burnet, *Own Time*, ii. 84-5: 'I am not sure, if this was laid, or if it happened by accident'; A.S. Turberville, 'The House of Lords under Charles II', part I, *EHR* 40 (1929), 413; [Denzil Holles], *The Case stated concerning the Judicature of the House of Peers in the point of Appeals* (London, 1675); *Debates of the House of Commons, From the Year 1667 to the Year 1694, collected by the Hon. Anchitel Grey, Esq* . . . (10 vols., London, 1769), iv. 52. See appendix I for Holles's authorship. Lacey, *Dissent and Parliamentary Politics*, p. 296 n. 29, mentions that Holles was the 'great friend' of Fagg, but Holles's arguments actually supported Shirley's right of appeal.

4 *Ibid.*, pp. 80, 297, n. 41; Register of the Privy Council, PRO, PC 2/65, f. 87:

When Parliament next met in February 1677 after fifteen months' prorogation, a group of the opposition led by Shaftesbury tried to force a dissolution by arguing that a prorogation of more than twelve months was illegal.[1] Shaftesbury and Holles tried to persuade the Catholic Lords to join them, and Burnet says Holles wrote a book on the subject 'but a fit of the gout kept him out of the way'. The King and Lords suspected his authorship of one of the anonymous pamphlets which Parliament condemned as 'seditious', but were unable to establish the charge. Dr. Nicholas Cary, Holles's physician, admitted under questioning that Holles's servant had brought him the book, but he equivocated about the author. Holles challenged the Lords to make a specific charge, but none dared enter the lists against him.[2]

Meanwhile in October 1677 the announcement of the betrothal of William of Orange and Mary, daughter of James, was viewed in France as a dangerous alteration of England's foreign policy. Louis feared that Charles might employ an army against France, which he tried to prevent by using the parliamentary opposition who likewise feared a standing army, believing the King might use it at home. Holles and Russell negotiated with the French ambassador in January 1678 but although some of the English opposition received French money, Holles refused. (He was tempted by a portrait of Louis set in diamonds, feeling that he was still owed a present from his earlier refusal of his ambassadorial gift in 1666). The French ambassador found Holles very embittered against the Court and ministry, and deeply suspicious of Charles raising troops in April 1678: 'He is apprehensive the court will always adhere to the design of governing more absolutely than the laws of England admit'.[3]

At the end of 1678 the political atmosphere changed when Oates 'discovered' the Popish Plot. Shaftesbury supported all the evidence,

---

HMC Portland MSS., iii. 353.

1 Haley, *Shaftesbury*, p. 412.

2 *Original Papers: Containing the Secret History of Britain*, ed. J. Macpherson (2 vols., London, 1775), i. 79-80; Burnet, *Own Time*, ii. 117. *LJ*, xiii. 55 (1 Mar. 1677); *The Life, Diary, and Correspondence of Sir William Dugdale*, ed. W. Hamper, (London, 1827), p. 403; 'though he [Cary] refused to name him, and when the King asked him if he would say it was not my Lord Holles, he would not say so neither'. Marvell, *Poems and Letters*, ii. 177-8 (3 Mar. 1677). There is a manuscript on the prorogation in Holles's hand; Sheff. C.L., W.W.M., MSS vol. 15, 'The Grand Question concerning the Prorogation of this Parliamt for a yeare & 3 months stated & discussed'. I have been unable to find a printed copy. Two other pamphlets on the subject have been attributed to Holles, for a discussion of which see appendix 1.

3 Dalrymple, *Memoirs*, ii. 260-1; Haley, *Shaftesbury*, pp. 443-5, doubts Shaftesbury's involvement.

but Burnet says that 'Lord Holles had more temper than I expected from a man of his heat'[1] An intermediary, Sir John Baber, suggested to Holles that the King's chief minister Danby would agree to the dissolution of the Parliament, but Holles thought 'this pleasant news' was 'but golden dreams' until Danby came privately to him one night. Negotiations proceeded on the basis of the King and Danby agreeing that if the opposition would save Danby, the King would dissolve Parliament and make other concessions. Holles hoped that they could 'procure moneys in London . . . for the disbandment of the army'. However, the King delayed, then dissolved Parliament without mentioning these terms. He gave Danby a pardon and advanced him in the peerage. Although Charles had not kept to his bargain, Holles thought they should save Danby because he had obtained the dissolution of the hated Cavalier Parliament[2] But although he favoured lenient treatment of Danby, the King's pardon raised a constitutional issue he could not ignore. Charles, fearing that his pardon would be pronounced illegal without the bishops' support, and attempting to maintain the view that they were one of the three estates, refused to allow them to withdraw from the Lords. Holles opposed the bishops' right to vote, undertaking the argument 'with great vehemence'. He published a book anonymously justifying the bishops' exclusion and quoting a variety of authorities to show that the bishops were not a separate estate. Holles's second work on the subject was published posthumously[3]

Charles attempted to conciliate the opposition by reorganising his Privy Council[4] On 21 April 1679 he announced the new names: Shaftesbury was its president, and Holles a member, although he rarely attended[5] It was soon apparent that this new Council was as

---

1 Burnet, *Own Time,* ii. 171.

2 Lacey, *Dissent and Parliamentary Politics,* pp. 95-6, 128-9, 303 n. 113. Morrice was Holles's chaplain. Burnet, *Own Time,* ii. 187-8, does not mention these terms, but says simply that the opposition undertook to save Danby if he obtained the dissolution of Parliament, the exile of the Duke of York, and retired himself.

3 Burnet, *Own Time,* ii. 219-20; [Denzil Holles], *A Letter of a Gentleman to his Friend, shewing that the Bishops are not to be judges in Parliament in cases capital* (London, 1679), pp. 98-103, cites James I, Charles I (Answer to the Nineteen Propositions), Stephen Gardiner and Sir Henry Finch. For discussion of Holles's authorship, see Appendix I. *Lord Holles his Remains: being a second letter to a friend, concerning the judicature of the Bishops in Parliament* (London, 1682).

4 This is generally believed to have been on the advice of Sir William Temple, although the French ambassador Barrillon believed that Monmouth, Sunderland, Holles and the Duchess of Portsmouth had promoted the plan; E.R. Turner, 'The privy council of 1679', *EHR* 30 (1915), 257.

5 Holles attended only four times and these attendances were within the first month of his appointment; Register of the Privy Council, PRO, PC 2/68, f. 143.

unwieldy as the old, and the current joke was that 'they are called the private council, because everything of moment is kept private from them'. The opposition also found themselves unpopular. As in the 1640s the Commons suspected those who accepted offices: 'Court and country livery can never be worn together'.[1] In addition to sowing distrust of the opposition leaders, Charles managed to wean some of them from more extreme policies on the question of the Duke of York. At the end of April he offered to limit the power of a future Catholic monarch, and although his sincerity was doubtful, his proposal divided the opposition. While Shaftesbury believed limitations would be ineffective, Holles, according to the French ambassador, accepted the notion of limitations on a future monarch:

> He is very moderate on the subject of the Duke of York, and declares he cannot consent to his exclusion; but, at the same time he is of opinion that the power of a Catholic King of England should be limited.[2]

Thus in the context of the exclusion crisis, Holles's unwillingness to exclude James places him with the moderates, and his willingness to accept a Catholic king contrasts strangely with his dread of Popery. James wrote of Holles as a friend:

> I have long looked on him as very much my friend, and when so ever it has come in my way to talk of him have always said it, and that I knew him to be a man of as great honour as any man living, though in some things we did not agree.[3]

Even so, Holles was still a Parliamentarian, and signed a petition in December 1679 for the King to meet his newly elected Parliament. In January the French ambassador said that Holles

> would like to see both sides restrain themselves within legitimate limits, and would be satisfied to see England governed according to the laws which are established here.[4]

Holles's willingness to compromise on exclusion won him no following in the House of Lords.

---

1 *The Memoirs . . . of Sir John Reresby . . . of Thrybergh Bart., M.P. for York, &c. 1634-1689,* ed. J.J. Cartwright, (London, 1875), p. 167; Roberts, *Growth of Responsible Government,* p. 233. Later in 1679 Charles prorogued and then dissolved Parliament in defiance of his Council's advice, and when the time came for the new Parliament Charles announced to his Council he would prorogue it until 26 January 1680 'and desired nobody to speak therein'; G. Davies, 'Council and cabinet; 1679-88', *EHR* 37 (1922), 50-1.

2 Jones, *The First Whigs,* pp. 64-5; Dalrymple, *Memoirs,* ii. 261.

3 Holles voted in March for the prosecution of five Catholic Lords; Lacey, *Dissent and Parliamentary Politics,* p. 123. Bodl., Clarendon 87, ff. 321-321v., 29 Jan. 1680.

4 Lacey, *Dissent and Parliamentary Politics,* pp. 135-6, 324 n. 61.

Although Holles commanded respect during the 1670s as one of the leaders of the opposition party, the French ambassador and Holles himself overestimated his importance. Apart from other leaders, such as Annesley, Manchester, Robartes and Wharton, the Whig party was dominated by Shaftesbury. Holles was old, and his attacks of gout kept him away from the House. His personal prestige from his long career in Parliament was great: 'he had much knowledge and was very well acquainted with all parliamentary records', according to Burnet. However, his vast pride made him unable to bear contradiction, which may explain his lack of a personal following and his limited political influence at the end of his life.[1]

[1] When Shaftesbury was annotating his list of the Lords and Commons in 1677-8, on a scale from 'www' to 'vile' he inscribed only 'ww' for 'moderately worthy' after Holles's name; K.H.D. Haley 'Shaftesbury's lists of lay peers and members of the Commons, 1677-8', *BIHR* 43 (1970), 95; Jones, *The First Whigs*, p. 35; Burnet, *Supplement*, p. 63.

CONCLUSION

Judging by the shaky signature Holles appended to a codicil to his will in January 1680, he was already failing, and soon after, on 17 February 1680, he died, aged eighty-one years. His political activity continued to his last days, and he died in good repute. Morrice, his former chaplain, said that

> as great respects and honour [were] paid to his memory by the town and country as hath ever been known, and more coaches and horsemen attended his corpse out of the City than (as it's said) has ever been seen.[1]

He was succeeded by his sole surviving son, Francis, and survived by his third wife. His title died out with his grandson, Denzil, in 1693. His estates fell to his great-nephew, John Holles, subsequently Duke of Newcastle.

In the last years of his life Holles was a man out of his time. Few of his contemporaries from the Civil Wars, the period of his greatest importance, survived, and fewer still from the parliaments of the 1620s. Holles's generation had passed, and in his last years he was a solitary monument to distant and stirring times. To his allies in the parliamentary opposition, and later to the Whigs, he was a useful transitional figure because he demonstrated that opposition to the Crown could be conservative and respectable. Gradually an image of a patriot in a classical mould took shape, as Burnet wrote of him as one who 'never changed his principles for above sixty years, in which he made a considerable figure in the world, and had the soul of an old stubborn Roman in him'.[2] In 1699 his eventual heir, John Duke of Newcastle, erected a monument to his memory in St. Peter's Church Dorchester which enshrined in marble this conception of the Whig patriot.[3] Holles reclines upon a marble cushion clad in the garb of the Roman patriot, tunic and sandals, topped incongruously with a full-bottomed wig.

Holles's Parliamentarianism and his Protestantism were the qualities which appealed to the Whigs. He had believed in the independence and authority of Parliament, and had adhered to these principles throughout the changing circumstances of the seventeenth century. Although he never abandoned the view that Parliament might lawfully resist the King, he combined his Parliamentarianism with service and loyalty to

1   Dr Williams Library, Morrice, i. 256.

2   Burnet, *Supplement*, p. 63. See also Burnet, *Own Time*, i. 175: 'He was faithful and firm to his side, and never changed through the whole course of his life'.

3   The monument is described in Hutchins, *Dorset*, ii. 383-4.

the Crown. He opposed Charles I and fought against him, but he had nothing to do with the regicide, nor with the republican regime, and his respectability was confirmed when Charles II took him into his Privy Council and ennobled him. The Whigs had no cause to hesitate in revering one who had been so acceptable to the monarchy. As for Holles's Protestantism, his Puritanism precluded any fears of Roman Catholicism, while his detestation of fanatical, sect-type Puritanism dissociated him from dangerous extremists.

The Whigs' appreciation of Holles's adherence to principle throughout the vicissitudes of his sixty years of political life would have surprised his contemporaries during the Civil Wars, who remembered rather his alterations. A martyr to the parliamentary cause from the 1620s, in the van of the fiery spirits in 1640, he changed within a few months of the outbreak of the war to a supporter of peace with the King, one who tried to opt out of the war altogether. Once an enemy of the Scots, he later became their friend and ally; the Royalists, who had thought of him as 'the man of mischief'[1] in 1642, were referring to him as 'a sure card', one of themselves, in 1645.

Did Holles defend constant principles through changing circumstances? As a politician, Holles obviously perceived that there was more than one way out of the woods; some shifts of view and emphasis could not be avoided if he were to survive dramatic changes of political circumstances. His alterations were not prompted by any obvious self-interest. He had a strict conception of honour which made him endeavour to appear well in his own eyes and in the eyes of the world. Although this image of complete disinterestedness was quite self-consciously maintained, he did not in fact appear to his contemporaries as an opportunist, and no elaborate defence of him against the charge of time-serving is required. Some of the contradictions in his sixty years of political life are explicable in terms of the cooling of youthful radicalism. His bad temper and pride also burnt hot at particular crises, giving way to a cooler position later. Yet other contrasts are more apparent than real.

Holles was unlucky in the time of his death, since there was no one around who could pass any meaningful comments on the span of his political career. Those who had known him well and been his allies during the period of his greatest importance, the Civil Wars, had died, and those who knew him at his death had no real understanding of the times through which he had lived. He seems to have inspired little love

1   Quoted in P.L. Ralph, *Sir Humphery Mildmay: Royalist Gentleman Glimpses of the English Scene 1633-1652* (New Brunswick, 1947), p. 159.

or affection among his contemporaries. Perhaps they were repelled by his sense of personal rectitude. Walpole, in the eighteenth century, argued that Holles's very success had made him unattractive; unlike the unfortunate who failed, he needed no man's sympathy.[1]

Holles was not a very subtle politician, nor was he a successful one in any particular political crisis. His holding down the Speaker in 1629 was a memorable act, but it was also unconstitutional, disapproved of by many other Parliamentarians, and landed him in the Tower. He was not able to use his position among the parliamentary leaders nor his personal prestige and authority to solve the constitutional crisis between King and Parliament in 1641-2, and in 1647 his attempt to settle the kingdom failed, and he was forced to flee. While Pym is remembered as a politician *par excellence,* quietly controlling the Commons to a greater extent than any other leader was to do, Holles seems to have been too impatient to make plans, to lobby, to work quietly and unobtrusively. At one time he favoured a bold dramatic solution to the Civil Wars by making his own private overtures to the King, a solution which was totally unparliamentary, and ultimately unrealistic, for the problems posed by the Civil Wars could not be solved by one man's private initiative.

Nevertheless, although Holles was not the most successful politician in any particular situation, in the long run he succeeded: he survived. While other politicians from the time of the Civil Wars were either dead or disgraced in 1660, Holles was still involved, and in a position to make contributions which might be heeded. He was still relevant to politics in a way that many who had sided with Parliament were not. Although he was no political thinker, but remained constant to the ideas of the 1620s and the first two years of the Long Parliament and was thus incapable of new inspiration to solve the problems posed by the defeat of the King and the settlement of the nation in 1647, in the long term his conservative ideals of a balance between King and Parliament, return to the old and known ways, were those accepted with relief by the nation at large at the Restoration. Holles and his limited political philosophy were thus in the mainstream of English political life. He represents a continuing strand of ideals, and was associated with the enduring elements of the English revolution.

1 Walpole, *Works,* i. 392.

Appendix I

THE ATTRIBUTION OF ANONYMOUS WORKS TO HOLLES.

Two manuscript parliamentary diaries for the Parliament of 1628[1] have been attributed to Holles. F.H. Relf discussed their authorship in 1918, and concluded that the external evidence of the bookplate of 'John Duke of Newcastle' suggested either a Pelham or a Holles, of which there were both in the 1628 Parliament: 'One would like to think that the diary was written by the latter, the Denzil Holles who in the next session made himself so well known. The handwriting bears out this supposition to some extent'.[2] Professor Robert Johnson, who is currently editing the diaries of 1628 for the Yale Parliamentary Diaries Project, feels he has no evidence to go further than Relf's statement.

Various points have been made about diaries, some of them contradictory. For example, Relf said the diaries were especially valuable for committee meetings, whereas Johnson says that there are practically no committee reports.[3] Mr. J.P. Ferris who transcribed the diary for Professor Johnson remarked upon the diarist's interest in matters affecting the western counties. Professor Johnson has drawn attention to the fact that the diarist did not attend on Good Friday, and that the text suggests a lawyer, or one interested in matters of law, one more apt to quote Coke or Selden than, say, Sir John Eliot, and one who in the citation of legal precedents is more accurate than many others. Relf said that the diarist possessed the rare talent of putting the gist of debate into a few words.

If these diaries were by Holles, they would offer some interesting information about him. To attribute the diaries to Holles on the basis of these characteristics would, however, be to engage in tautology, and the only evidence seems to be handwriting. Unfortunately the British Library had no aid to offer on this point. My sole contribution to the question is to suggest that a manuscript of Miscellanea in the

---

1   These diaries are catalogued as follows: BL, Harl. 5324, 'Short notes of what passed in the House of Commons, April and May 1628, &c in a Paper book'. BL, Harl. 2313, 'An oblong book . . . wherein I find Brief and cursory Notes, taken in the Commons-house of Parliament the 26th, 27, and 28 of March 1627, as I take it: and then beginning again at 31 August 1627, carried on for a much longer space of time'.

2   Relf, *Petition of Right,* pp. 70-1.

3   These points from Professor Johnson are from personal correspondence 24 Nov. 1968 and 13 Mar. 1970.

Duke of Portland's collection which dates to about 1616 could be identified as Denzil Holles's on the basis of internal evidence,[1] and that the handwriting of the Miscellanea is not dissimilar to that of the diaries. Nevertheless, extant letters of Denzil's for the later 1620s reveal a more flowing hand than either the Miscellanea, or the diaries.

Several anonymous printed works have been attributed to Holles. Some of these, which relate to questions of parliamentary judicature, aroused such political contention at their publication that the House of Commons investigated their authorship. Holles's authorship was never proven, and the evidence is inconclusive. For an understanding of Holles's political views the question of attribution is not crucial, since his views are known from other sources, but what is of interest is whether he was, in fact, the author of works which aroused such political controversy that they contributed to the King's decision to prorogue his Parliament.

Stylistically, these works are poor compared with Holles's *Memoirs*. Possibly some arose from conference activity, but the points of parliamentary procedure and precedents make dull reading, and the arguments do not carry the same emotional conviction as some of his earlier works.

In the following account, the anonymous works and the sources for the attribution are discussed chronologically.

> *The Grand Question concerning the Judicature of the House of Peers stated and argued, and the case of T. Skinner, complaining of the East India Company, which gave occasion to that question related, . . .* (1669.)

Various contemporaries attributed this work to Lord Holles. A newsletter mentions 'the Lord Holles hath writ a book', Lindenou refers to 'a quite curious book said to have been written by Lord Holles', and Colbert accepted Holles's authorship without question, saying that Charles and his ministers were very annoyed with him.[2]

Later writers, such as Robert Atkyns, Moule, Hargrave, Halkett and Laing, and Firth, have accepted Holles's authorship with varying degrees of certitude.[3]

---

1 See above, p. 13, n.6.

2 BL, Add. 36916, ff. 143, 144, [newsletter], 5 Oct. 1669; *The First Triple Alliance. The Letters of Christopher Lindenou, Danish Envoy to London 1668-1672*, trans. & ed. W. Westergaard (New Haven, 1947), p. 168; PRO, French transcripts, PRO 31/3/123, f. 20. Colbert à de Lionne, 24 Oct. 1669. See also *HMC*, Report VII. 488.

3 Sir Robert Atkyns, *A Treatise of the True and Ancient Jurisdiction of the House of Peers* (London, 1699), pp. 1-4, 35; T. Moule, *Bibliotheca Heraldica*

The Case Stated Concerning the Judicature of the House of Peers in the Point of Appeals (1675).

There is a manuscript version of this which is in different hands, none, so far as can be seen, Holles's.[1] In the House of Commons in 1675 Sir Thomas Meeres cited 'Lord Holles's last book' and was reproved by the Speaker.[2]

This work is usually attributed to Holles, although Hargrave mentions that some suggest the Earl of Anglesey was the author.[3]

The Case stated of the Jurisdiction of the House of Lords In the point of Impositions (London, 1676).

A manuscript among the papers of Sir Richard Temple mentions Holles's authorship of this work as a fact 'sufficiently known', and points out to the reader, lest he be biased by Holles's 'great honour, ability, and experience', that it was 'a work began in his declining age'.[4]

Later writers have generally accepted Holles's authorship.[5] For example, Palmer, editing the work in 1836, observed that it had 'always been ascribed to Denzil Lord Holles, a nobleman of splendid talents'.[6]

The Long Parliament dissolved (1676)
Some Considerations Upon the Question whether the Parliament is Dissolved By its Prorogation for 15 months? (1676)

Halkett and Laing attributed both *The Long Parliament dissolved* and *Some Considerations* to Holles, which Firth accepted, suggesting

Magnae Britanniae. An Analytical Catalogue of Books on Genealogy, Heraldry, Nobility, Knighthood and Ceremonies (London, 1882), pp. 220-1; Francis Hargrave, manuscript notes on his copy of *The Grand Question*, now in the British Library; S. Halkett and J. Laing, *Dictionary of Anonymous and Pseudonymous English Literature* (6 vols., revised edn., Edinburgh, 1926-1932), ii. 410; Firth, *DNB*, Holles article.

1 BL, Harl. 6810, ff. 115-133. There are a number of manuscripts in this volume relating to political issues in which Holles was interested.

2 Grey, *Debates*, iv. 52.

3 Halkett and Laing, *Dictionary of Anonymous and Pseudonymous English Literature*, i. 290. F. Hargrave, Preface to Matthew Hale, *The Jurisdiction of the Lords House, or Parliament, considered according to ancient records* (London, 1796), p. clxx.

4 BL, Stow 304, f. 113, 'Observations upon My Lord Holles's Book, or Notes in order to a Conference'. There is an erased reference to Holles's authorship of the work in Stow 300.

5 Firth, *DNB*, Holles article.

6 *Tracts on Law, Government, and other Political Subjects*, ed. J. Palmer (London, 1836).

that the two pamphlets were probably the same,[1] but in fact they are quite different and it is unlikely Holles was the author of either. One Browne was fined 1000 marks for writing *The Long Parliament dissolved*.[2]

The House of Lords named a committee to investigate two publications about the prorogation. In their report, the Lords declared that they had examined *Some Considerations, The Long Parliament dissolved*, and *The Grand Question concerning the Prorogation*. Both the King and the Lords had questioned Dr Nicholas Cary, Holles's physician, as to the authorship of *The Grand Question*, but he returned equivocal answers. The Lords fined him for his refusal to answer. Holles was not in the House at the time of Cary's examination.[3] All the evidence points to Holles's authorship of *The Grand Question concerning the prorogation* which I have not seen published. Burnet says Holles wrote a book on the subject, and the manuscript of *The Grand Question* is in Holles's holograph.[4]

> *A Letter to Monsieur Van- - - - B- - - - de M- - - - At Amsterdam, written Anno 1676.*

Various copies and different editions of this work in the British Library and the Bodleian Library are attributed to Holles,[5] and writers from Collins onwards, have accepted the work as Holles's.[6] I have found no contemporary evidence to authenticate the publication, and the ideas expressed therein are more trenchantly critical of the Stuarts than those Holles expressed elsewhere. For example, the author argues that had it not been for Parliament in the middle of three weak Princes 'we would not taken one true step, nor struck one true stroke, since Queen Elizabeth'. Consequently Holles's authorship appears doubtful.

> *A Letter of a Gentleman to his Friend, showing that the Bishops Are not to be judges in Parliament in Cases Capital* (1679).

Burnet says Holles opposed the bishops' voting on the legality of Danby's pardon in 1679 'with great vehemence' and wrote upon the

---

1 Halkett and Laing, *Dictionary of Anonymous and Pseudonymous English Literature*, iii. 392, v. 306; Firth, *DNB*, Holles article. There is a manuscript version of *Some Considerations* in BL, Harl. 6810, f. 102.

2 Burnet, *Own Time*, ii. 116n.

3 *LJ*, xiii. 42, 49, 54-5; *HMC* Report IX, 70-2; Dugdale, *Diary*, pp. 403-5.

4 Burnet, *Own Time*, ii. 117; Sheff. C.L., W.W.M., MSS vol. 15.

5 For example, Bodl., Firth 1 10; Pamphlet B. 136 (published 1691). BL, 1712 edn. published as *The British Constitution Considered*.

6 Collins, *Historical collections*, pp. 152-6; *Catalogue of the Library of the London Institution* (4 vols., London, 1840), ii. 551; Halkett and Laing, *Dictionary of Anonymous and Psuedonymous English Literature*, iii. 290.

subject.[1]   Holles's authorship is authenticated by the posthumous publication in his name of a second letter on the issue.[2]

The work has been generally accepted as Holles's.[3]

> *Lord Holles his Remains: being a second letter to a friend, concerning the judicature of the Bishops in Parliament in vindication of what he wrote in his first, and in answer to a book since published against it . . .* (London, 1682).

The preface informed the reader that he would recognise the work as 'the genuine product' of Holles's large soul, and added that there was 'other sufficient proof of its being authentic' from persons who had known Holles. There is, among some Baxter papers, a manuscript version of the work in Holles's hand with corrections in the same hand.[4]

---

1   Burnet, *Own Time*, ii. 224.

2   See *Lord Holles his Remains* (1682).

3   Halkett and Laing, *Dictionary of Anonymous and Pseudonymous English Literature*, iii. 272; Firth, *DNB*, Holles article.

4   Original papers of Richard Baxter, the Nonconformitst, BL, Egerton 2570, ff. 136-149.

Appendix II

HOLLES'S WEALTH

Unfortunately there are not estate papers available to study how Denzil Holles gained his wealth nor to reveal its extent. Such estate papers as there are relate chiefly to the period after 1693 when his grandson, Denzil, died a minor and the estate passed to John, Earl of Clare and later Duke of Newcastle. By this date the composition of the estate had changed.

Estimates of Denzil's wealth at his death in 1680 vary. One petition of creditors to the Holles estate claimed that he had land worth £5,000 *per annum*, leases worth £1,000 *per annum*, and also possessed 'a magnificent and noble personal estate in money, debts, plate, jewels, rich hangings, pictures, books, arrears of rent and likewise arrears of salaries and pensions from the Crown to the value of twenty thousand pounds and upwards'.[1] Another group of creditors claimed he was worth £3,000 *per annum* with goods worth £50,000 and upwards.[2] Four years after Denzil's death, his son Francis set out his financial position for a marriage settlement, and although the composition of the estates differed, Francis's income gives a rough guide to the position of his father. He estimated his total annual income as £4,646, and among his assets he mentioned £12,000 worth of timber, several mansion houses 'fit for any gentleman to live in' and some advowsons of ministers' livings.[3]

By 1693 when the estates passed to John Earl of Clare they were encumbered with debt to the tune of £35,000 with interest of nearly £4,000 *per annum*, and much of the land was mortgaged.[4] Although a private act was passed in 1697 to settle the debts of the estate, creditors were still petitioning for settlement eighteen years later.[5] These creditors list debts of Francis Holles, but it is not clear whether they were his own or inherited.[6]

The chief source of Holles's wealth was land. His embassy in France

1 Nott. U.L., Ne D 570 a, petition to Parliament, n.d.
2 Nott. U.L., Ne D 570 c.
3 Nott. C.R.O., DD 4 P 54/81.
4 Nott. C.R.O., DD 4 P 40/21, 22, 23. Some of the mortgages date to 1662-1673.
5 Nott. U.L., Ne D 570, a, c, d, f.
6 Nott. C.R.O., DD 4 P 40/22.

does not appear to have been profitable. He had no great office, although there may have been pickings from his post as one of the trustees for the Queen's jointure lands. His landed estate was built up chiefly by two good marriages. His first wife, Dorothy, was the sole heiress of Sir Francis Ashley whose estate was worth £1,200 *per annum*; his second wife Jane had been twice married and he enjoyed her extensive jointure lands during her lifetime. Holles himself purchased and leased various lands, consolidating his estate. The bulk of his property was in the counties Sussex, Surrey, Wiltshire, Dorset, and Hertfordshire and he probably owned a house in London.[1] One of the few extant accounts of his estate for 1676-80 shows income from the sale of wool as well as rentals.[2]

1 Mentioned in BL, Add. 32679, f. 12, Holles to his son Francis, 8 Apr./29 Mar. 1664.
2 An Abstract of the Receipts and Payments Yearly of Nicholas Bowdidg . . . 1675-1680, Nott. C.R.O., DD 4 P 54/126.

INDEX

Cheeke, Robert, 184
Chesterfield, Earl of, *see* Stanhope, Philip
Cheynell, Francis, 125
Chillingworth, William, 61-2
Christ's College, Cambridge, 5, 14
Church of England, restoration of, 194-7; *see also* Episcopacy
Clare, Earls of, *see* Holles, John, 1st Earl; Holles, John, 2nd Earl
Clarendon, Earl of, *see* Hyde, Edward
clergy, secular employment of, 47, 49, 50, 60-1
Clifton, Sir Gervase, 37n
Clotworthy, Sir John, 1st Viscount Massereene, 36, 68, 100, 104, 117, 129, 131-2, 141n, 152, 156, 164, 166 & n, 167, 179
Coke, Sir Edward, 8, 18
Coke, Sir John, 20, 71, 72
Coke, Thomas, 61, 175, 181
Colbert, Jean Baptiste, 199, 202
Collins, Arthur, 1-2, 168
colonization, 27-8, 35 & n
Comenius (Jan Amos Komensky), 35
committee for the Admiralty, 164-5
committee of both kingdoms, 102-3, 114, 127, 128
committee for Irish affairs, 150
committee of safety, 102
committees, *see also* Commons, House of
Common Prayer, Book of, 31, 58, 195
Commons, House of; committees, 53; conferences, 53-4, 73; elections, 31, 122, 183-4, 188; messengers of, 42n, 55; Speaker of, 21; *see also* Finch, Sir John; Lenthall, William; Grimston, Sir Harbottle
Compton, Henry, Bishop of London, 209
Constantine, William, 183 & n
Convention (1660), elections, 188; meetings, 188-90, 192-3, 195-6
Conway, Edward, 2nd Viscount Conway, 91, 97, 99
Conyers, Sir John, 97
Cook, John, 160, 168n
Cooper, Anthony Ashley, 1st Earl of Shaftesbury; and Holles, 120 & n, 144 & n, 205; political activity, 187, 188, 195, 212, 215, 216, 217 & n
Corbett, Miles, 116
Coryton, William, 21
Cotton, Mrs, sister to Monson, 118
Council of State (1660), 185, 186-7
'Court', 10, 11-12, 16, 214, 216

covenant (May 1642), 91, 94
Covenant, Solemn League and, 99-100, 101, 102, 107, 111, 127, 129, 130, 152, 159, 177, 210
Coventry, Henry, 190-1, 205-6, 207
Covert, Sir Walter, 71
Cranfield, Lionel, Earl of Middlesex, 11
Cranford, James, 114-5
Crew, John, 111
Crispe, Sir Nicholas, 90
Cromwell, Oliver, 3, 104, 105, 141 & n, 142n, 175, 185; and Holles, 107-8, 129, 136, 168, 171, 182; political activity, 140, 152, 165
Culpepper, Sir John, 49, 54n
Customs' Farmers, 20, 45, 55, 86

Damner, Edward, 209n
Damner, John, 209n
Danby, Earl of, see Osborne, Sir Thomas
Deare, Edward, 184
Declaration (30 March 1647), 142-3, 146
Declaration, King's (1660), 196
Declaration of Indulgence (1672), 211
Defence of the Militia Ordinance, 71
Delamer, Lord, see Booth, George
Denbigh, Earl of, see Feilding, Basil
Dendy, Sergeant-at-Arms, 65
Derby, Earl of, see Stanley, James
Dering, Sir Edward, 49 & n
Devereux, Robert, Earl of Essex, 40, 136; and army 70-1, 78, 80-2, 87, 88, 90, 101, 103-4, 106-7; and parliamentary opposition, 34, 48; and peace party, 93, 96, 97, 104, 107, 110, 134; see also 'Essex's party'
D'Ewes, Sir Symonds, 20, 68, 89, 91; comments on Holles, 84, 96; and peace party, 87, 88, 100; and religious issues, 48-9, 50, 58
Digby family, 30
Digby, Lord George, 31, 36, 39n, 47n, 65, 67 & n; Holles attacks, 59-60; Holles accused of corresponding with, 116, 119, 120 & n; intercepted letters of, 114-5, 127
Digby, John, 1st Earl of Bristol, 40, 44, 48, 59-60
Digges, Sir Dudley, 18
Dorchester, co. Dorset, 16, 27, 31-2, 79, 96-7, 162, 175n, 188; see also Dorset
Dorislaus, Dr., 90
Dorset, 27, 30-1, 71, 78, 96, 104, 174, 182
Downing, Sir George, 201, 207

233

Fowke, Alderman John, 145n, 158
Frederick, Elector Palatine, 14
Freke, John (husband to Jane Shirley), 71, 182n
Freke, John (son to Jane Shirley), 184
Freke, Thomas (son to Jane Shirley), 184, 204 & n
Fuller, Thomas, 71n

Gerard, Sir Gilbert, 35, 187, 188
Gibbons, John (servant of Holles's), 181-2
Gibbs, Alderman William, 158
Glover, Henry, 184
Glyn, John, 44, 54n, 68, 85, 90, 92, 95, 96, 117, 122n, 179; one of
    'eleven members', 152, 164, 166
Gondomar, Count of, 9
Goodwin, Colonel Arthur, 93
Goodwin, Robert, 59
Gower, Stanley, 175n, 184, 209
Graham, James, Marquis of Montrose, 111-12, 128
Grand Remonstrance, 26n, 59, 60, 62
Graves, Colonel Richard, 147
Gray's Inn, 5, 14
Great Seal, Parliament's, 89, 190, 192
Grenville, John, Earl of Bath, 91
Greville, Robert, Lord Brooke, 34, 35, 81
Grey, Henry, Earl of Stamford, 161
Grimston, Sir Harbottle, 175, 189
Gurdon, John, 35, 113, 118, 131

Halifax, Marquis of; *see* Savile, Sir George
Hamer, Sir Thomas, 128
Hamilton, William, 2nd Duke of Hamilton, 113n
Hampden, John, 34, 35, 41, 49, 50, 51, 63-8, 87n, 91; his regiment,
    81
Hardy, Nathaniel, 159
Harley, Sir Edward, 142, 152, 164, 179, 198
Harley, Sir Robert, 50, 70, 87, 95, 184
Harrington, John, 131, 132
Harris, John, 160
Harrison, Thomas, 193-4
Hartlib, Samuel, 35
Haselrig, Sir Arthur, 63, 67, 167, 171, 172 & n, 185n; *see also* 'Five
    Members'
Hastings, Henry, 31
Hatton, Lady Elizabeth (wife of Sir Edward Coke), 8-9, 14, 15

Holles, John, 1st Earl of Clare (father of Denzil), life and political
career, 5-16, 23-4; marriage, 6; will, 28-9
Holles, John, 2nd Earl of Clare, 13-16, 17, 23-4, 28-9; in Civil War,
69, 85 & n, 97, 99, 146; at Restoration, 187n, 188; mentioned, 91,
93n, 119, 204
Holles, Thomas (uncle of Denzil), 85
Holles, Sir William, 5
Hopton, Sir Ralph, 42n, 79
Hotham, Captain John, 84, 122n
Hotham, Sir John, 34, 54n, 72
Howard, Theophilus, 2nd Earl of Suffolk, 31
Hudson, Michael, 128
Hyde, Edward, 43, 86-7; comments on Holles, 32-3, 34, 38, 51, 111,
143, 165n, 182; during Civil War, 110, 111; in Long Parliament,
41-2, 48, 54n, 57, 61; Restoration and after, 186, 192, 196,
199, 200, 203, 206, 212
Hyde, Sir Nicholas, Chief Justice of King's Bench, 23

Ince, Peter, 184 & n
Inchiquin, Murrough O'Brien, Lord, 95n, 141-2
Independents in Assembly, 102, 105-6
'Independent' party, 101, 105-6, 109-10, 111, 114, 119, 140, 146,
148, 157, 165-6, 174; Holles's account of, 160-1; see also parties
Inns of Court, 63
Ireland, 130, 141-2; revolt (1641), 57, 59, 60, 62, 139
Ireton, Henry, 4, 143

James I, 9, 11n, 14; office holding under, 7-12
James II, 216
Jephson, William, 95
Jermyn, Henry, Lord, 180
Jesop, William, 189
Joyce, Cornet George, 146 & n

Keeling, Lord Chief-Justice of King's Bench (1671), 211
Kendrick, Alderman John, 145n
Kimbolton, Lord, see Montagu, Edward
King's Bench, 23, 24-25, 26

Lambe, Ezekias (servant of Holles), 97n, 182-3
Lambert, John, 188
Lanark, Earl of, see Hamilton, William, Duke of Hamilton
Laud, William, Archbishop of Canterbury, 37, 39, 46
Lechmere, Nicholas, 183n

240

Roe, Sir Thomas, 54
'root and branch' petition, 45-6; *see also* Episcopacy
Rothes, Earl of, *see* Leslie, John
Rous, Francis, 87, 157 & n
Royalist lands, sales of, 133, 144
Royalist uprisings, 180-1, 182
Royalists, in Long Parliament, 57, 58; and Restoration, 186, 188-91
Rudyard, Sir Benjamin, 70
Ruggle, George, 14
Rupert, Prince, 81
Russell, Francis, 4th Earl of Bedford (1593-1641), 34, 38, 40, 41
Russell Richard, 209 & n
Russell, William, Duke of Bedford, 79, 88, 97, 99, 146, 187
Russell, William, Lord, 214
Rutherford, Samuel, 124
Rutland, Earl of, *see* Manners, John

St. John, Oliver, 34, 35-6, 40, 51n, 54n, 87, 128; Holles's views of, 115, 168, 171-2; and middle group, 100-2, 104-6; and Restoration, 187
St. Margaret's, Westminster, 46
Sabran, M. de (French ambassador), 101, 106n, 109 & n, 111, 113
Salisbury, Earl of, *see* Cecil, William
Salway, Humphery, 118
Savile, Sir George, Marquis of Halifax, 212, 213
Savile, Thomas, 1st Viscount, 40, 108, 109; 'Savile affair' (1645), 114-20, 122, 123
Saye and Sele, Viscount, *see* Fiennes, William
Scot, Thomas, 156
Scotland and Scots, Bishops wars of, 31, 32; and Long Parliament before war, 42, 43-51; Charles visits, 54, 55, 58; enter Civil War, 92-100 peace party hostility to, 99-100, 102; allied with peace party, 105-8, 112-4, 118; at Uxbridge, 111; Presbyterian campaign, 121-7; departure of, 127-34; *see also* Covenant, Solemn League and; Presbyterian church government; Scots' Army
Scots' Army, 43-4, 100, 105; flight of Charles to, 126, 128-9; payment of, 131-4; invades (1648), 173-5
secluded members, 177; readmitted, 185
Sedgewick, Obadiah, 80, 125
Selden, John, 21, 44, 45
Seton, Charles, 2nd Earl of Dunfermline, 147
Seymour, William, Marquis of Hertford, 40, 78, 79